# HARBINGER

# RENEGADES

JOSHUA DYSART | BARRY KITSON | LEE GARBETT | MATTHEW CLARK

D1410300

# CONTENTS

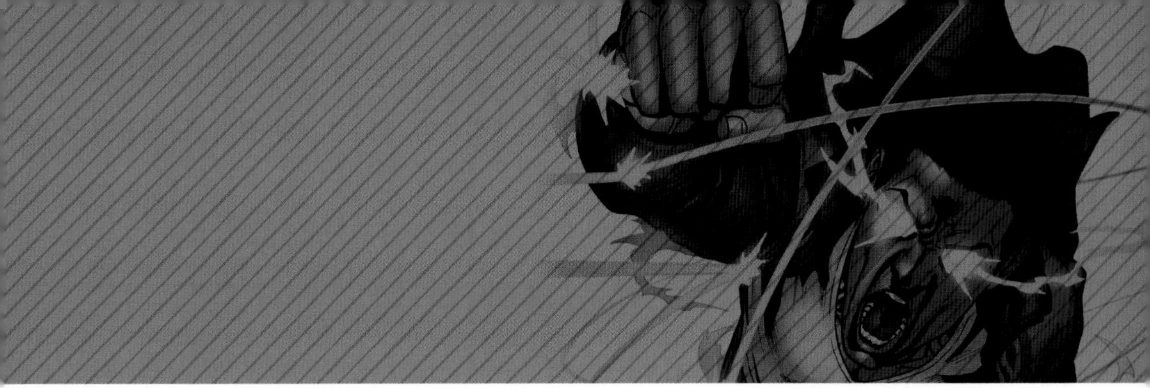



*Collection Cover Art:* Mico Suayan

**VALIANT.**

**Peter Cuneo**
Chairman

**Dinesh Shamdasani**
CEO and Chief Creative Officer

**Gavin Cuneo**
CFO and Head of Strategic Development

**Fred Pierce**
Publisher

**Warren Simons**
VP Executive Editor

**Walter Black**
VP Operations

**Hunter Gorinson**
Marketing and Communications Manager

**Atom! Freeman**
Sales Manager

**Travis Escarfullery**
Production and Design Manager

**Rian Hughes/Device**
Trade Dress and Book Design

**Jody LeHeup**
Associate Editor

**Josh Johns**
Assistant Editor

**Peter Stern**
Operations Coordinator

**Ivan Cohen**
Collection Editor

**Steve Blackwell**
Collection Designer

**Russell Brown**
President, Consumer Products,
Promotions & Ad Sales

**Jason Kothari**
Vice Chairman

Harbinger®: Renegades.
Published by Valiant Entertainment, LLC. Office of Publication:
424 West 33rd Street, New York, NY 10001. Compilation copyright
© 2013 Valiant Entertainment, Inc. All rights reserved. Contains
materials originally published in single magazine form as
Harbinger #6-7, Copyright ©2012 and Harbinger #8-10 Copyright
©2013 Valiant Entertainment, Inc. All rights reserved. All
characters, their distinctive likenesses and related indicia featured
in this publication are trademarks of Valiant Entertainment, Inc.
The stories, characters, and incidents featured in this publication
are entirely fictional. Valiant Entertainment does not read or accept
unsolicited submissions of ideas, stories, or artwork. Printed in
the USA. Second Printing. ISBN:9781939346025.

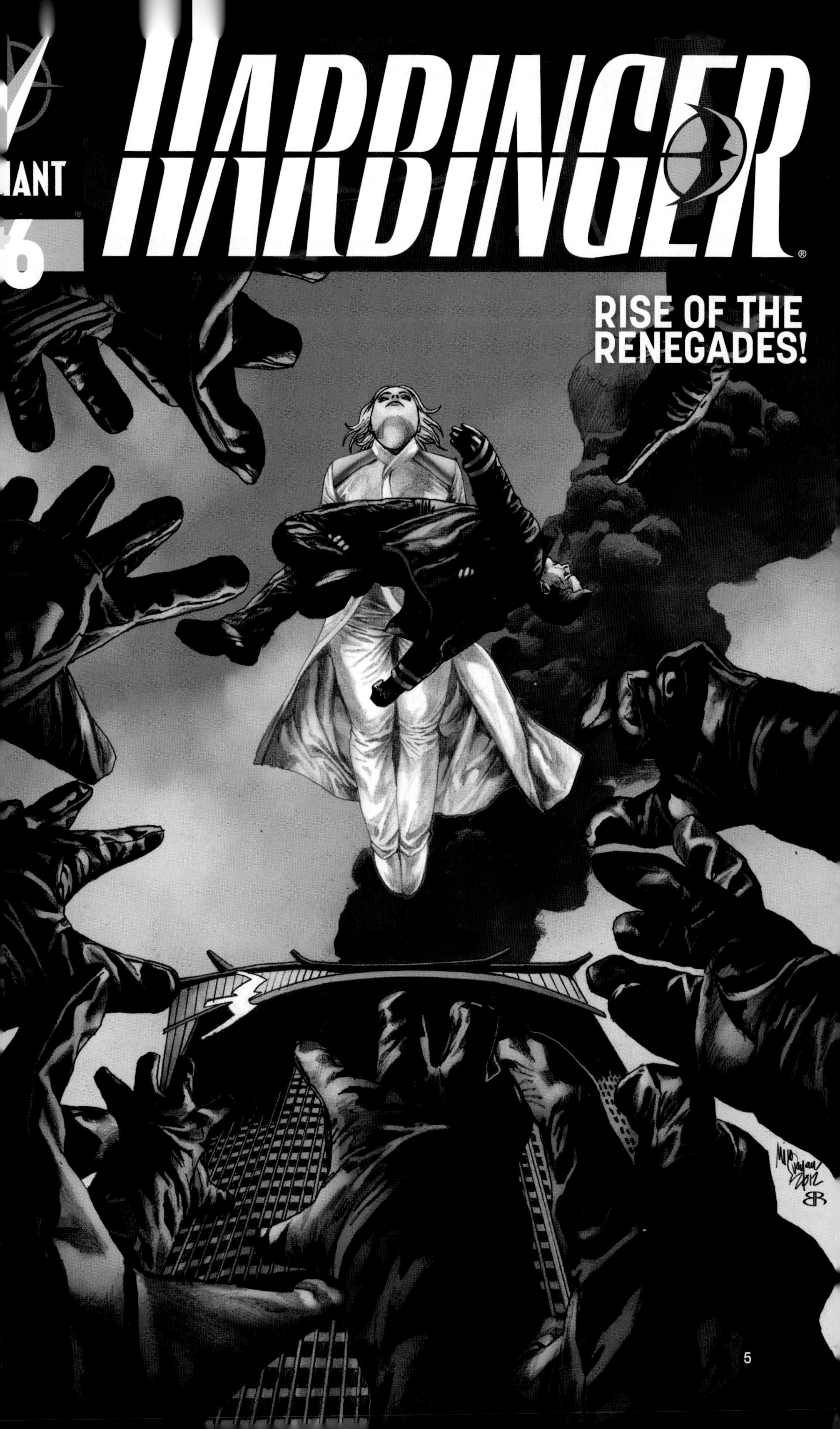
VALIANT
6
HARBINGER
RISE OF THE RENEGADES!

# HARBINGER

*OUR STORY SO FAR...*

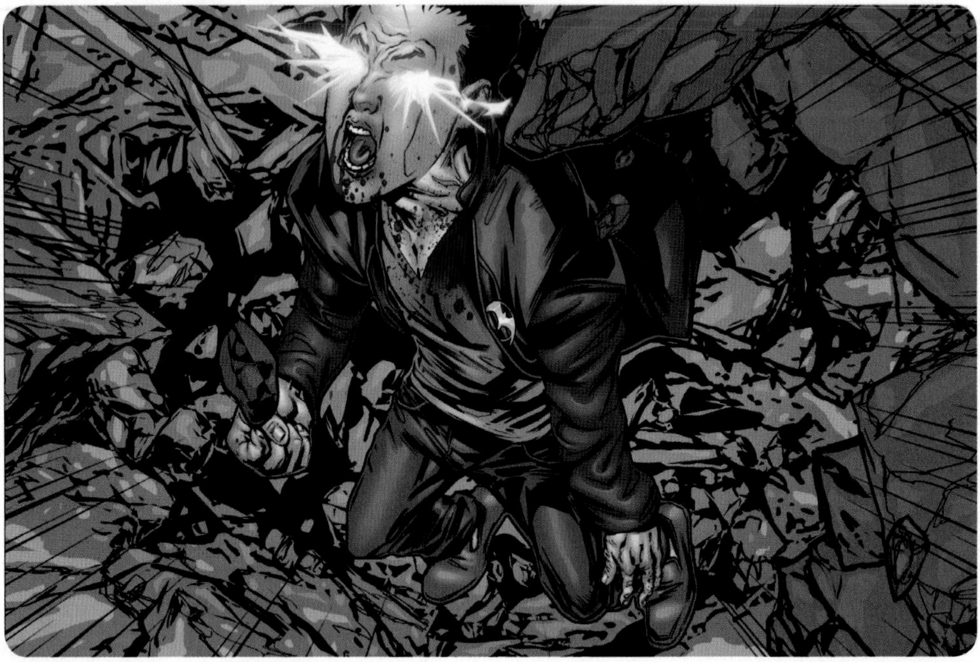

Toyo Harada is the world's most powerful psionic and founder of the Harbinger Foundation, an organization that helps individuals with powerful abilities shape the future. One of those individuals is an immensely powerful teenage psionic named Peter Stanchek. A street kid on the run from the law, Peter was clearly out of control--robbing pharmacies, popping pills to quiet the voices in his head, and squatting in foreclosed homes with his only friend in the world, a drug-addled mental patient named Joe Irons.

With Harada's guidance, Peter recognized the danger he represented to himself and others and agreed to join the Foundation, hoping Harada could give him a better understanding of his unique abilities. In return, Harada promised to take care of Joe. Once at the organization, Peter learned that Harada had been subjecting people with the potential to be psiots to a surgical activation process that left one in four dead. Peter was horrified by Harada's cavalier attitude to the loss of human life, and left the Foundation. However, unwilling to lose his prized pupil, Harada attempted to break Peter's spirit by ordering the murder of Peter's friend Joe and making it look like an accidental overdose. Unfortunately for Harada, the plan backfired, and after discovering the truth, Peter turned on his would-be mentor. The psionic battle that ensued was brutal, leaving Peter beaten and on the brink of death. Peter managed to escape only with the help of high-flying Faith Herbert, a young psiot that Peter had telepathically activated only days earlier.

Before he joined the school, one of Peter's many bad decisions was to telepathically force his childhood friend Kris Hathaway to fall in love with him. Peter eventually freed Kris from his control the night he left to join the Foundation, but he left her confused and enraged...

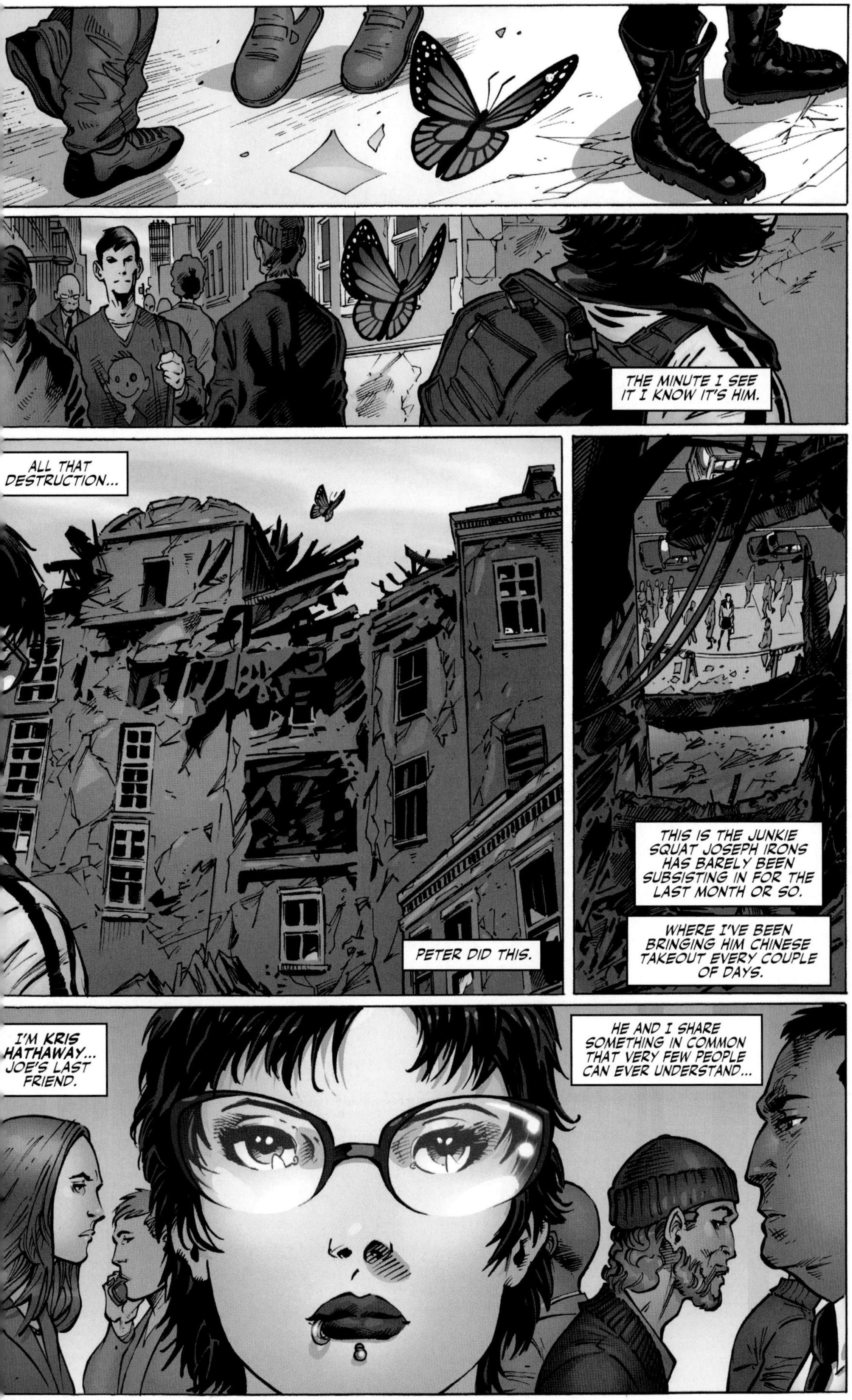
THE MINUTE I SEE IT I KNOW IT'S HIM.
ALL THAT DESTRUCTION...
PETER DID THIS.
THIS IS THE JUNKIE SQUAT JOSEPH IRONS HAS BARELY BEEN SUBSISTING IN FOR THE LAST MONTH OR SO.
WHERE I'VE BEEN BRINGING HIM CHINESE TAKEOUT EVERY COUPLE OF DAYS.
I'M KRIS HATHAWAY... JOE'S LAST FRIEND.
HE AND I SHARE SOMETHING IN COMMON THAT VERY FEW PEOPLE CAN EVER UNDERSTAND...

A HISTORY WITH PETER STANCHEK.

HI, KRIS, IT'S ME...

JOE SAYS PETER'S GOT SOME KIND OF SUPER PSYCHIC POWERS. I BELIEVE HIM...

FALL IN LOVE WITH ME, KRIS.

I HAVE TO. OTHERWISE NOTHING MAKES ANY SENSE.

LIKE HOW MY HEART FELL THROUGH A TRAPDOOR IN MY CHEST AT THE BLINK OF AN EYE.

HOW I WA CONSUME FOLDED DC TO NOTHIN NO SELF NO FUTUR NO HOPE: NO FREE W

NOTHING BUT THE OVERWHELMING IDEA OF PE

NOW I KNOW WHY THEY CALL IT "FALLING" IN LOVE.

WHEN HE FREED ME FROM HIS SPELL IT FELT LIKE AN INFLATED BALLOON INSIDE ME HAD POPPED.

A SENSE OF EMOTIONAL FULLNESS WAS SUDDENLY GONE. LEAVING NOTHING BL HOLLOW, ANGRY, EMPTINES:

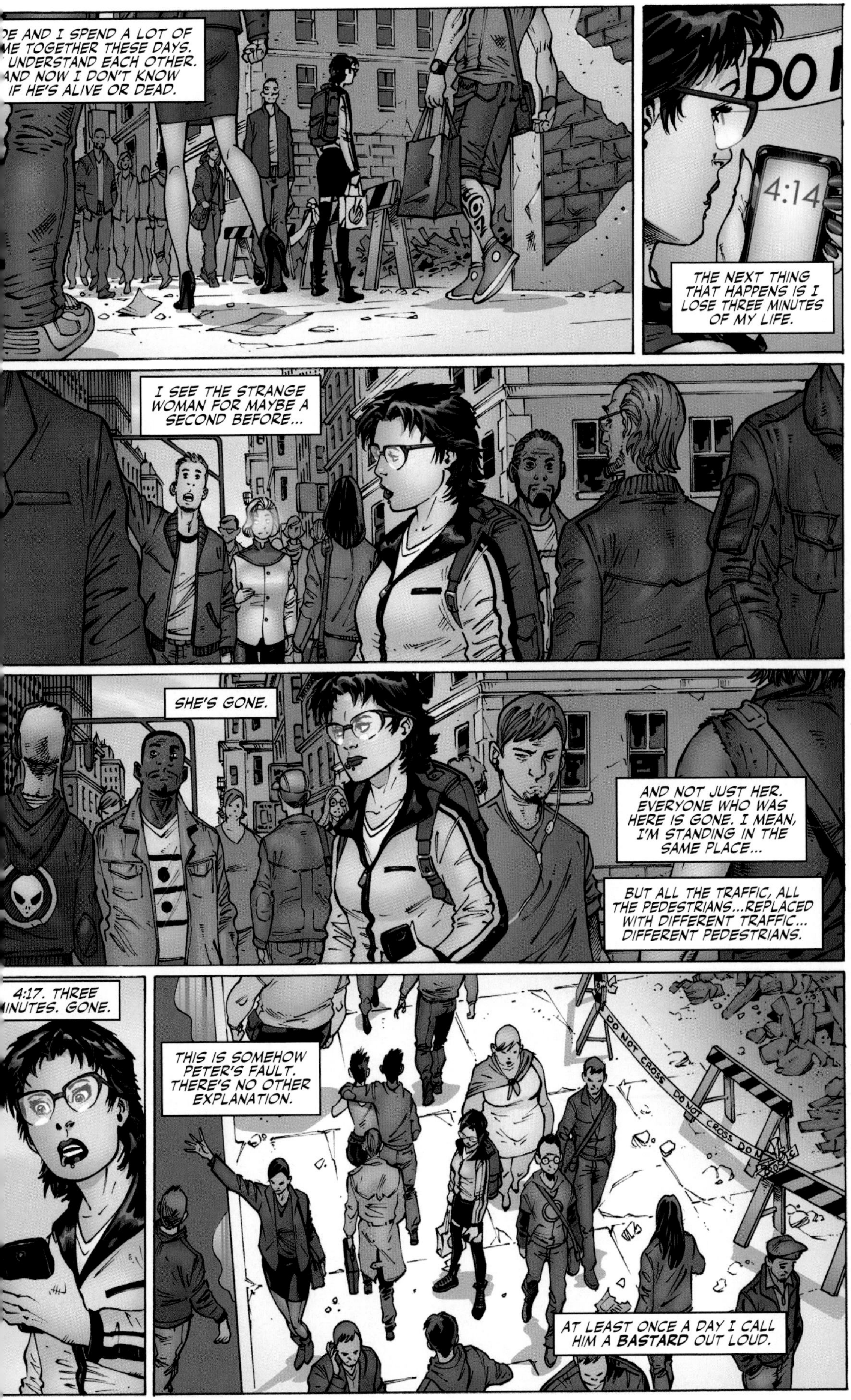
DE AND I SPEND A LOT OF
ME TOGETHER THESE DAYS.
UNDERSTAND EACH OTHER.
AND NOW I DON'T KNOW
IF HE'S ALIVE OR DEAD.
DO N
4:14
THE NEXT THING THAT HAPPENS IS I LOSE THREE MINUTES OF MY LIFE.
I SEE THE STRANGE WOMAN FOR MAYBE A SECOND BEFORE...
SHE'S GONE.
AND NOT JUST HER. EVERYONE WHO WAS HERE IS GONE. I MEAN, I'M STANDING IN THE SAME PLACE...
BUT ALL THE TRAFFIC, ALL THE PEDESTRIANS...REPLACED WITH DIFFERENT TRAFFIC... DIFFERENT PEDESTRIANS.
4:17. THREE
INUTES. GONE.
THIS IS SOMEHOW PETER'S FAULT. THERE'S NO OTHER EXPLANATION.
DO NOT CROSS
DO NOT CROSS
AT LEAST ONCE A DAY I CALL HIM A BASTARD OUT LOUD.

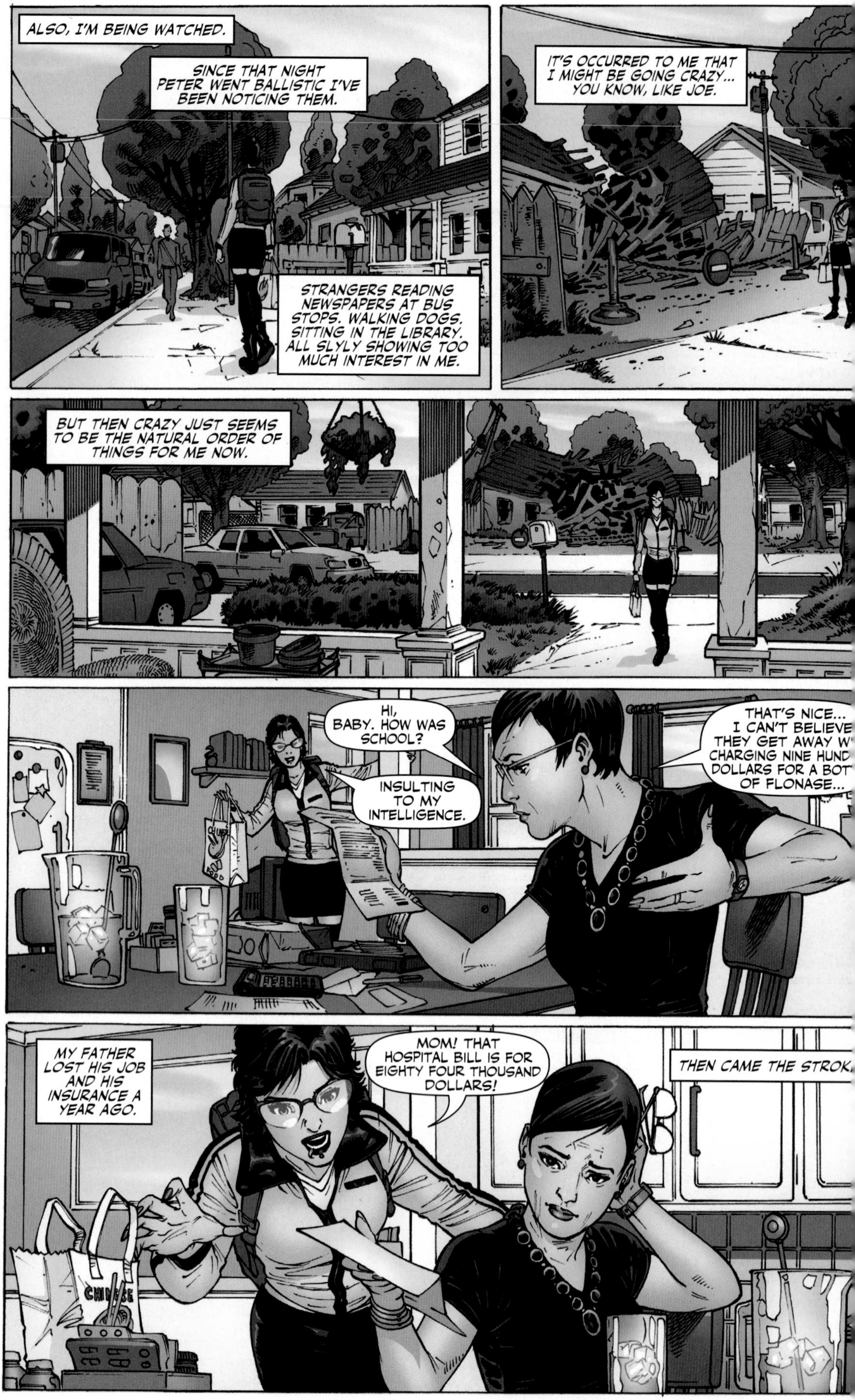
ALSO, I'M BEING WATCHED.
SINCE THAT NIGHT PETER WENT BALLISTIC I'VE BEEN NOTICING THEM.
STRANGERS READING NEWSPAPERS AT BUS STOPS. WALKING DOGS. SITTING IN THE LIBRARY. ALL SLYLY SHOWING TOO MUCH INTEREST IN ME.
IT'S OCCURRED TO ME THAT I MIGHT BE GOING CRAZY... YOU KNOW, LIKE JOE.
BUT THEN CRAZY JUST SEEMS TO BE THE NATURAL ORDER OF THINGS FOR ME NOW.
HI, BABY. HOW WAS SCHOOL?
INSULTING TO MY INTELLIGENCE.
THAT'S NICE... I CAN'T BELIEVE THEY GET AWAY W CHARGING NINE HUND DOLLARS FOR A BOT OF FLONASE...
MY FATHER LOST HIS JOB AND HIS INSURANCE A YEAR AGO.
MOM! THAT HOSPITAL BILL IS FOR EIGHTY FOUR THOUSAND DOLLARS!
THEN CAME THE STROK

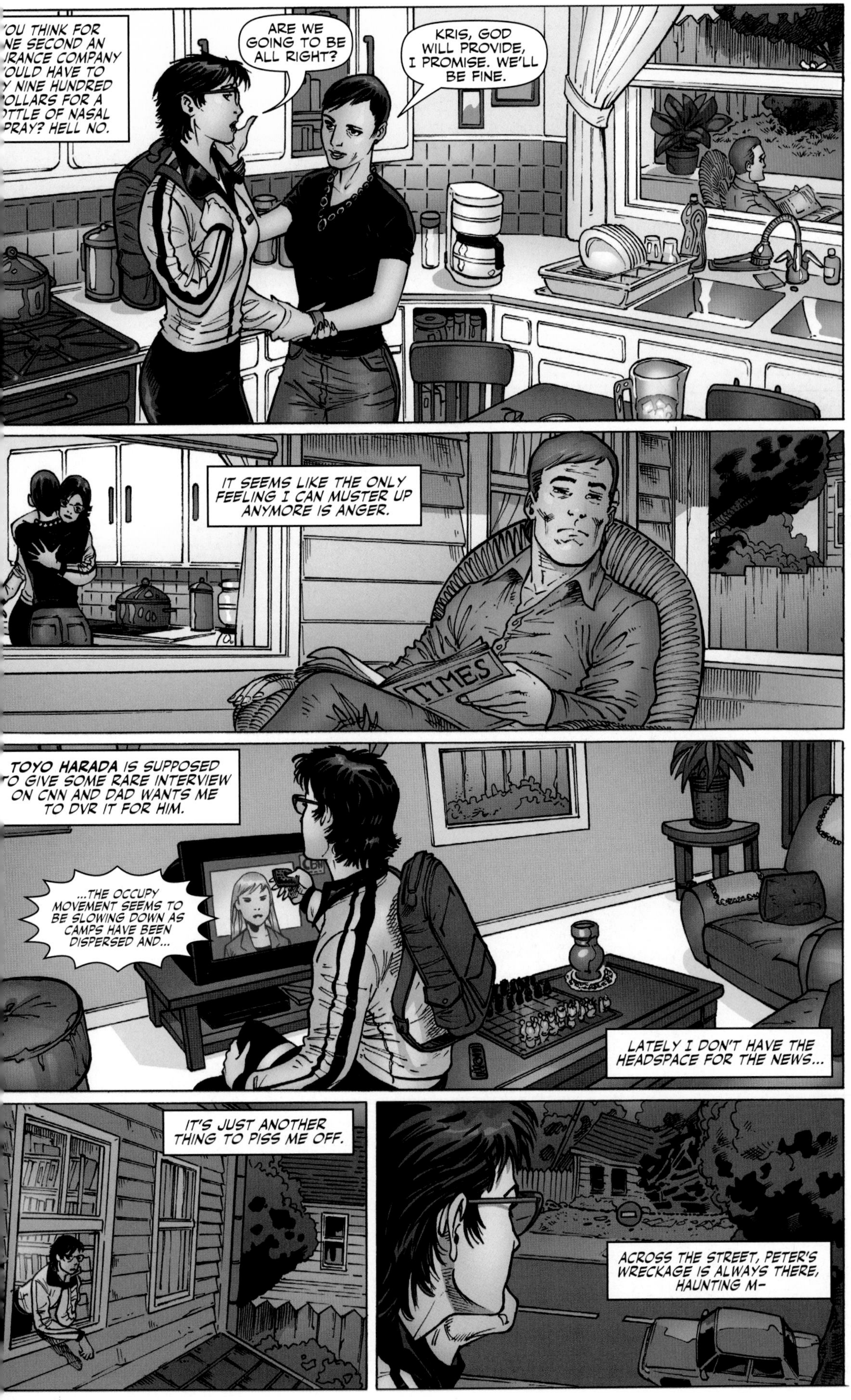

YOU THINK FOR ONE SECOND AN INSURANCE COMPANY WOULD HAVE TO PAY NINE HUNDRED DOLLARS FOR A BOTTLE OF NASAL SPRAY? HELL NO.
ARE WE GOING TO BE ALL RIGHT?
KRIS, GOD WILL PROVIDE, I PROMISE. WE'LL BE FINE.
IT SEEMS LIKE THE ONLY FEELING I CAN MUSTER UP ANYMORE IS ANGER.
TIMES
TOYO HARADA IS SUPPOSED TO GIVE SOME RARE INTERVIEW ON CNN AND DAD WANTS ME TO DVR IT FOR HIM.
...THE OCCUPY MOVEMENT SEEMS TO BE SLOWING DOWN AS CAMPS HAVE BEEN DISPERSED AND...
LATELY I DON'T HAVE THE HEADSPACE FOR THE NEWS...
IT'S JUST ANOTHER THING TO PISS ME OFF.
ACROSS THE STREET, PETER'S WRECKAGE IS ALWAYS THERE, HAUNTING M–

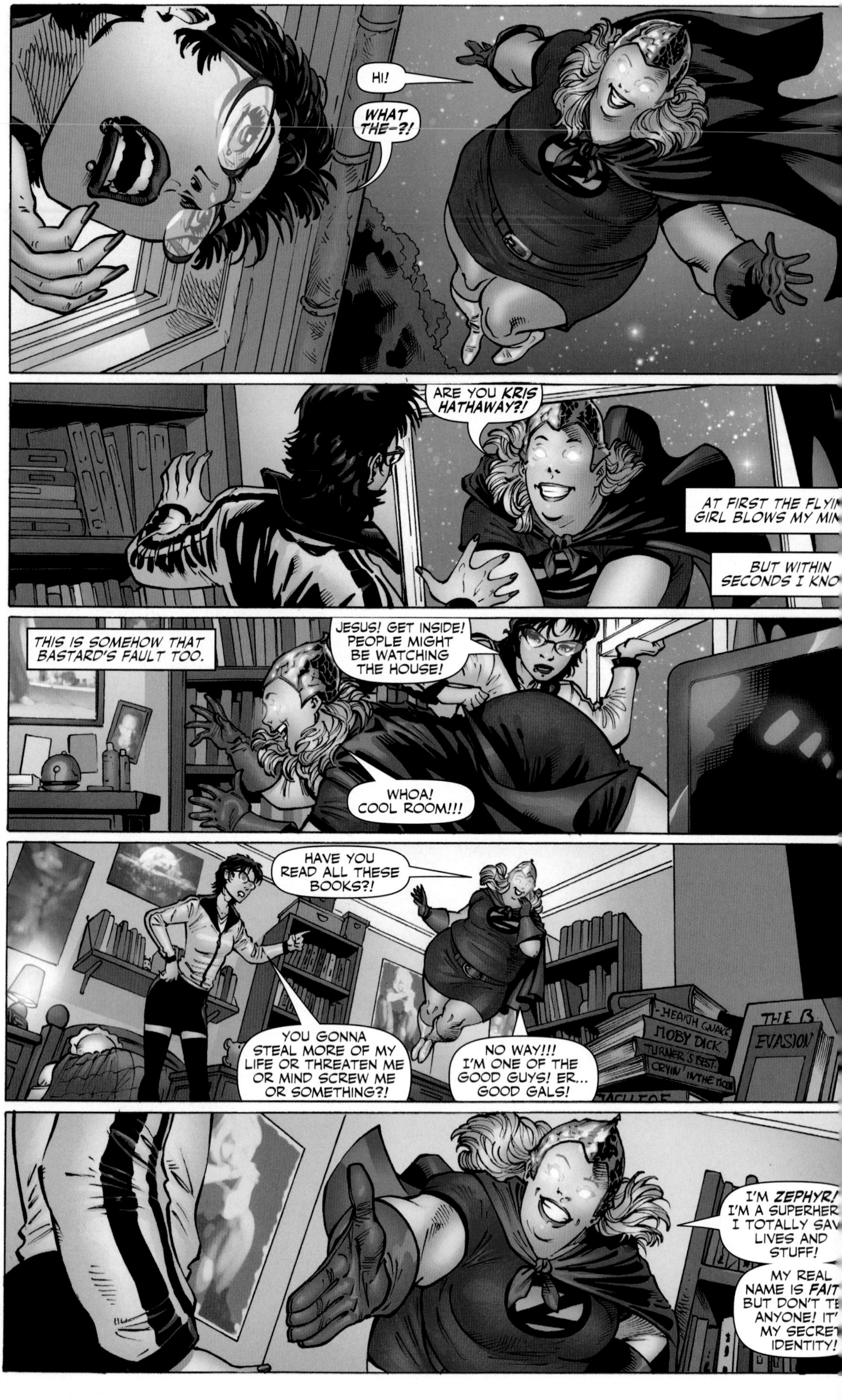
HI!
WHAT THE-?!
ARE YOU KRIS HATHAWAY?!
AT FIRST THE FLYIN
GIRL BLOWS MY MIN
BUT WITHIN SECONDS I KNO
THIS IS SOMEHOW THAT BASTARD'S FAULT TOO.
JESUS! GET INSIDE! PEOPLE MIGHT BE WATCHING THE HOUSE!
WHOA! COOL ROOM!!!
HAVE YOU READ ALL THESE BOOKS?!
YOU GONNA STEAL MORE OF MY LIFE OR THREATEN ME OR MIND SCREW ME OR SOMETHING?!
NO WAY!!! I'M ONE OF THE GOOD GUYS! ER... GOOD GALS!
MOBY DICK
EVASION
I'M ZEPHYR! I'M A SUPERHER I TOTALLY SAV LIVES AND STUFF!
MY REAL NAME IS FAIT BUT DON'T TE ANYONE! IT' MY SECRET IDENTITY!

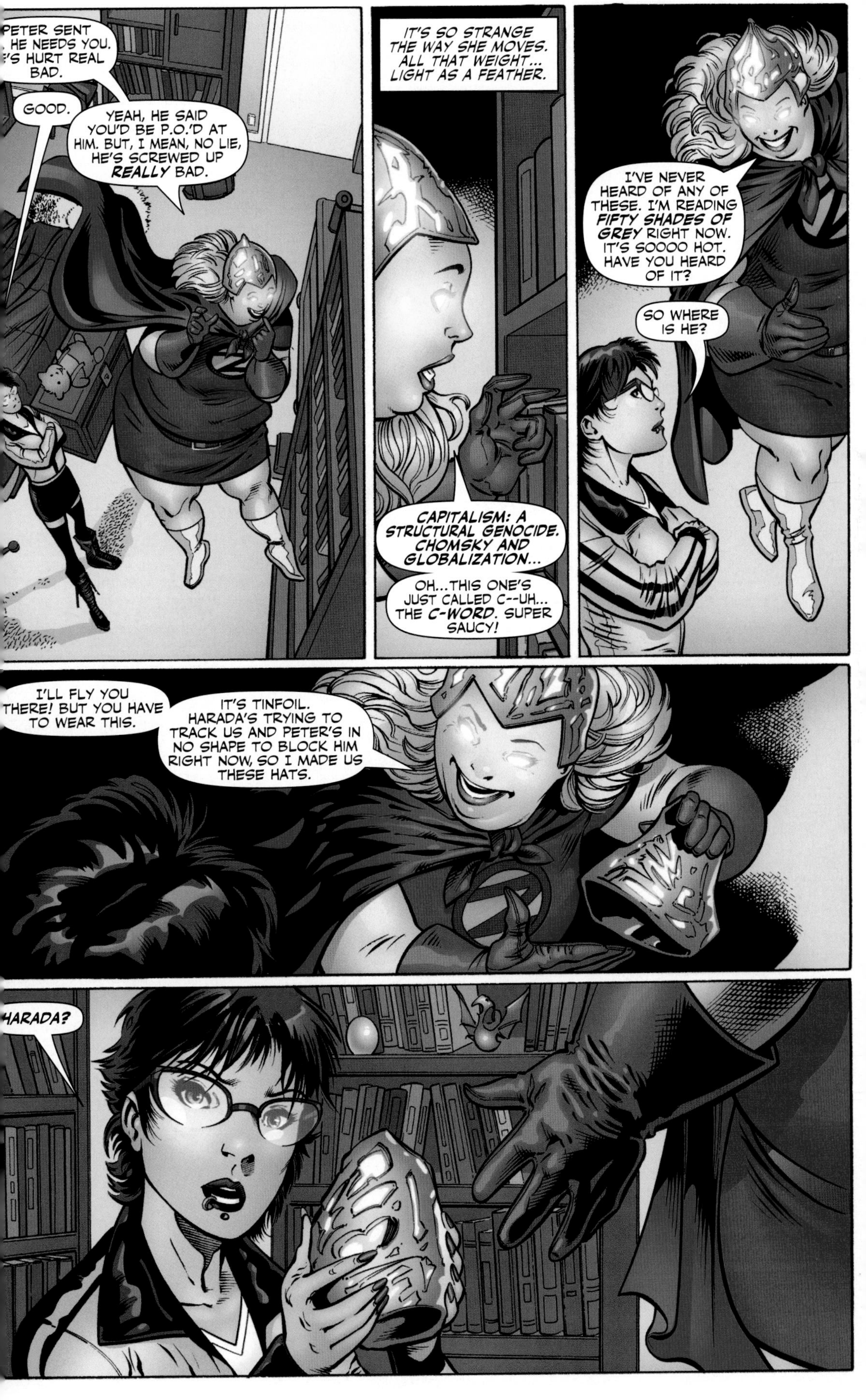
PETER SENT . HE NEEDS YOU. 'S HURT REAL BAD.
GOOD.
YEAH, HE SAID YOU'D BE P.O.'D AT HIM. BUT, I MEAN, NO LIE, HE'S SCREWED UP REALLY BAD.
IT'S SO STRANGE THE WAY SHE MOVES. ALL THAT WEIGHT... LIGHT AS A FEATHER.
CAPITALISM: A STRUCTURAL GENOCIDE. CHOMSKY AND GLOBALIZATION...
OH...THIS ONE'S JUST CALLED C--UH... THE C-WORD. SUPER SAUCY!
I'VE NEVER HEARD OF ANY OF THESE. I'M READING FIFTY SHADES OF GREY RIGHT NOW. IT'S SOOOO HOT. HAVE YOU HEARD OF IT?
SO WHERE IS HE?
I'LL FLY YOU THERE! BUT YOU HAVE TO WEAR THIS.
IT'S TINFOIL. HARADA'S TRYING TO TRACK US AND PETER'S IN NO SHAPE TO BLOCK HIM RIGHT NOW, SO I MADE US THESE HATS.
HARADA?

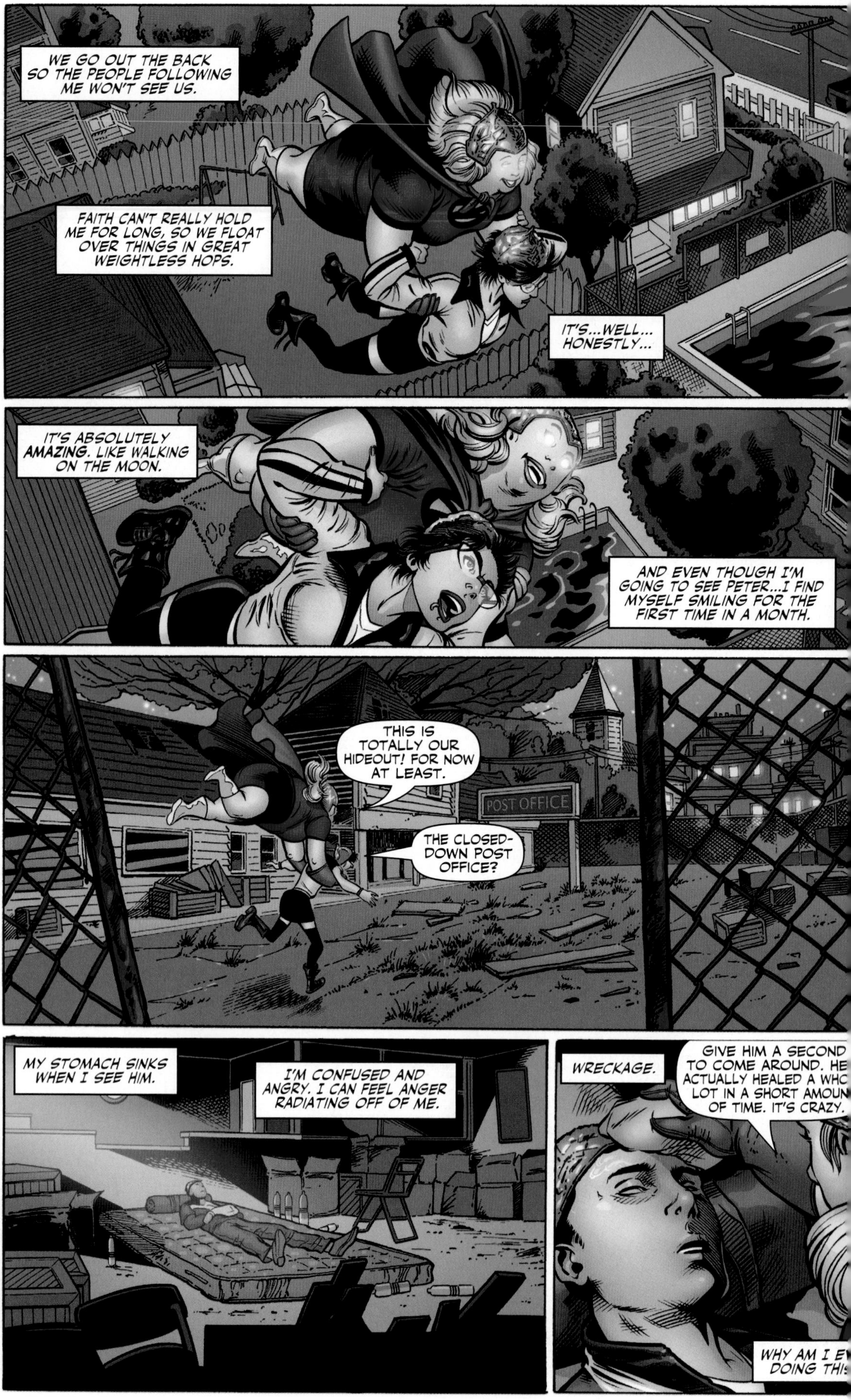
WE GO OUT THE BACK SO THE PEOPLE FOLLOWING ME WON'T SEE US.
FAITH CAN'T REALLY HOLD ME FOR LONG, SO WE FLOAT OVER THINGS IN GREAT WEIGHTLESS HOPS.
IT'S...WELL... HONESTLY...
IT'S ABSOLUTELY **AMAZING**. LIKE WALKING ON THE MOON.
AND EVEN THOUGH I'M GOING TO SEE PETER...I FIND MYSELF SMILING FOR THE FIRST TIME IN A MONTH.
THIS IS TOTALLY OUR HIDEOUT! FOR NOW AT LEAST.
POST OFFICE
THE CLOSED-DOWN POST OFFICE?
MY STOMACH SINKS WHEN I SEE HIM.
I'M CONFUSED AND ANGRY. I CAN FEEL ANGER RADIATING OFF OF ME.
WRECKAGE.
GIVE HIM A SECOND TO COME AROUND. HE ACTUALLY HEALED A WHO LOT IN A SHORT AMOUN OF TIME. IT'S CRAZY.
WHY AM I E DOING THI

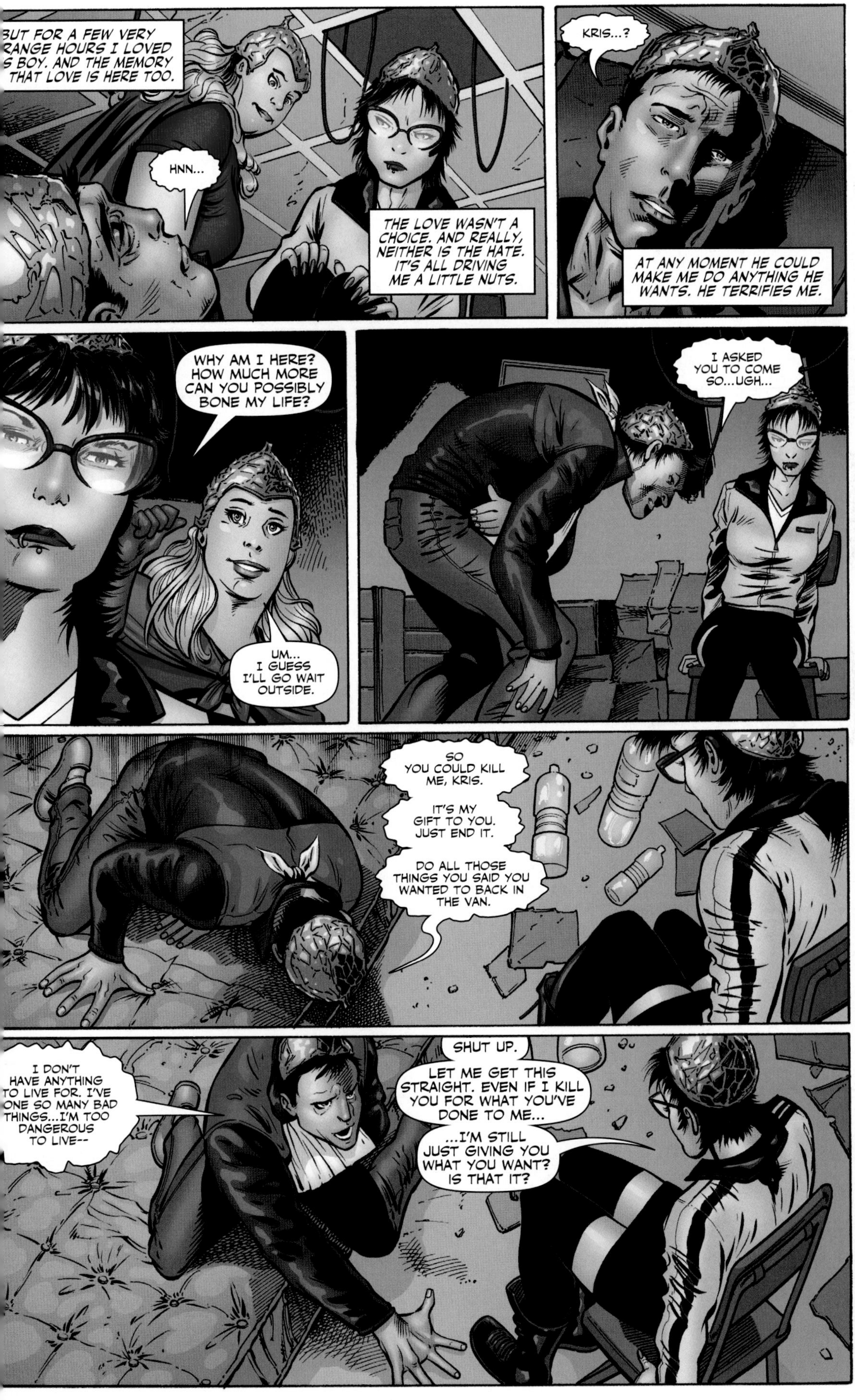

BUT FOR A FEW VERY RANGE HOURS I LOVED S BOY. AND THE MEMORY THAT LOVE IS HERE TOO.
HNN...
THE LOVE WASN'T A CHOICE. AND REALLY, NEITHER IS THE HATE. IT'S ALL DRIVING ME A LITTLE NUTS.
KRIS...?
AT ANY MOMENT HE COULD MAKE ME DO ANYTHING HE WANTS. HE TERRIFIES ME.
WHY AM I HERE? HOW MUCH MORE CAN YOU POSSIBLY BONE MY LIFE?
UM... I GUESS I'LL GO WAIT OUTSIDE.
I ASKED YOU TO COME SO...UGH...
SO YOU COULD KILL ME, KRIS.
IT'S MY GIFT TO YOU. JUST END IT.
DO ALL THOSE THINGS YOU SAID YOU WANTED TO BACK IN THE VAN.
I DON'T HAVE ANYTHING TO LIVE FOR. I'VE ONE SO MANY BAD THINGS...I'M TOO DANGEROUS TO LIVE--
SHUT UP.
LET ME GET THIS STRAIGHT. EVEN IF I KILL YOU FOR WHAT YOU'VE DONE TO ME...
...I'M STILL JUST GIVING YOU WHAT YOU WANT? IS THAT IT?

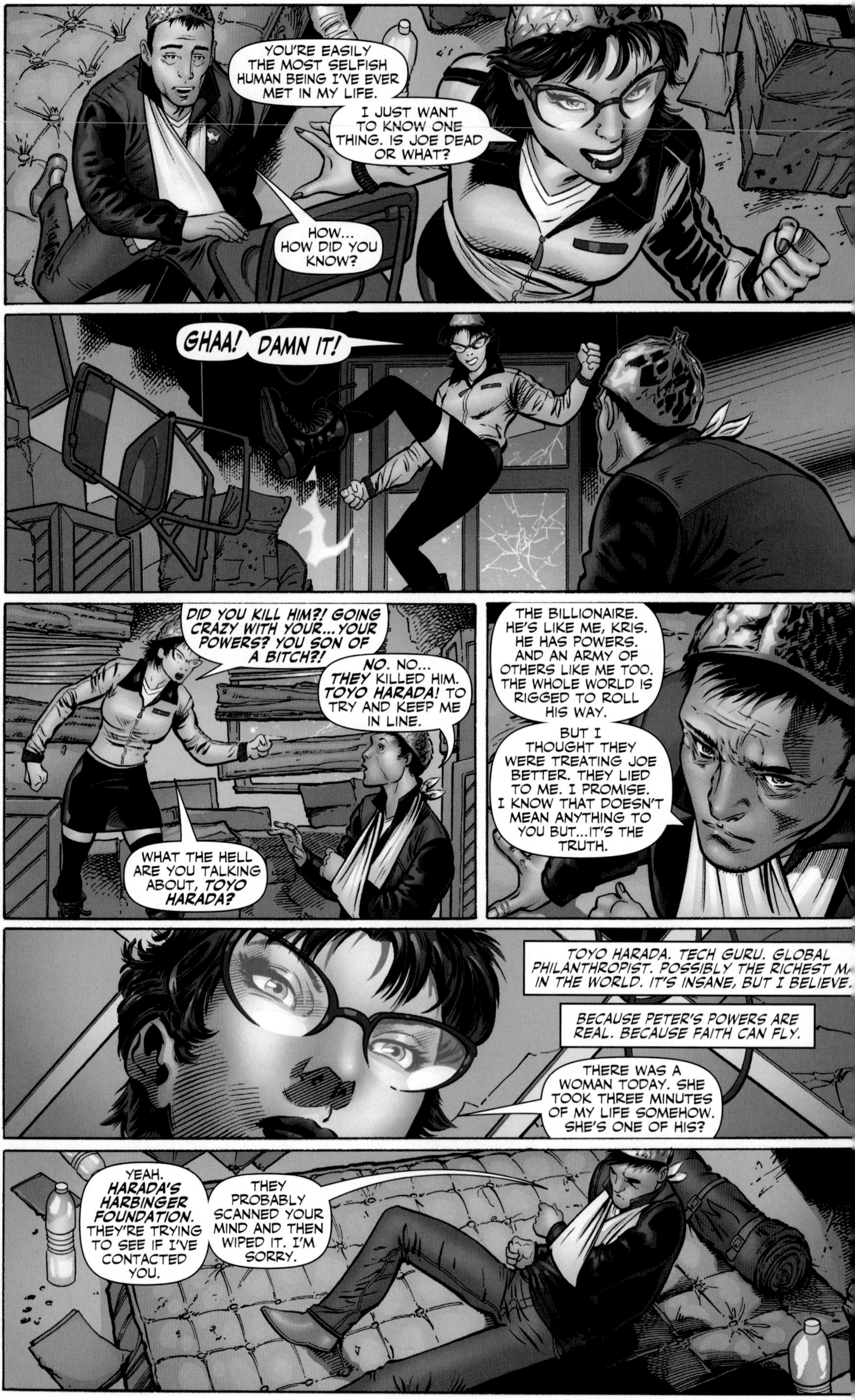

YOU'RE EASILY THE MOST SELFISH HUMAN BEING I'VE EVER MET IN MY LIFE.
I JUST WANT TO KNOW ONE THING. IS JOE DEAD OR WHAT?
HOW... HOW DID YOU KNOW?
GHAA!
DAMN IT!
DID YOU KILL HIM?! GOING CRAZY WITH YOUR...YOUR POWERS? YOU SON OF A BITCH?!
NO. NO... THEY KILLED HIM. TOYO HARADA! TO TRY AND KEEP ME IN LINE.
WHAT THE HELL ARE YOU TALKING ABOUT, TOYO HARADA?
THE BILLIONAIRE. HE'S LIKE ME, KRIS. HE HAS POWERS. AND AN ARMY OF OTHERS LIKE ME TOO. THE WHOLE WORLD IS RIGGED TO ROLL HIS WAY.
BUT I THOUGHT THEY WERE TREATING JOE BETTER. THEY LIED TO ME. I PROMISE. I KNOW THAT DOESN'T MEAN ANYTHING TO YOU BUT...IT'S THE TRUTH.
TOYO HARADA. TECH GURU. GLOBAL PHILANTHROPIST. POSSIBLY THE RICHEST MA IN THE WORLD. IT'S INSANE, BUT I BELIEVE.
BECAUSE PETER'S POWERS ARE REAL. BECAUSE FAITH CAN FLY.
THERE WAS A WOMAN TODAY. SHE TOOK THREE MINUTES OF MY LIFE SOMEHOW. SHE'S ONE OF HIS?
YEAH. HARADA'S HARBINGER FOUNDATION. THEY'RE TRYING TO SEE IF I'VE CONTACTED YOU.
THEY PROBABLY SCANNED YOUR MIND AND THEN WIPED IT. I'M SORRY.

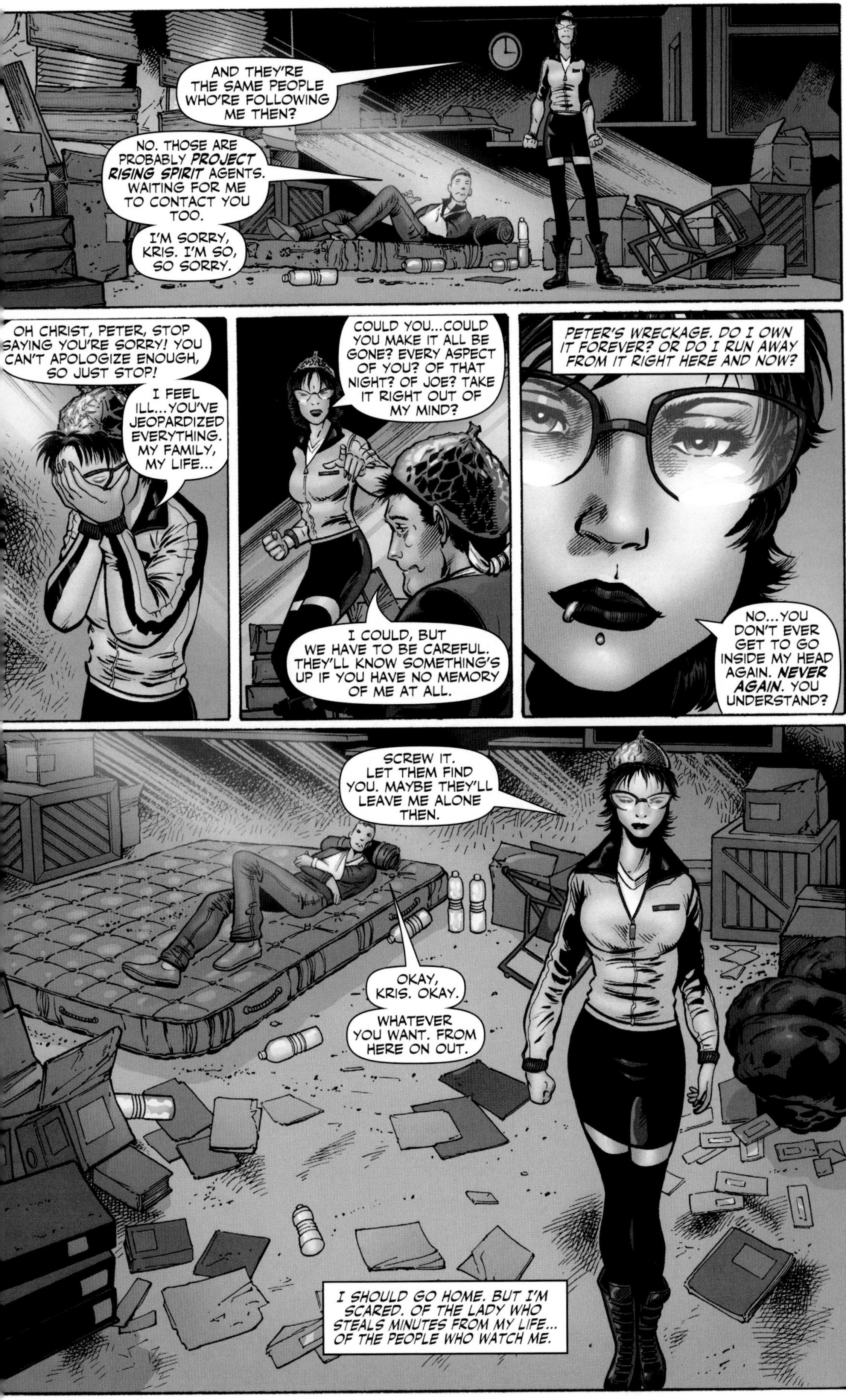
AND THEY'RE THE SAME PEOPLE WHO'RE FOLLOWING ME THEN?
NO. THOSE ARE PROBABLY PROJECT RISING SPIRIT AGENTS. WAITING FOR ME TO CONTACT YOU TOO.
I'M SORRY, KRIS. I'M SO, SO SORRY.
OH CHRIST, PETER, STOP SAYING YOU'RE SORRY! YOU CAN'T APOLOGIZE ENOUGH, SO JUST STOP!
I FEEL ILL...YOU'VE JEOPARDIZED EVERYTHING. MY FAMILY, MY LIFE...
COULD YOU...COULD YOU MAKE IT ALL BE GONE? EVERY ASPECT OF YOU? OF THAT NIGHT? OF JOE? TAKE IT RIGHT OUT OF MY MIND?
I COULD, BUT WE HAVE TO BE CAREFUL. THEY'LL KNOW SOMETHING'S UP IF YOU HAVE NO MEMORY OF ME AT ALL.
PETER'S WRECKAGE. DO I OWN IT FOREVER? OR DO I RUN AWAY FROM IT RIGHT HERE AND NOW?
NO...YOU DON'T EVER GET TO GO INSIDE MY HEAD AGAIN. NEVER AGAIN. YOU UNDERSTAND?
SCREW IT. LET THEM FIND YOU. MAYBE THEY'LL LEAVE ME ALONE THEN.
OKAY, KRIS. OKAY.
WHATEVER YOU WANT. FROM HERE ON OUT.
I SHOULD GO HOME. BUT I'M SCARED. OF THE LADY WHO STEALS MINUTES FROM MY LIFE... OF THE PEOPLE WHO WATCH ME.

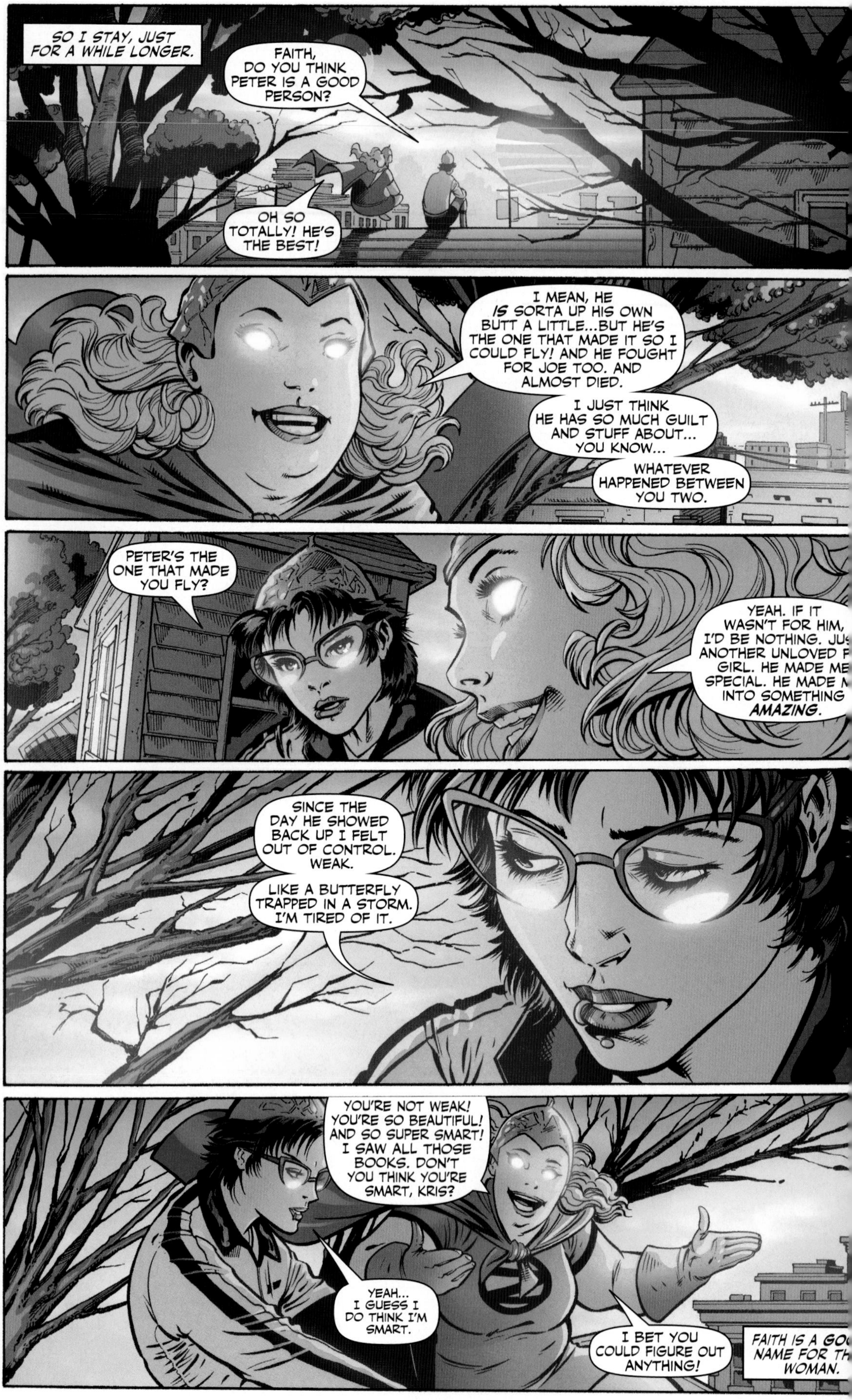
SO I STAY, JUST FOR A WHILE LONGER.
FAITH, DO YOU THINK PETER IS A GOOD PERSON?
OH SO TOTALLY! HE'S THE BEST!
I MEAN, HE *IS* SORTA UP HIS OWN BUTT A LITTLE...BUT HE'S THE ONE THAT MADE IT SO I COULD FLY! AND HE FOUGHT FOR JOE TOO. AND ALMOST DIED.
I JUST THINK HE HAS SO MUCH GUILT AND STUFF ABOUT... YOU KNOW...
WHATEVER HAPPENED BETWEEN YOU TWO.
PETER'S THE ONE THAT MADE YOU FLY?
YEAH. IF IT WASN'T FOR HIM, I'D BE NOTHING. JUS ANOTHER UNLOVED GIRL. HE MADE ME SPECIAL. HE MADE INTO SOMETHING ***AMAZING***.
SINCE THE DAY HE SHOWED BACK UP I FELT OUT OF CONTROL. WEAK.
LIKE A BUTTERFLY TRAPPED IN A STORM. I'M TIRED OF IT.
YOU'RE NOT WEAK! YOU'RE SO BEAUTIFUL! AND SO SUPER SMART! I SAW ALL THOSE BOOKS. DON'T YOU THINK YOU'RE SMART, KRIS?
YEAH... I GUESS I DO THINK I'M SMART.
I BET YOU COULD FIGURE OUT ANYTHING!
FAITH IS A GO NAME FOR TH WOMAN.

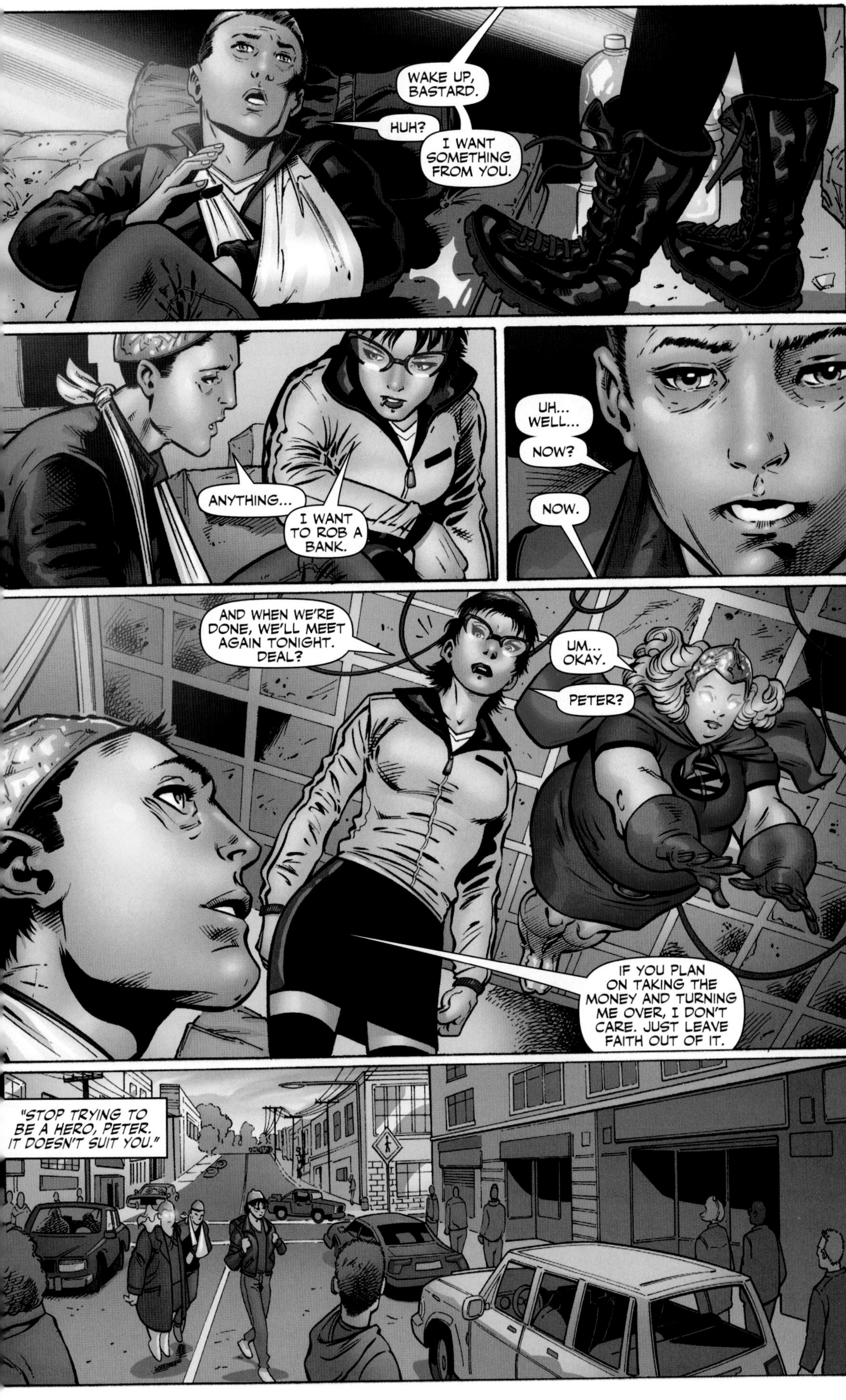
WAKE UP, BASTARD.
HUH?
I WANT SOMETHING FROM YOU.
ANYTHING...
I WANT TO ROB A BANK.
UH... WELL...
NOW?
NOW.
AND WHEN WE'RE DONE, WE'LL MEET AGAIN TONIGHT. DEAL?
UM... OKAY.
PETER?
IF YOU PLAN ON TAKING THE MONEY AND TURNING ME OVER, I DON'T CARE. JUST LEAVE FAITH OUT OF IT.
"STOP TRYING TO BE A HERO, PETER. IT DOESN'T SUIT YOU."

OPEN UP.

DO EVERYTHING SHE SAYS.

HELLO, CITIZENS OF THE NATION WITH MORE VIOLENT LABOR DISPUTES THAN ANY OTHER IN THE WESTERN WORLD!

HAND OVER THE CASH, PLEASE.

YES, MA'AM.

COULD IT BE ARGUED THAT I'M LETTING PETER DO TO OTHERS WHAT HE DID TO ME? MAYBE.

I DON'T THINK THE EMOTIONAL VIOLATION IS THE SAME THOUGH. NOT EVEN CLOSE.

DON'T WORRY. IT'S NOT REALLY YOUR MONEY AND IT WASN'T GOING TO TRICKLE DOWN ANYWAY.

THAT'S HOW I JUSTIFY IT ANYWAY.

FORGET.

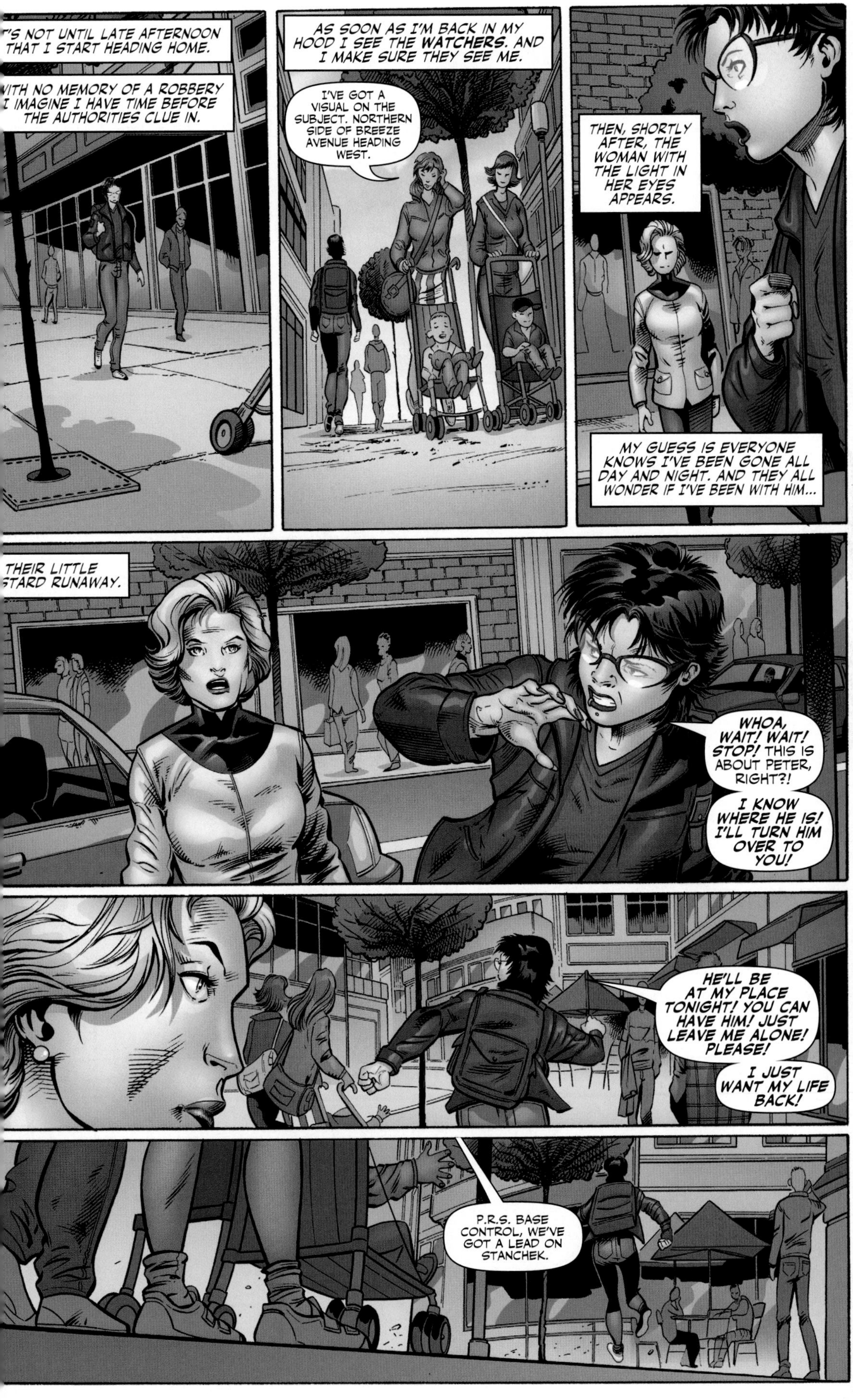
'S NOT UNTIL LATE AFTERNOON THAT I START HEADING HOME.
ITH NO MEMORY OF A ROBBERY I IMAGINE I HAVE TIME BEFORE THE AUTHORITIES CLUE IN.
AS SOON AS I'M BACK IN MY HOOD I SEE THE WATCHERS. AND I MAKE SURE THEY SEE ME.
I'VE GOT A VISUAL ON THE SUBJECT. NORTHERN SIDE OF BREEZE AVENUE HEADING WEST.
THEN, SHORTLY AFTER, THE WOMAN WITH THE LIGHT IN HER EYES APPEARS.
MY GUESS IS EVERYONE KNOWS I'VE BEEN GONE ALL DAY AND NIGHT. AND THEY ALL WONDER IF I'VE BEEN WITH HIM...
THEIR LITTLE STARD RUNAWAY.
WHOA, WAIT! WAIT! STOP! THIS IS ABOUT PETER, RIGHT?!
I KNOW WHERE HE IS! I'LL TURN HIM OVER TO YOU!
HE'LL BE AT MY PLACE TONIGHT! YOU CAN HAVE HIM! JUST LEAVE ME ALONE! PLEASE!
I JUST WANT MY LIFE BACK!
P.R.S. BASE CONTROL, WE'VE GOT A LEAD ON STANCHEK.

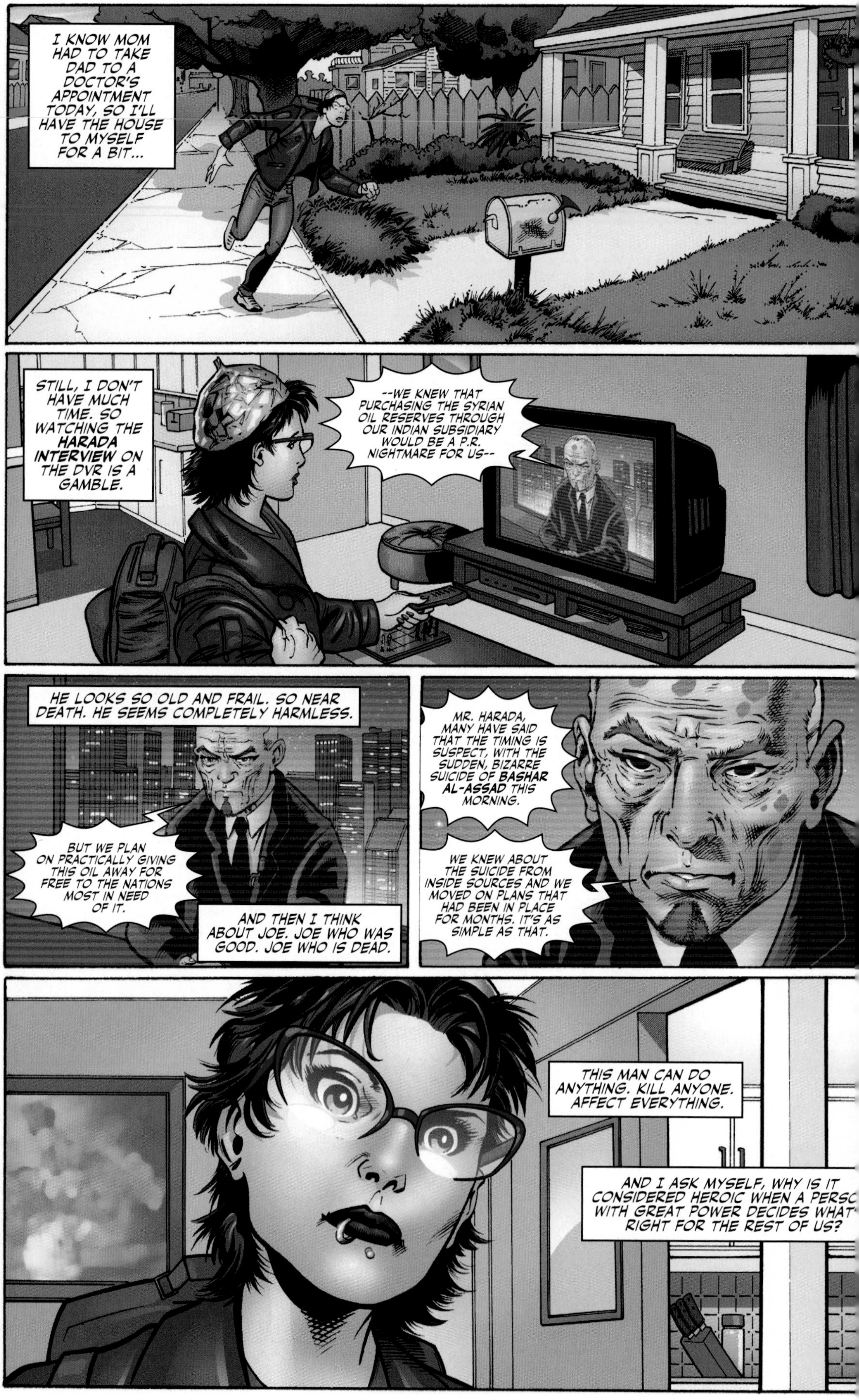
I KNOW MOM HAD TO TAKE DAD TO A DOCTOR'S APPOINTMENT TODAY, SO I'LL HAVE THE HOUSE TO MYSELF FOR A BIT...
STILL, I DON'T HAVE MUCH TIME. SO WATCHING THE HARADA INTERVIEW ON THE DVR IS A GAMBLE.
--WE KNEW THAT PURCHASING THE SYRIAN OIL RESERVES THROUGH OUR INDIAN SUBSIDIARY WOULD BE A P.R. NIGHTMARE FOR US--
HE LOOKS SO OLD AND FRAIL. SO NEAR DEATH. HE SEEMS COMPLETELY HARMLESS.
BUT WE PLAN ON PRACTICALLY GIVING THIS OIL AWAY FOR FREE TO THE NATIONS MOST IN NEED OF IT.
AND THEN I THINK ABOUT JOE. JOE WHO WAS GOOD. JOE WHO IS DEAD.
MR. HARADA, MANY HAVE SAID THAT THE TIMING IS SUSPECT, WITH THE SUDDEN, BIZARRE SUICIDE OF BASHAR AL-ASSAD THIS MORNING.
WE KNEW ABOUT THE SUICIDE FROM INSIDE SOURCES AND WE MOVED ON PLANS THAT HAD BEEN IN PLACE FOR MONTHS. IT'S AS SIMPLE AS THAT.
THIS MAN CAN DO ANYTHING. KILL ANYONE. AFFECT EVERYTHING.
AND I ASK MYSELF, WHY IS IT CONSIDERED HEROIC WHEN A PERSO WITH GREAT POWER DECIDES WHAT RIGHT FOR THE REST OF US?

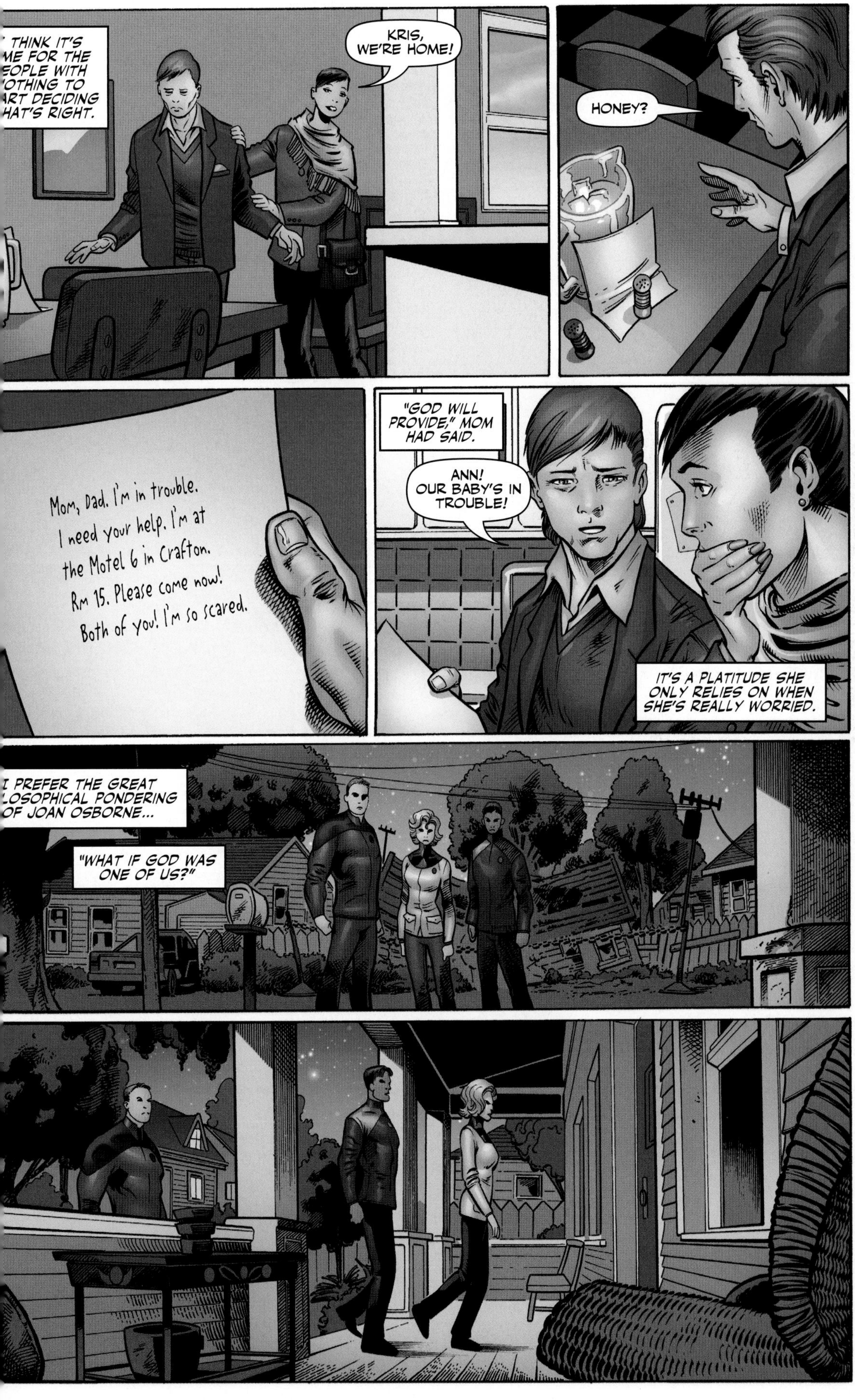
THINK IT'S ME FOR THE EOPLE WITH OTHING TO ART DECIDING HAT'S RIGHT.
KRIS, WE'RE HOME!
HONEY?
Mom, Dad. I'm in trouble. I need your help. I'm at the Motel 6 in Crafton. Rm 15. Please come now! Both of you! I'm so scared.
"GOD WILL PROVIDE," MOM HAD SAID.
ANN! OUR BABY'S IN TROUBLE!
IT'S A PLATITUDE SHE ONLY RELIES ON WHEN SHE'S REALLY WORRIED.
PREFER THE GREAT LOSOPHICAL PONDERING OF JOAN OSBORNE...
"WHAT IF GOD WAS ONE OF US?"

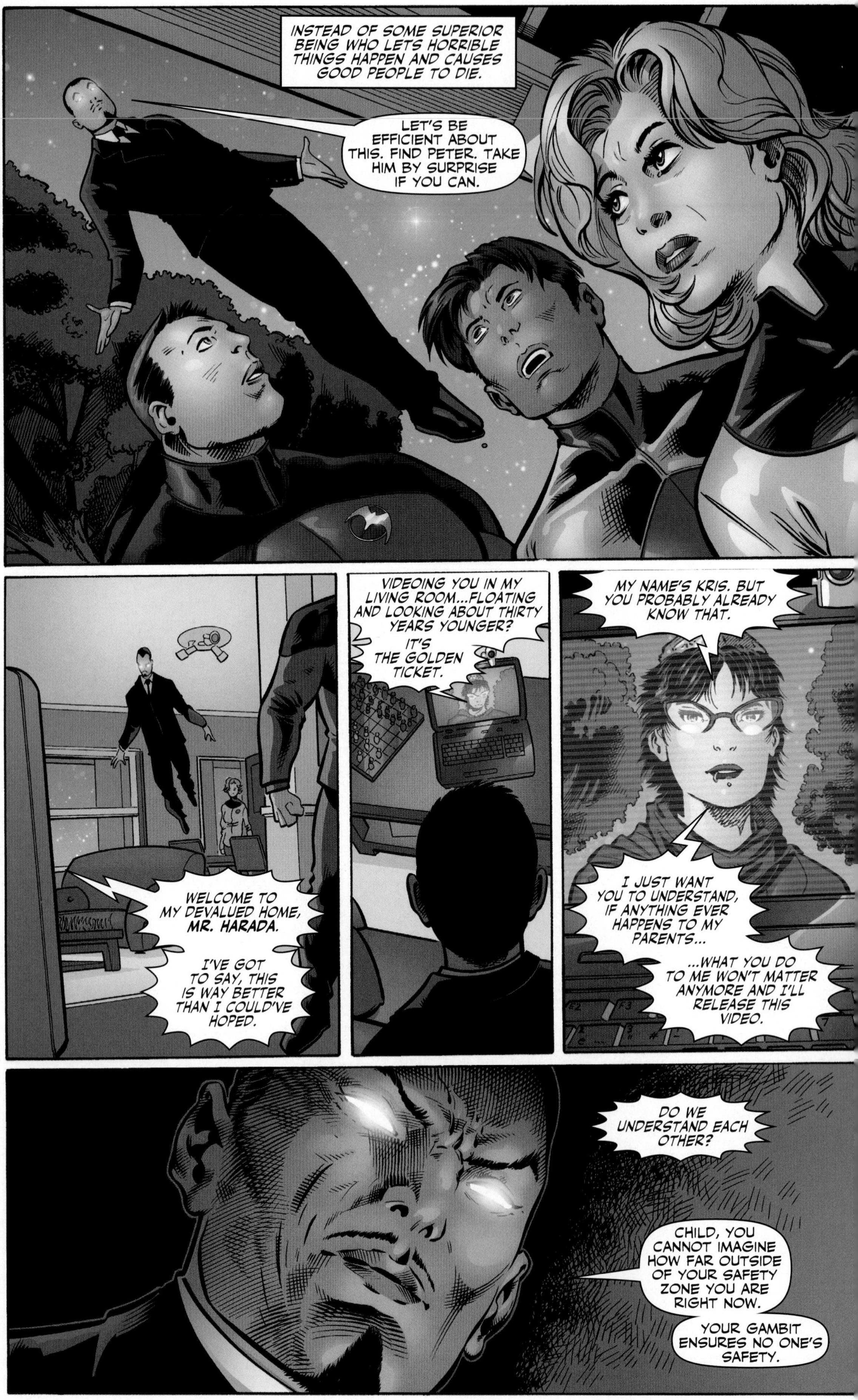
INSTEAD OF SOME SUPERIOR BEING WHO LETS HORRIBLE THINGS HAPPEN AND CAUSES GOOD PEOPLE TO DIE.
LET'S BE EFFICIENT ABOUT THIS. FIND PETER. TAKE HIM BY SURPRISE IF YOU CAN.
WELCOME TO MY DEVALUED HOME, **MR. HARADA.**
I'VE GOT TO SAY, THIS IS WAY BETTER THAN I COULD'VE HOPED.
VIDEOING YOU IN MY LIVING ROOM...FLOATING AND LOOKING ABOUT THIRTY YEARS YOUNGER?
IT'S THE GOLDEN TICKET.
MY NAME'S KRIS. BUT YOU PROBABLY ALREADY KNOW THAT.
I JUST WANT YOU TO UNDERSTAND, IF ANYTHING EVER HAPPENS TO MY PARENTS...
...WHAT YOU DO TO ME WON'T MATTER ANYMORE AND I'LL RELEASE THIS VIDEO.
DO WE UNDERSTAND EACH OTHER?
CHILD, YOU CANNOT IMAGINE HOW FAR OUTSIDE OF YOUR SAFETY ZONE YOU ARE RIGHT NOW.
YOUR GAMBIT ENSURES NO ONE'S SAFETY.

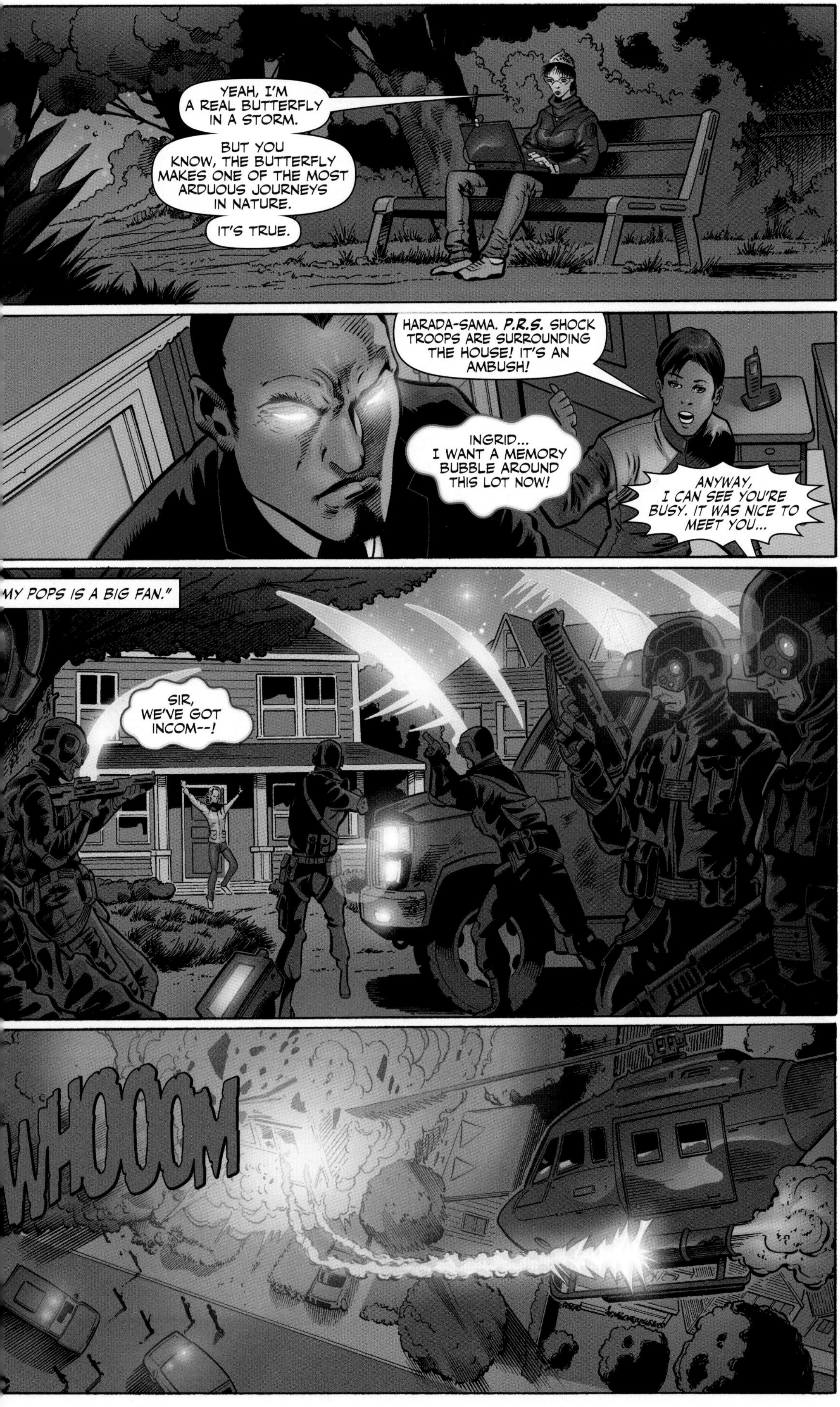

YEAH, I'M A REAL BUTTERFLY IN A STORM.
BUT YOU KNOW, THE BUTTERFLY MAKES ONE OF THE MOST ARDUOUS JOURNEYS IN NATURE.
IT'S TRUE.
HARADA-SAMA. P.R.S. SHOCK TROOPS ARE SURROUNDING THE HOUSE! IT'S AN AMBUSH!
INGRID... I WANT A MEMORY BUBBLE AROUND THIS LOT NOW!
ANYWAY, I CAN SEE YOU'RE BUSY. IT WAS NICE TO MEET YOU...
MY POPS IS A BIG FAN."
SIR, WE'VE GOT INCOM--!
WHOOOM

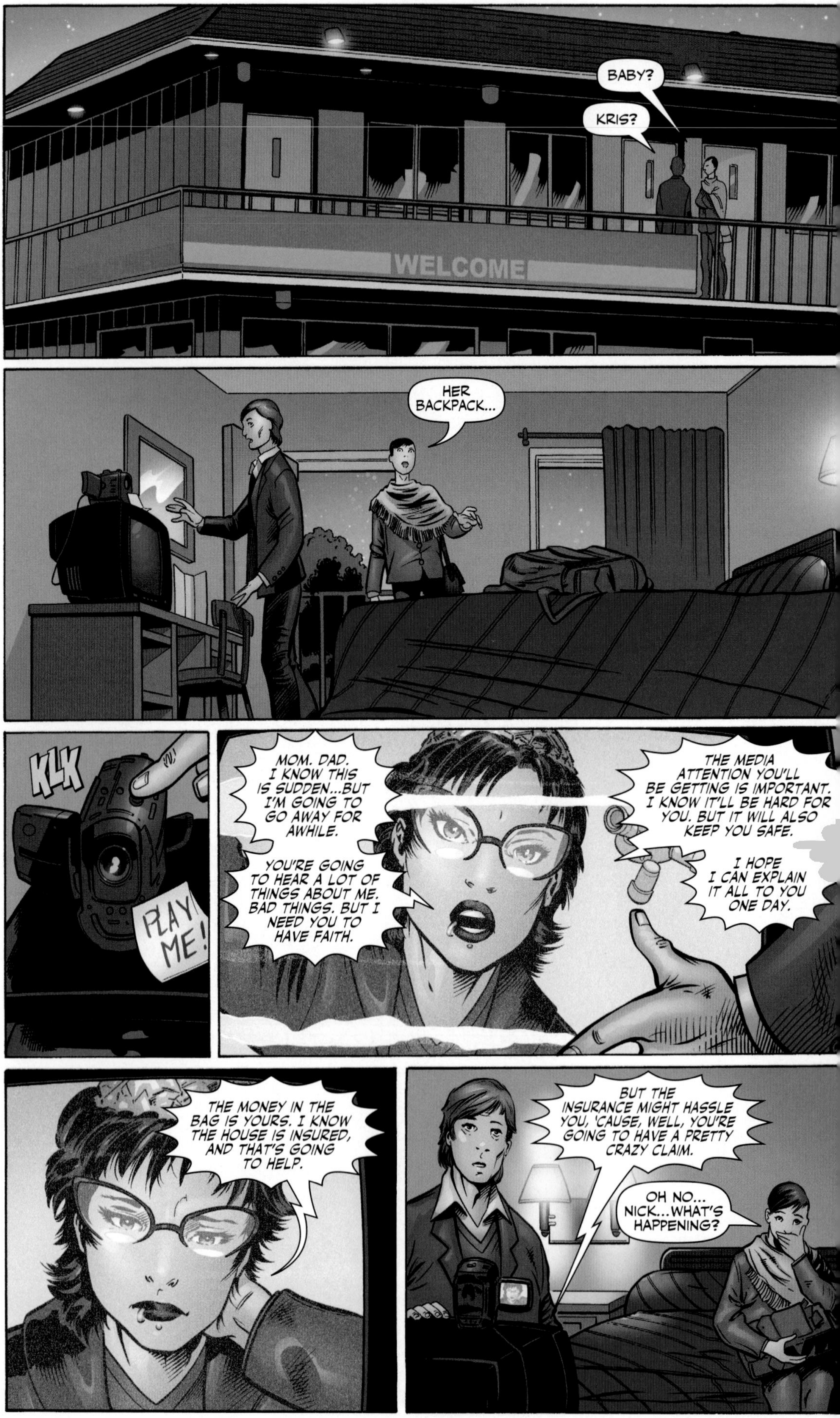
BABY?
KRIS?
HER BACKPACK...
KLK
PLAY ME!
MOM. DAD. I KNOW THIS IS SUDDEN...BUT I'M GOING TO GO AWAY FOR AWHILE.
YOU'RE GOING TO HEAR A LOT OF THINGS ABOUT ME. BAD THINGS. BUT I NEED YOU TO HAVE FAITH.
THE MEDIA ATTENTION YOU'LL BE GETTING IS IMPORTANT. I KNOW IT'LL BE HARD FOR YOU. BUT IT WILL ALSO KEEP YOU SAFE.
I HOPE I CAN EXPLAIN IT ALL TO YOU ONE DAY.
THE MONEY IN THE BAG IS YOURS. I KNOW THE HOUSE IS INSURED, AND THAT'S GOING TO HELP.
BUT THE INSURANCE MIGHT HASSLE YOU, 'CAUSE, WELL, YOU'RE GOING TO HAVE A PRETTY CRAZY CLAIM.
OH NO... NICK...WHAT'S HAPPENING?
WELCOME

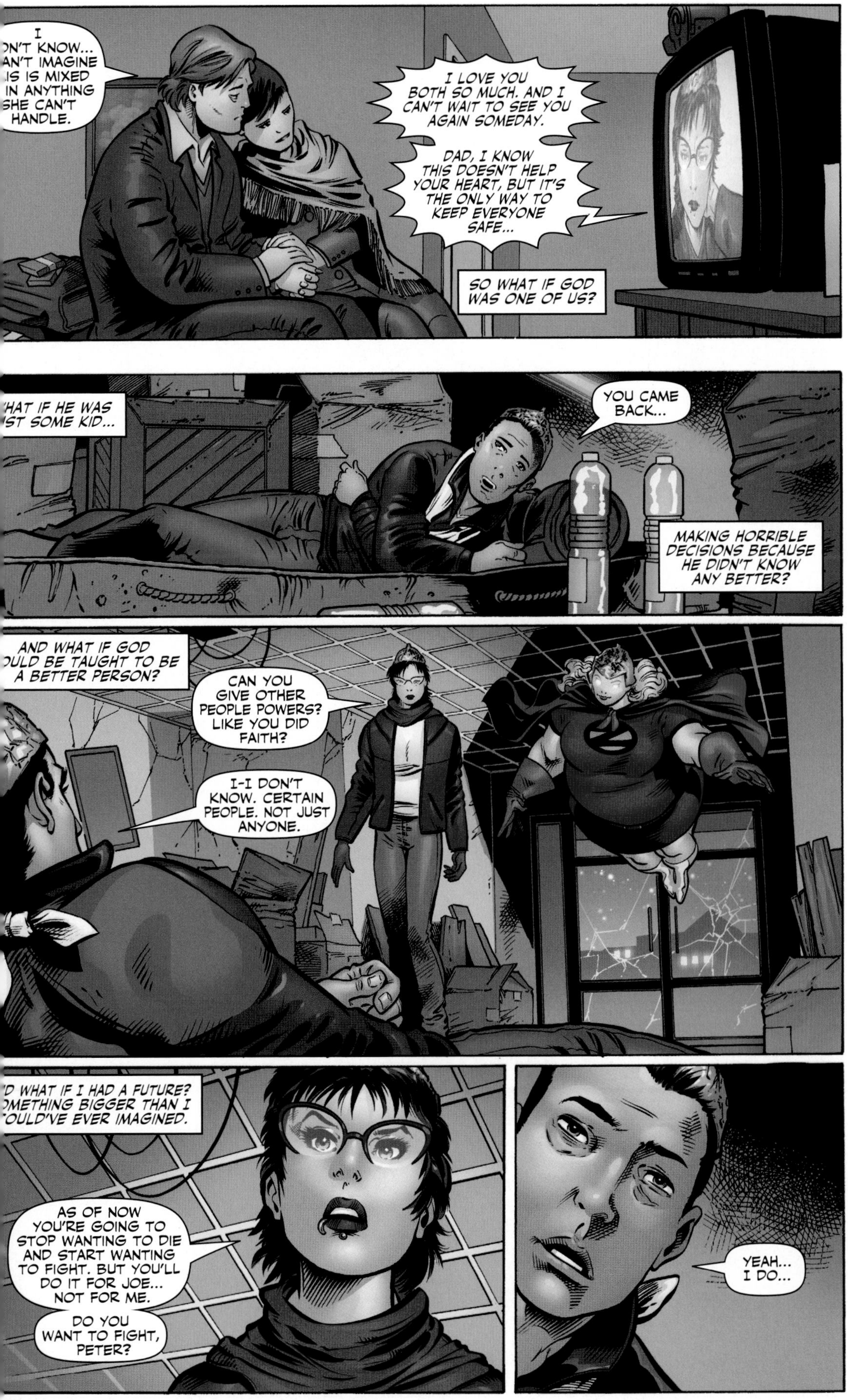

I
ON'T KNOW... AN'T IMAGINE IS IS MIXED IN ANYTHING SHE CAN'T HANDLE.
I LOVE YOU BOTH SO MUCH. AND I CAN'T WAIT TO SEE YOU AGAIN SOMEDAY.
DAD, I KNOW THIS DOESN'T HELP YOUR HEART, BUT IT'S THE ONLY WAY TO KEEP EVERYONE SAFE...
SO WHAT IF GOD WAS ONE OF US?
HAT IF HE WAS ST SOME KID...
YOU CAME BACK...
MAKING HORRIBLE DECISIONS BECAUSE HE DIDN'T KNOW ANY BETTER?
AND WHAT IF GOD OULD BE TAUGHT TO BE A BETTER PERSON?
CAN YOU GIVE OTHER PEOPLE POWERS? LIKE YOU DID FAITH?
I-I DON'T KNOW. CERTAIN PEOPLE. NOT JUST ANYONE.
D WHAT IF I HAD A FUTURE? OMETHING BIGGER THAN I OULD'VE EVER IMAGINED.
AS OF NOW YOU'RE GOING TO STOP WANTING TO DIE AND START WANTING TO FIGHT. BUT YOU'LL DO IT FOR JOE... NOT FOR ME.
DO YOU WANT TO FIGHT, PETER?
YEAH... I DO...

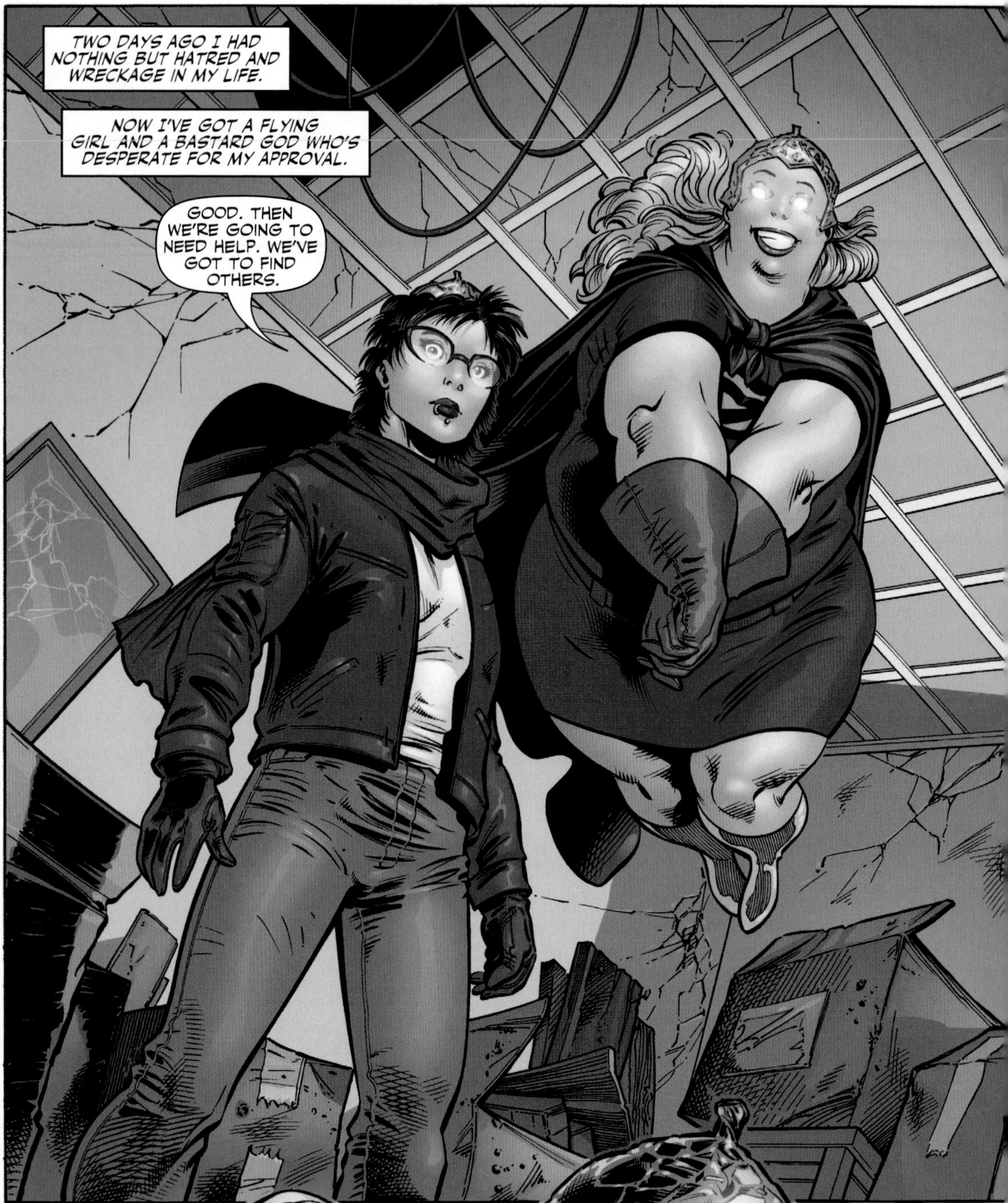
TWO DAYS AGO I HAD NOTHING BUT HATRED AND WRECKAGE IN MY LIFE.
NOW I'VE GOT A FLYING GIRL AND A BASTARD GOD WHO'S DESPERATE FOR MY APPROVAL.
GOOD. THEN WE'RE GOING TO NEED HELP. WE'VE GOT TO FIND OTHERS.

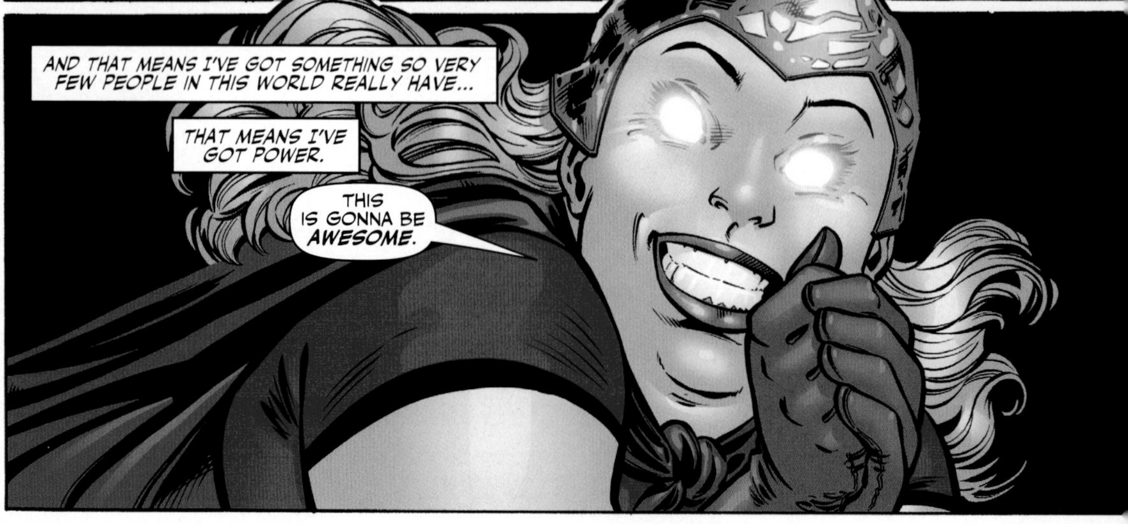
AND THAT MEANS I'VE GOT SOMETHING SO VERY FEW PEOPLE IN THIS WORLD REALLY HAVE...
THAT MEANS I'VE GOT POWER.
THIS IS GONNA BE **AWESOME**.

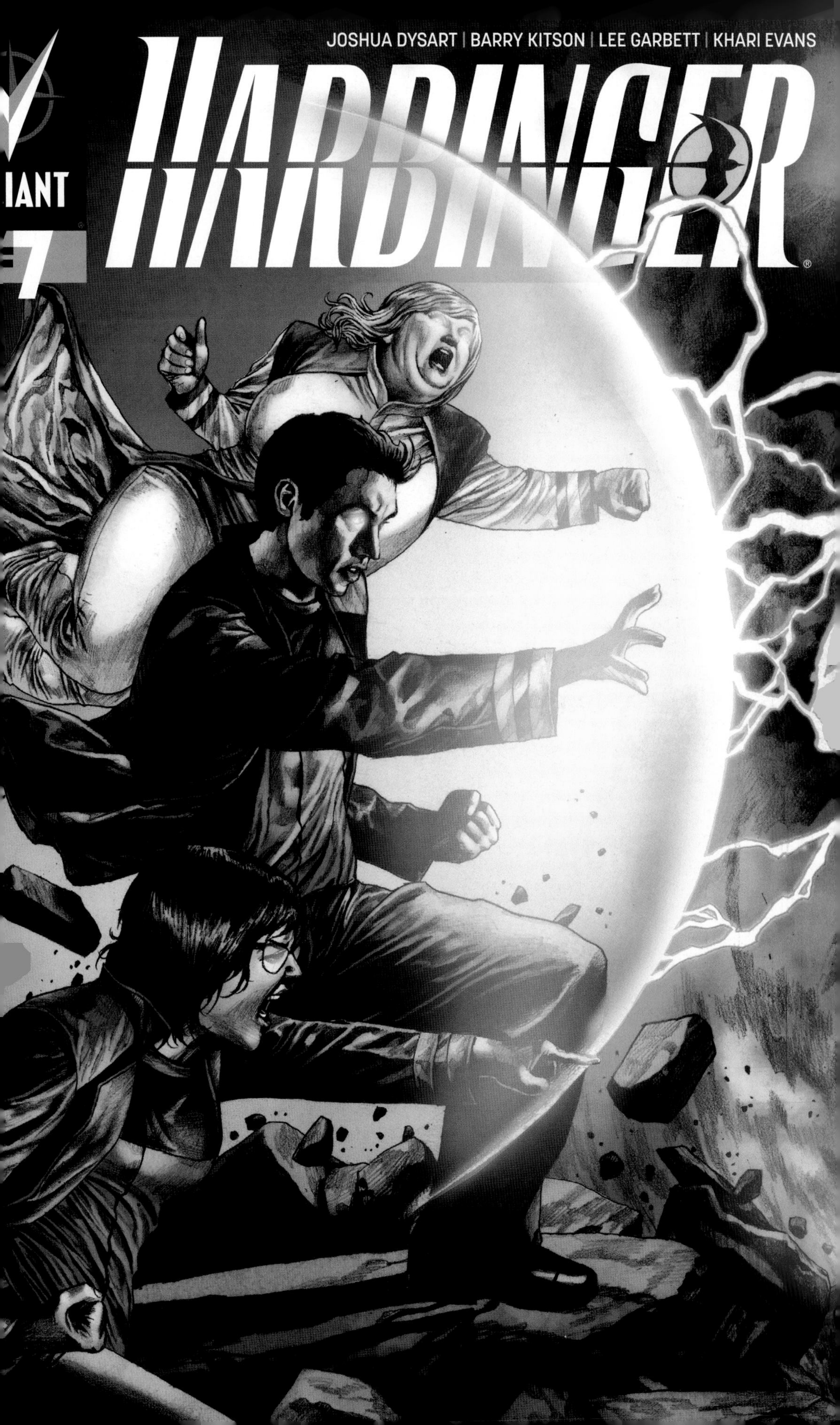
VALIANT
#7
JOSHUA DYSART | BARRY KITSON | LEE GARBETT | KHARI EVANS
HARBINGER

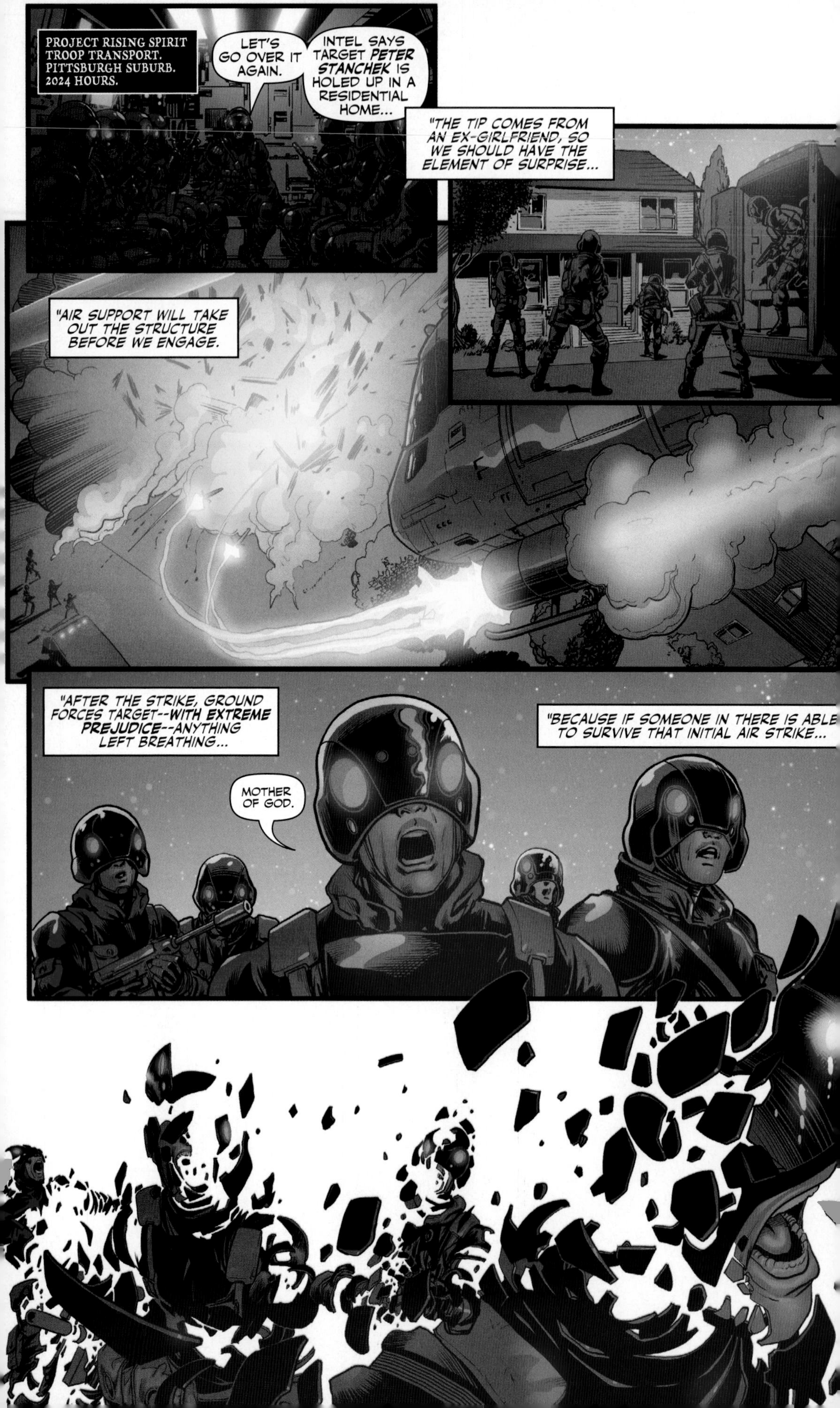

PROJECT RISING SPIRIT TROOP TRANSPORT. PITTSBURGH SUBURB. 2024 HOURS.
LET'S GO OVER IT AGAIN.
INTEL SAYS TARGET **PETER STANCHEK** IS HOLED UP IN A RESIDENTIAL HOME...
"THE TIP COMES FROM AN EX-GIRLFRIEND, SO WE SHOULD HAVE THE ELEMENT OF SURPRISE...
"AIR SUPPORT WILL TAKE OUT THE STRUCTURE BEFORE WE ENGAGE.
"AFTER THE STRIKE, GROUND FORCES TARGET--**WITH EXTREME PREJUDICE**--ANYTHING LEFT BREATHING...
"BECAUSE IF SOMEONE IN THERE IS ABLE TO SURVIVE THAT INITIAL AIR STRIKE...
MOTHER OF GOD.

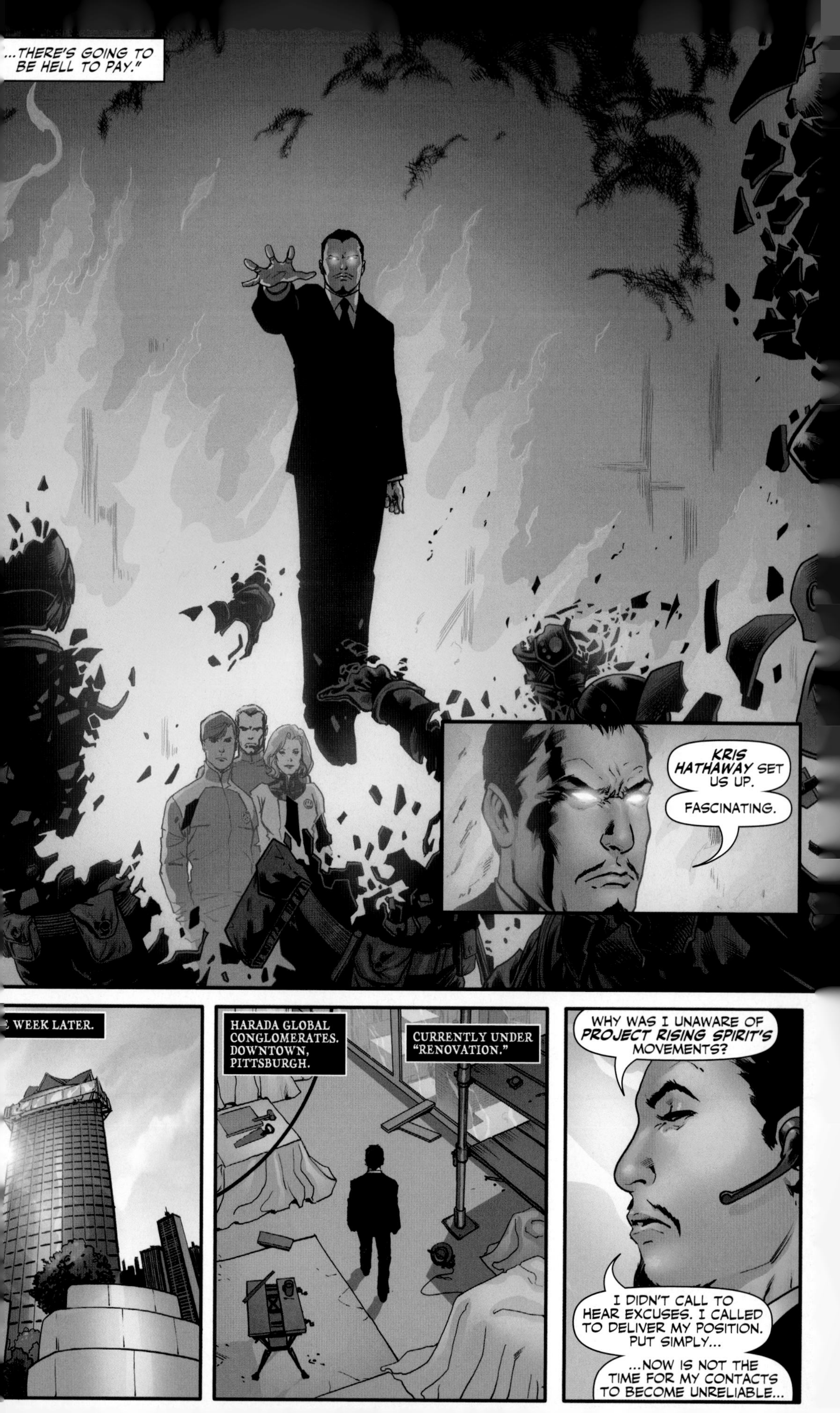

...THERE'S GOING TO BE HELL TO PAY."
KRIS HATHAWAY SET US UP.
FASCINATING.
WEEK LATER.
HARADA GLOBAL CONGLOMERATES. DOWNTOWN, PITTSBURGH.
CURRENTLY UNDER "RENOVATION."
WHY WAS I UNAWARE OF PROJECT RISING SPIRIT'S MOVEMENTS?
I DIDN'T CALL TO HEAR EXCUSES. I CALLED TO DELIVER MY POSITION. PUT SIMPLY...
...NOW IS NOT THE TIME FOR MY CONTACTS TO BECOME UNRELIABLE...

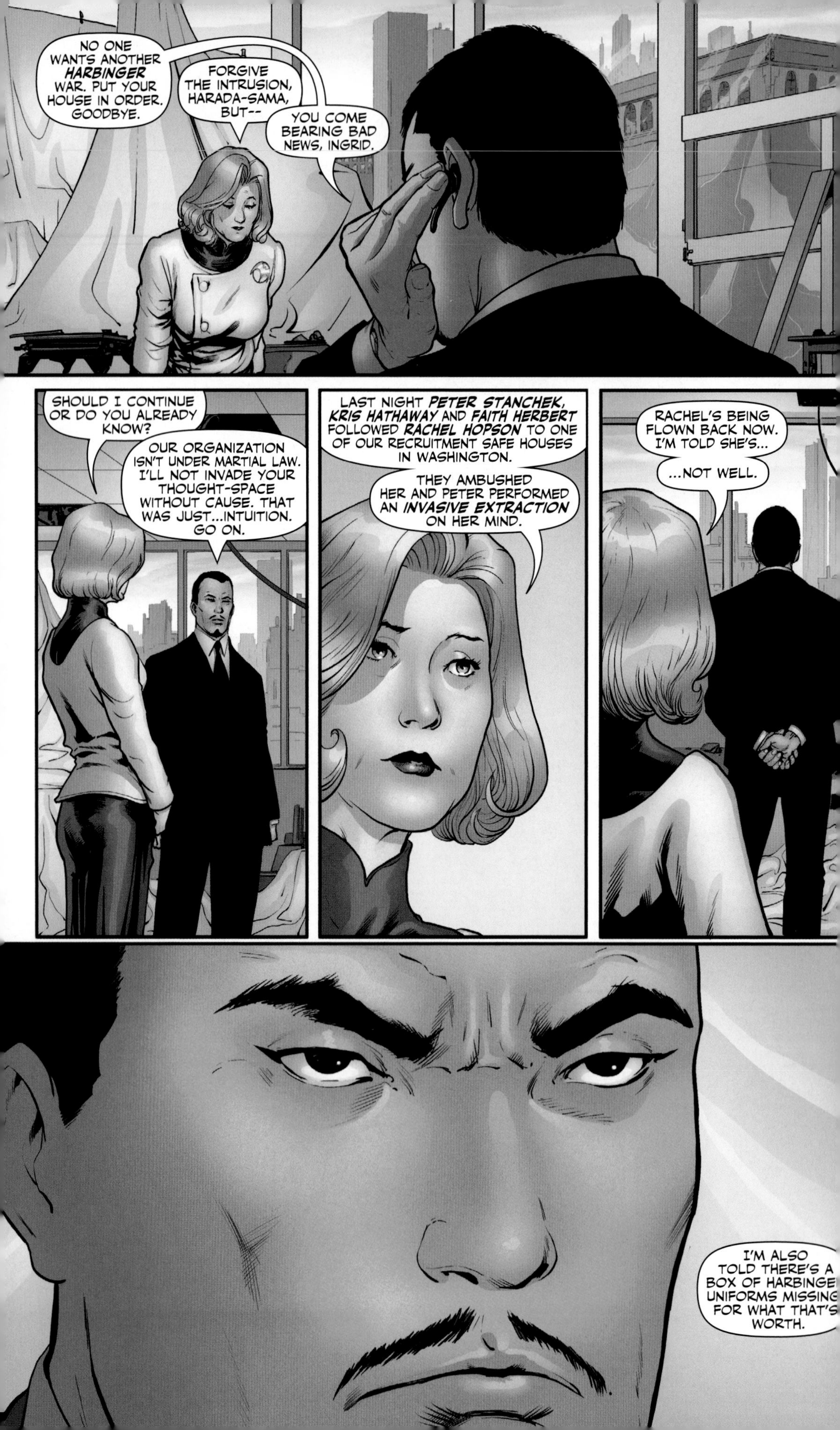
NO ONE WANTS ANOTHER HARBINGER WAR. PUT YOUR HOUSE IN ORDER. GOODBYE.
FORGIVE THE INTRUSION, HARADA-SAMA, BUT--
YOU COME BEARING BAD NEWS, INGRID.
SHOULD I CONTINUE OR DO YOU ALREADY KNOW?
OUR ORGANIZATION ISN'T UNDER MARTIAL LAW. I'LL NOT INVADE YOUR THOUGHT-SPACE WITHOUT CAUSE. THAT WAS JUST...INTUITION. GO ON.
LAST NIGHT PETER STANCHEK, KRIS HATHAWAY AND FAITH HERBERT FOLLOWED RACHEL HOPSON TO ONE OF OUR RECRUITMENT SAFE HOUSES IN WASHINGTON.
THEY AMBUSHED HER AND PETER PERFORMED AN INVASIVE EXTRACTION ON HER MIND.
RACHEL'S BEING FLOWN BACK NOW. I'M TOLD SHE'S...
...NOT WELL.
I'M ALSO TOLD THERE'S A BOX OF HARBINGE UNIFORMS MISSING FOR WHAT THAT'S WORTH.

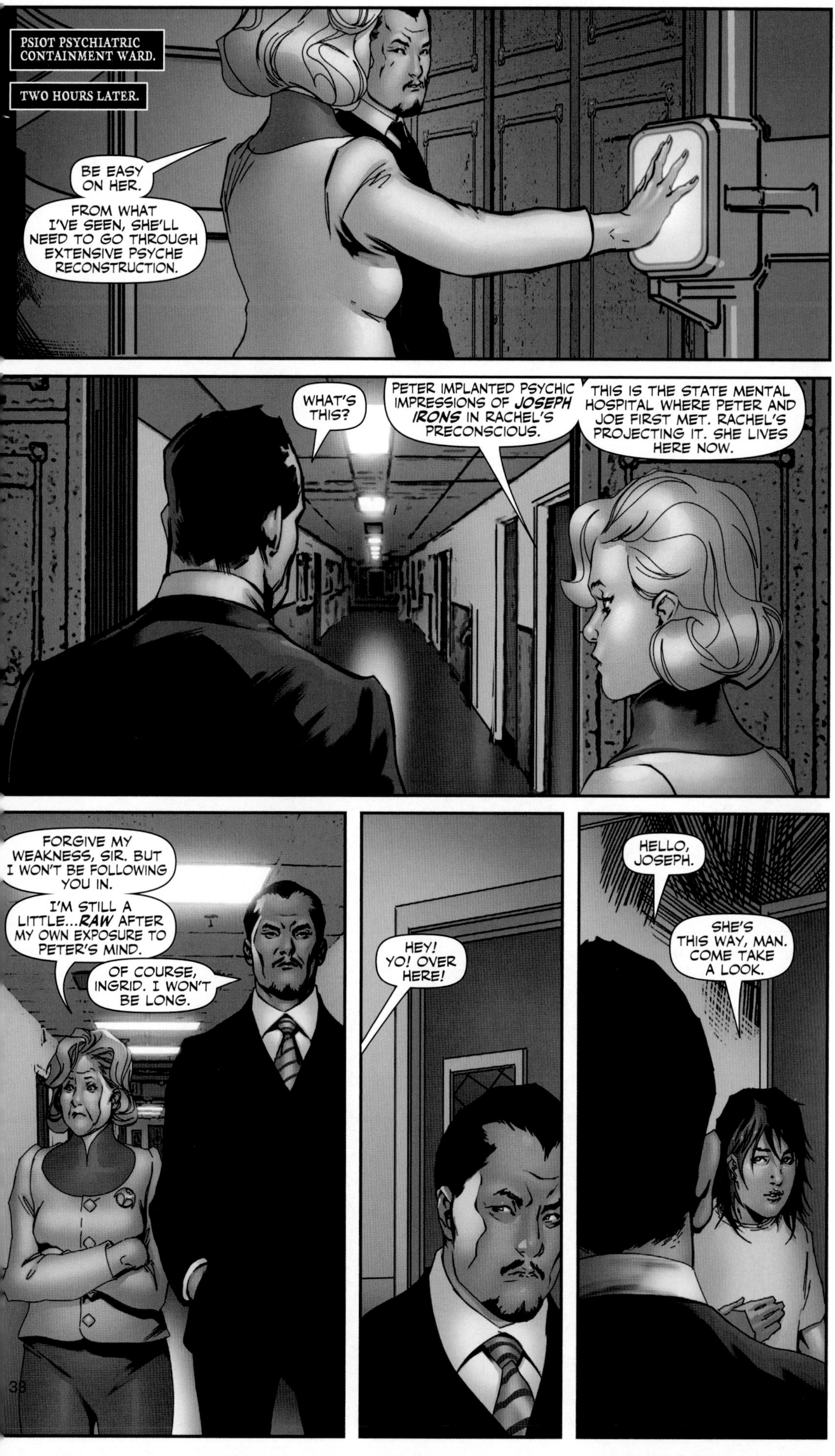
PSIOT PSYCHIATRIC CONTAINMENT WARD.
TWO HOURS LATER.
BE EASY ON HER.
FROM WHAT I'VE SEEN, SHE'LL NEED TO GO THROUGH EXTENSIVE PSYCHE RECONSTRUCTION.
WHAT'S THIS?
PETER IMPLANTED PSYCHIC IMPRESSIONS OF *JOSEPH IRONS* IN RACHEL'S PRECONSCIOUS.
THIS IS THE STATE MENTAL HOSPITAL WHERE PETER AND JOE FIRST MET. RACHEL'S PROJECTING IT. SHE LIVES HERE NOW.
FORGIVE MY WEAKNESS, SIR. BUT I WON'T BE FOLLOWING YOU IN.
I'M STILL A LITTLE...*RAW* AFTER MY OWN EXPOSURE TO PETER'S MIND.
OF COURSE, INGRID. I WON'T BE LONG.
HEY! YO! OVER HERE!
HELLO, JOSEPH.
SHE'S THIS WAY, MAN. COME TAKE A LOOK.

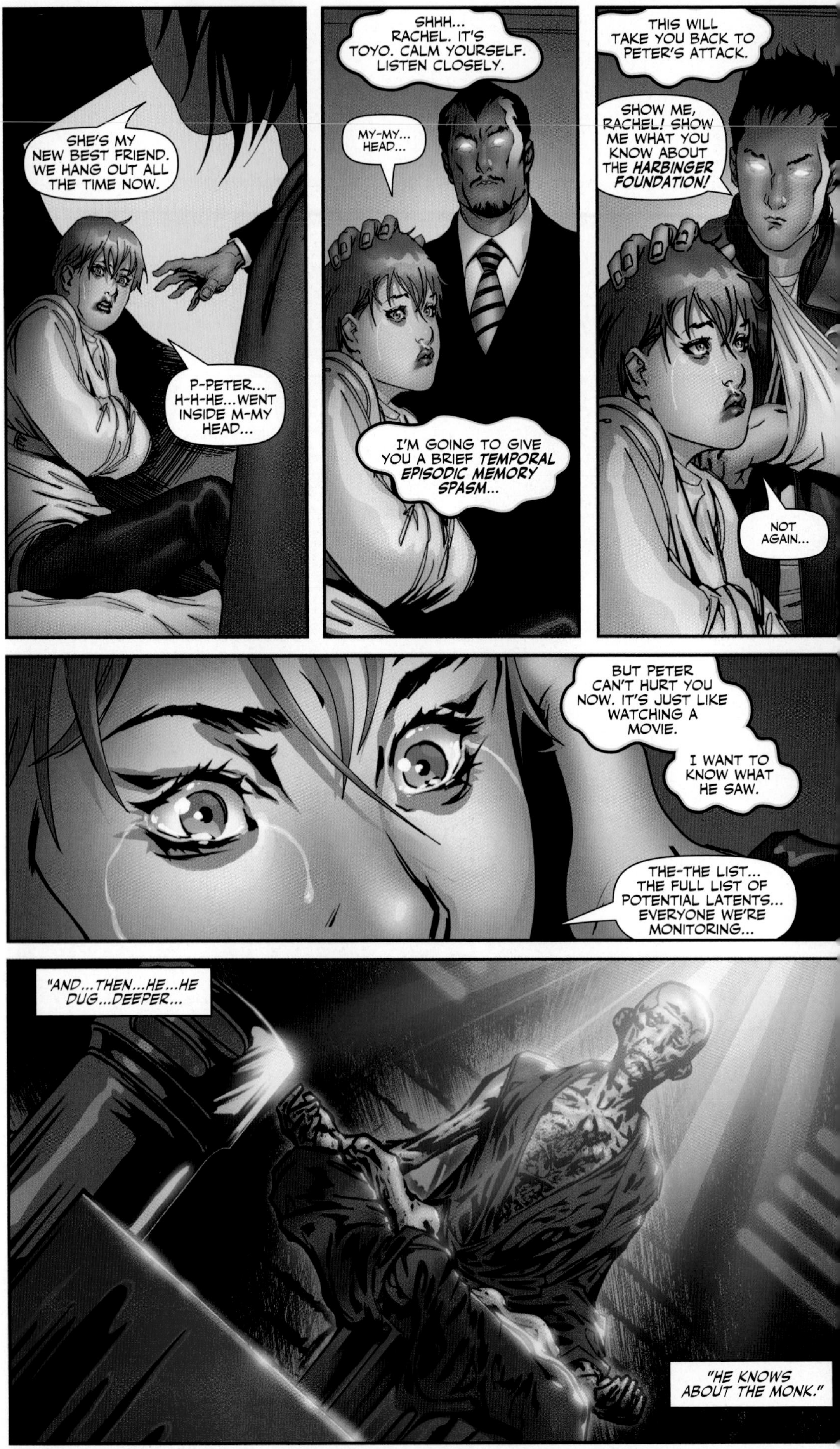
SHE'S MY NEW BEST FRIEND. WE HANG OUT ALL THE TIME NOW.
P-PETER... H-H-HE...WENT INSIDE M-MY HEAD...
SHHH... RACHEL. IT'S TOYO. CALM YOURSELF. LISTEN CLOSELY.
MY-MY... HEAD...
I'M GOING TO GIVE YOU A BRIEF TEMPORAL EPISODIC MEMORY SPASM...
THIS WILL TAKE YOU BACK TO PETER'S ATTACK.
SHOW ME, RACHEL! SHOW ME WHAT YOU KNOW ABOUT THE HARBINGER FOUNDATION!
NOT AGAIN...
BUT PETER CAN'T HURT YOU NOW. IT'S JUST LIKE WATCHING A MOVIE.
I WANT TO KNOW WHAT HE SAW.
THE-THE LIST... THE FULL LIST OF POTENTIAL LATENTS... EVERYONE WE'RE MONITORING...
"AND...THEN...HE...HE DUG...DEEPER...
"HE KNOWS ABOUT THE MONK."

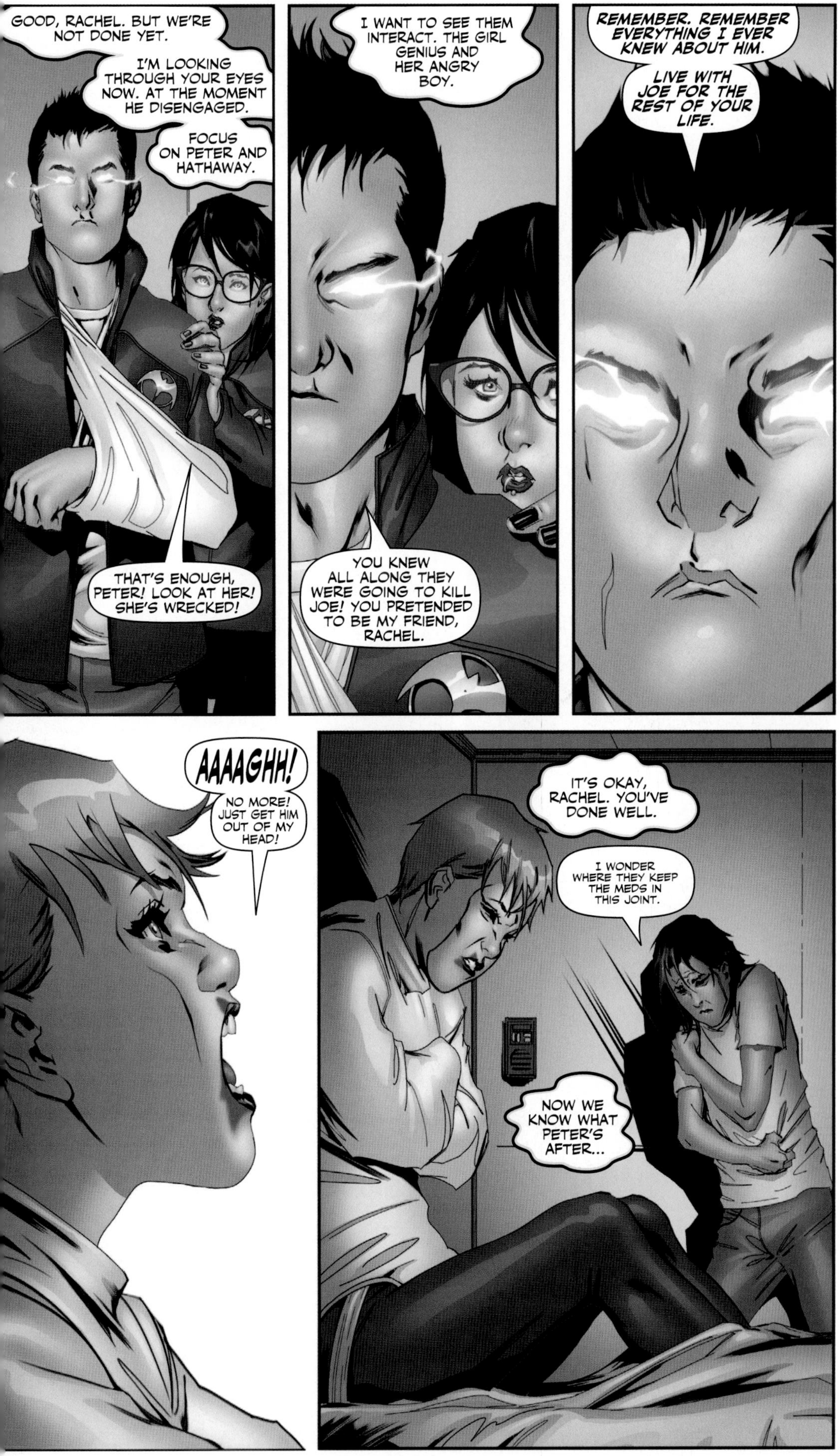

GOOD, RACHEL. BUT WE'RE NOT DONE YET.
I'M LOOKING THROUGH YOUR EYES NOW. AT THE MOMENT HE DISENGAGED.
FOCUS ON PETER AND HATHAWAY.
THAT'S ENOUGH, PETER! LOOK AT HER! SHE'S WRECKED!
I WANT TO SEE THEM INTERACT. THE GIRL GENIUS AND HER ANGRY BOY.
YOU KNEW ALL ALONG THEY WERE GOING TO KILL JOE! YOU PRETENDED TO BE MY FRIEND, RACHEL.
REMEMBER. REMEMBER EVERYTHING I EVER KNEW ABOUT HIM.
LIVE WITH JOE FOR THE REST OF YOUR LIFE.
AAAAGHH!
NO MORE! JUST GET HIM OUT OF MY HEAD!
IT'S OKAY, RACHEL. YOU'VE DONE WELL.
I WONDER WHERE THEY KEEP THE MEDS IN THIS JOINT.
NOW WE KNOW WHAT PETER'S AFTER...

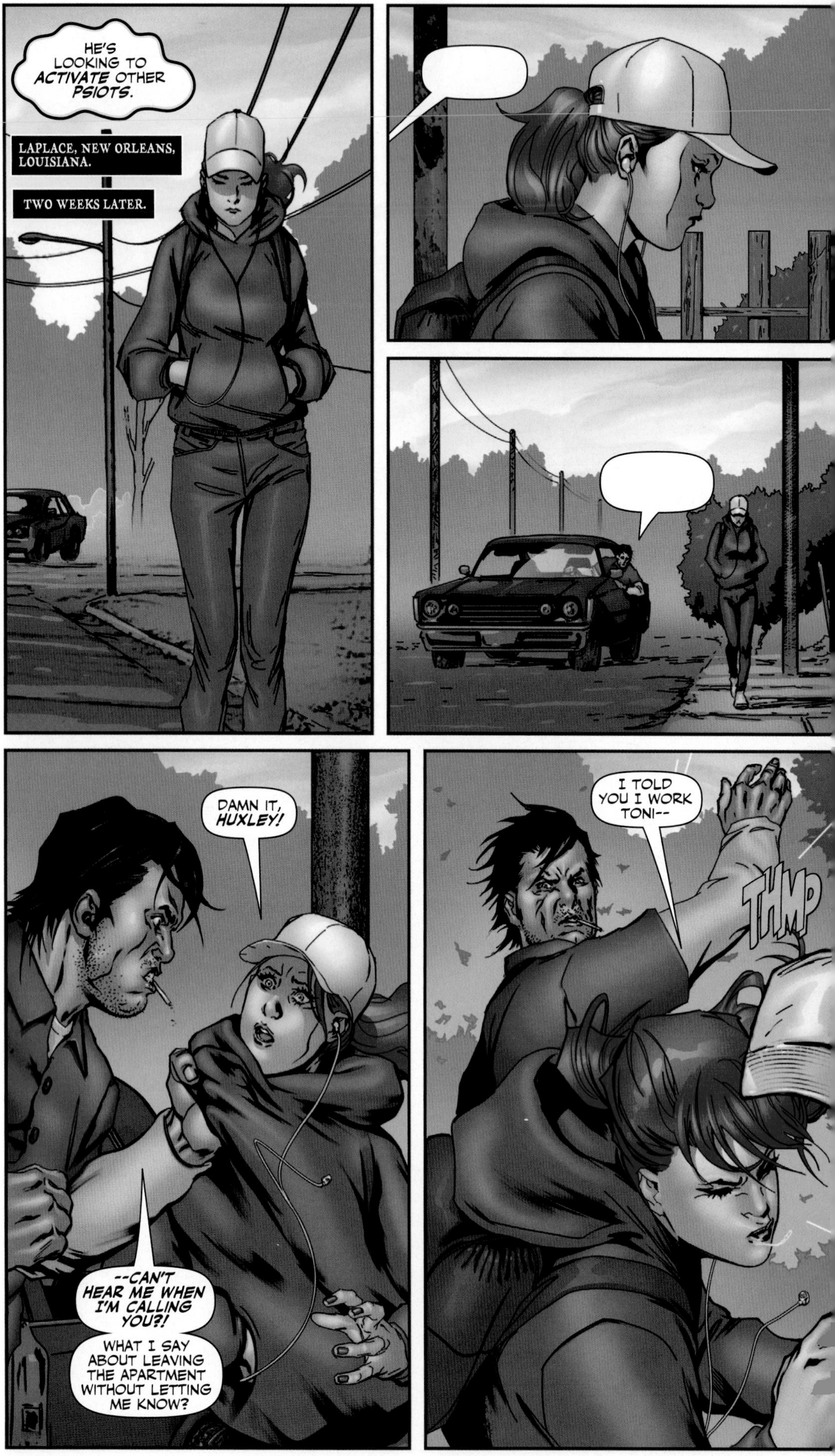
HE'S LOOKING TO ACTIVATE OTHER PSIOTS.
LAPLACE, NEW ORLEANS, LOUISIANA.
TWO WEEKS LATER.
DAMN IT, HUXLEY!
--CAN'T HEAR ME WHEN I'M CALLING YOU?!
WHAT I SAY ABOUT LEAVING THE APARTMENT WITHOUT LETTING ME KNOW?
I TOLD YOU I WORK TONI--
THMP

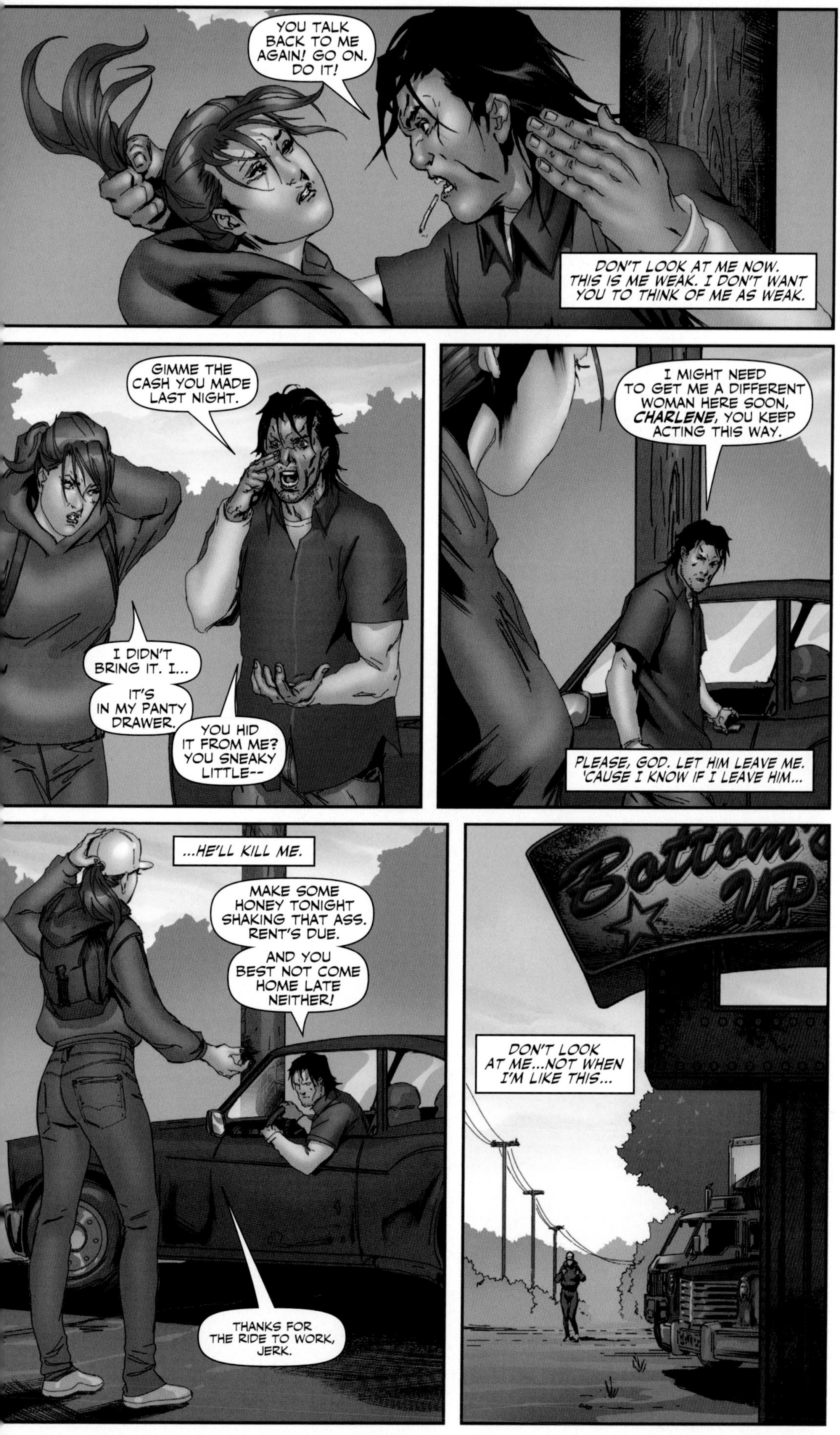
YOU TALK BACK TO ME AGAIN! GO ON. DO IT!
DON'T LOOK AT ME NOW. THIS IS ME WEAK. I DON'T WANT YOU TO THINK OF ME AS WEAK.
GIMME THE CASH YOU MADE LAST NIGHT.
I DIDN'T BRING IT. I...
IT'S IN MY PANTY DRAWER.
YOU HID IT FROM ME? YOU SNEAKY LITTLE--
I MIGHT NEED TO GET ME A DIFFERENT WOMAN HERE SOON, CHARLENE, YOU KEEP ACTING THIS WAY.
PLEASE, GOD. LET HIM LEAVE ME. 'CAUSE I KNOW IF I LEAVE HIM...
...HE'LL KILL ME.
MAKE SOME HONEY TONIGHT SHAKING THAT ASS. RENT'S DUE.
AND YOU BEST NOT COME HOME LATE NEITHER!
THANKS FOR THE RIDE TO WORK, JERK.
UP
DON'T LOOK AT ME...NOT WHEN I'M LIKE THIS...

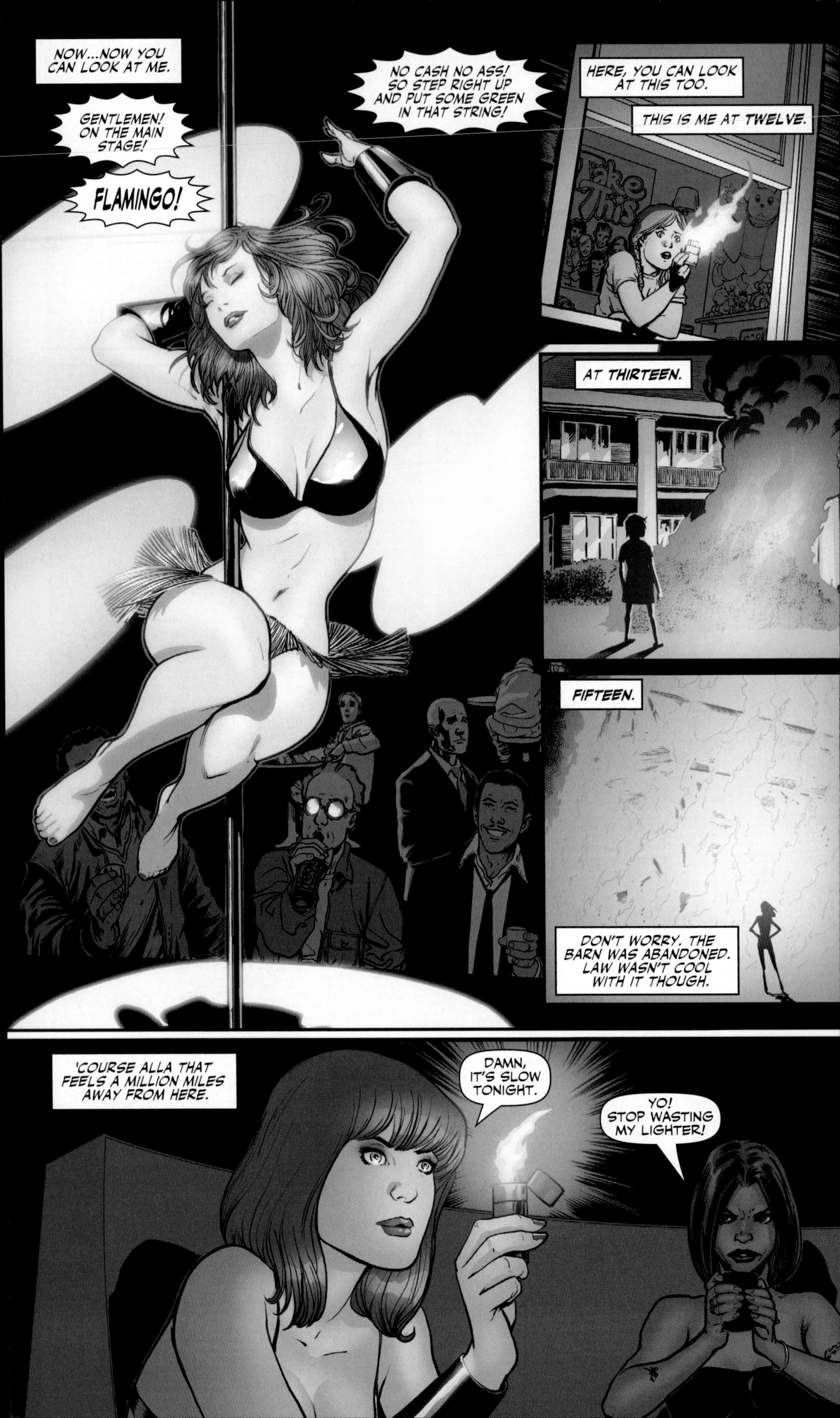
NOW...NOW YOU CAN LOOK AT ME.
GENTLEMEN! ON THE MAIN STAGE!
FLAMINGO!
NO CASH NO ASS! SO STEP RIGHT UP AND PUT SOME GREEN IN THAT STRING!
HERE, YOU CAN LOOK AT THIS TOO.
THIS IS ME AT TWELVE.
AT THIRTEEN.
FIFTEEN.
DON'T WORRY. THE BARN WAS ABANDONED. LAW WASN'T COOL WITH IT THOUGH.
'COURSE ALLA THAT FEELS A MILLION MILES AWAY FROM HERE.
DAMN, IT'S SLOW TONIGHT.
YO! STOP WASTING MY LIGHTER!

THIS PLACE IS DIIIIIRRRTY.

IT'S LIKE AN ANIMAL COGNITION EXPERIMENT. DO YOU SEE HER, PETER?

I DON'T EXACTLY KNOW WHAT I'M LOOKING FOR YET.

OOOHHHH...SO THAT'S WHAT FAKIES LOOK LIKE.

THERE SHE IS.

THIS ISN'T WHAT I HAD IN MIND WHEN I SAID WE NEEDED HELP.

MAN, THAT KID OVER THERE IS REALLY SCOPING ME OUT...I THINK I'M GONNA GO TALK TO THEM.

GOOD LUCK GETTING PAID THERE. THAT'S THE STRANGEST TABLE I'VE SEEN IN HERE IN AGES.

HI, Y'ALL! WANT SOME COMPANY?

YOU'RE SOOOO PRETTY.

SURE, SIT. WHAT'S OBSERVATION WITHOUT INTERACTION? BAD DATA, I SAY.

HA! I DON'T KNOW WHAT THAT MEANS, BUT I'LL TAKE IT!

WELL, THERE GOES THE "WORKING YOUR WAY THROUGH LAW SCHOOL" THEORY.

BITCH.

HEY HON, I'M *FLAMINGO*.

SERIOUSLY? *FLAMINGO?* THAT'S YOUR STAGE NAME? WHAT IS THIS, VEGAS IN THE FIFTIES?

RIGHT. GOT IT. YOU'RE BETTER THAN ME. SORRY I BOTHERED YOU--

WAIT, PLEA... IT'S COOL...W JUST A LITTL... EDGE. WE' NEVER DONE BEFORE...

I'M PETER... AND YOU'RE *CHARLENE DUPRE.*

CRAP. I SHOULD TOTALLY DENY MY NAME...

BUT THERE'S SOMETHING ABOUT THIS BOY.

SOMETHING ABOUT HIS SAD EYES.

OKAY. SO WHAT GIVES? YOU DON'T LOOK LIKE A JUVIE P.O.

THIS JUST GETS BETTER A BETTER.

HEY! YOU BETTER SLOW YOUR ROLL, CHICK, OR THIS IS GONNA GET REAL. GOT IT?

"SLOW YOUR ROLL"? WOW. TURNS OUT THERE'S SOMETHING INTERESTING IN THERE AFTER ALL.

BOTH OF YOU! CHILL OUT!

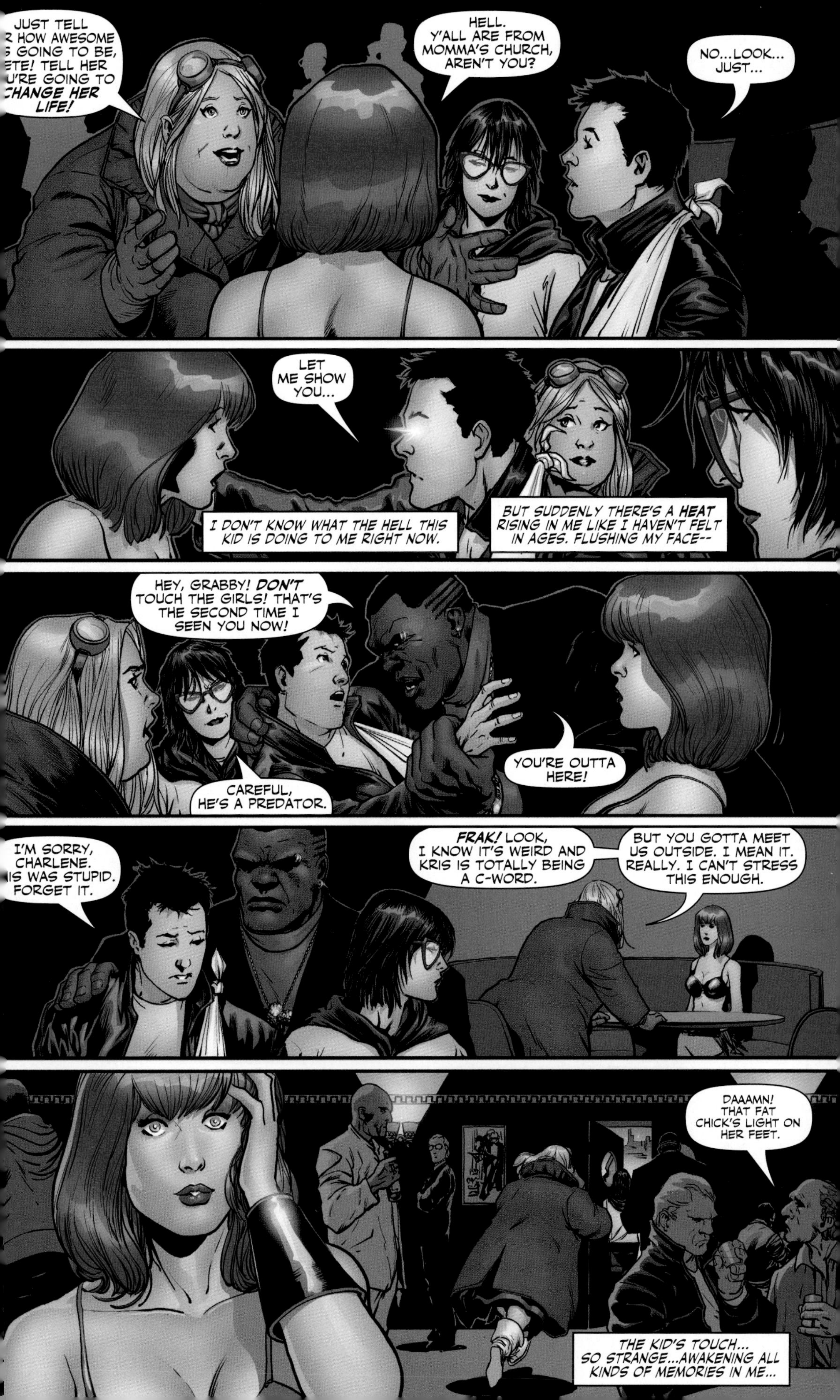
JUST TELL
R HOW AWESOME
S GOING TO BE,
ETE! TELL HER
U'RE GOING TO
CHANGE HER
LIFE!
HELL.
Y'ALL ARE FROM
MOMMA'S CHURCH,
AREN'T YOU?
NO...LOOK...
JUST...
LET
ME SHOW
YOU...
I DON'T KNOW WHAT THE HELL THIS
KID IS DOING TO ME RIGHT NOW.
BUT SUDDENLY THERE'S A HEAT
RISING IN ME LIKE I HAVEN'T FELT
IN AGES. FLUSHING MY FACE--
HEY, GRABBY! DON'T
TOUCH THE GIRLS! THAT'S
THE SECOND TIME I
SEEN YOU NOW!
YOU'RE OUTTA
HERE!
CAREFUL,
HE'S A PREDATOR.
I'M SORRY,
CHARLENE.
IS WAS STUPID.
FORGET IT.
FRAK! LOOK,
I KNOW IT'S WEIRD AND
KRIS IS TOTALLY BEING
A C-WORD.
BUT YOU GOTTA MEET
US OUTSIDE. I MEAN IT.
REALLY. I CAN'T STRESS
THIS ENOUGH.
DAAAMN!
THAT FAT
CHICK'S LIGHT ON
HER FEET.
THE KID'S TOUCH...
SO STRANGE...AWAKENING ALL
KINDS OF MEMORIES IN ME...

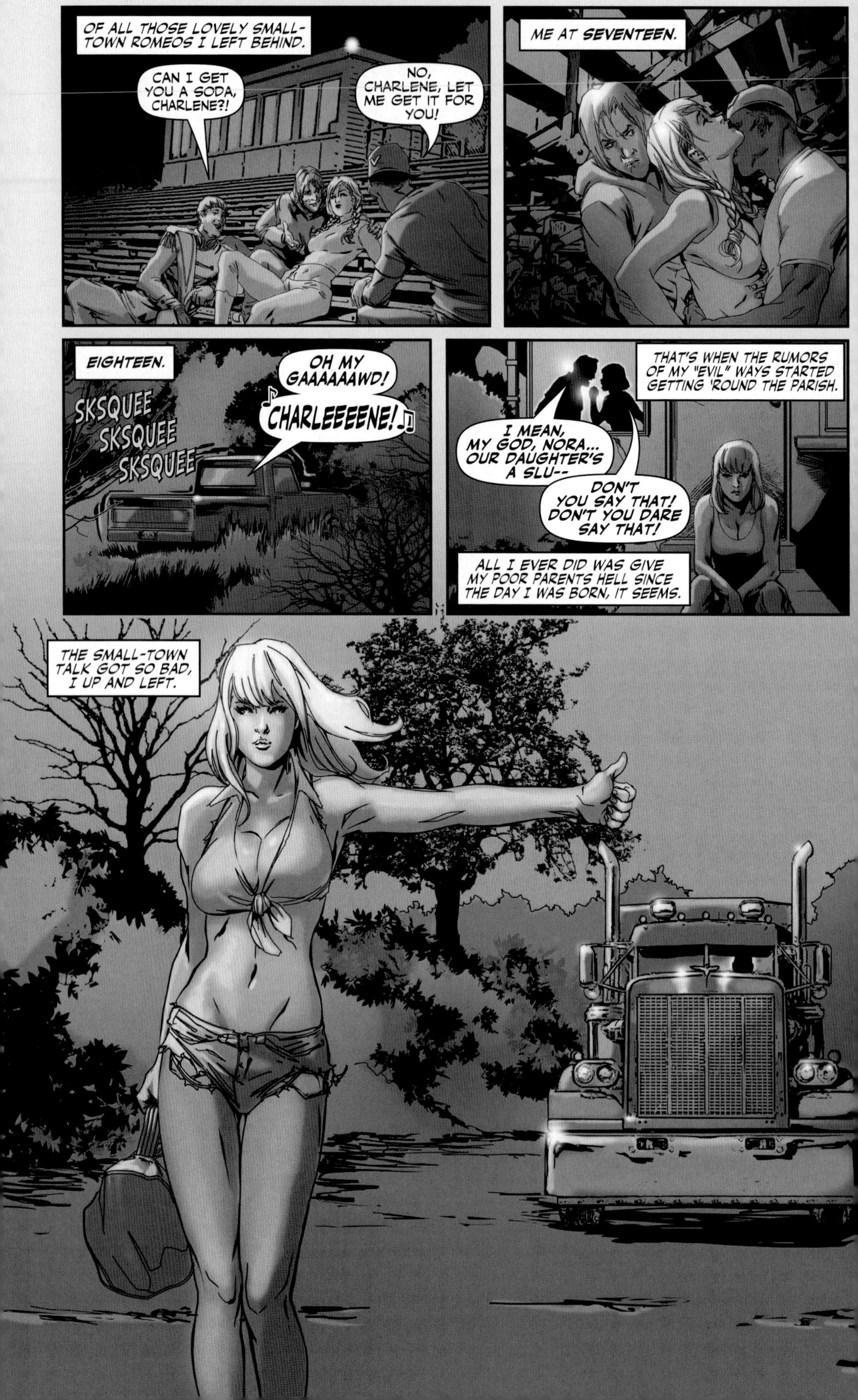
OF ALL THOSE LOVELY SMALL-TOWN ROMEOS I LEFT BEHIND.
CAN I GET YOU A SODA, CHARLENE?!
NO, CHARLENE, LET ME GET IT FOR YOU!
ME AT SEVENTEEN.
EIGHTEEN.
SKSQUEE SKSQUEE SKSQUEE
OH MY GAAAAAAWD!
CHARLEEEENE!
THAT'S WHEN THE RUMORS OF MY "EVIL" WAYS STARTED GETTING 'ROUND THE PARISH.
I MEAN, MY GOD, NORA... OUR DAUGHTER'S A SLU--
DON'T YOU SAY THAT! DON'T YOU DARE SAY THAT!
ALL I EVER DID WAS GIVE MY POOR PARENTS HELL SINCE THE DAY I WAS BORN, IT SEEMS.
THE SMALL-TOWN TALK GOT SO BAD, I UP AND LEFT.

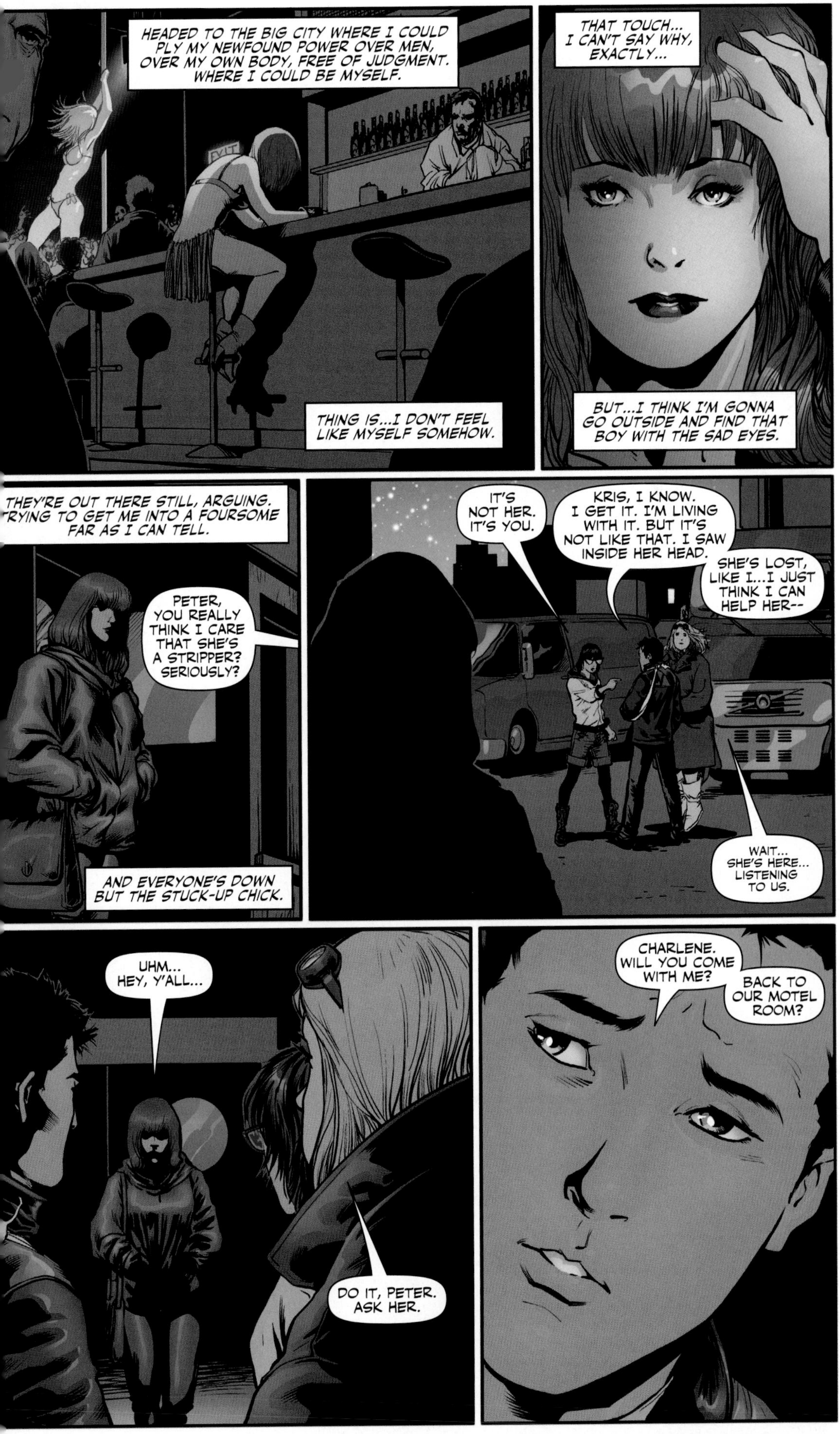
HEADED TO THE BIG CITY WHERE I COULD PLY MY NEWFOUND POWER OVER MEN, OVER MY OWN BODY, FREE OF JUDGMENT. WHERE I COULD BE MYSELF.
THING IS...I DON'T FEEL LIKE MYSELF SOMEHOW.
THAT TOUCH... I CAN'T SAY WHY, EXACTLY...
BUT...I THINK I'M GONNA GO OUTSIDE AND FIND THAT BOY WITH THE SAD EYES.
THEY'RE OUT THERE STILL, ARGUING. TRYING TO GET ME INTO A FOURSOME FAR AS I CAN TELL.
PETER, YOU REALLY THINK I CARE THAT SHE'S A STRIPPER? SERIOUSLY?
AND EVERYONE'S DOWN BUT THE STUCK-UP CHICK.
IT'S NOT HER. IT'S YOU.
KRIS, I KNOW. I GET IT. I'M LIVING WITH IT. BUT IT'S NOT LIKE THAT. I SAW INSIDE HER HEAD.
SHE'S LOST, LIKE I...I JUST THINK I CAN HELP HER--
WAIT... SHE'S HERE... LISTENING TO US.
UHM... HEY, Y'ALL...
DO IT, PETER. ASK HER.
CHARLENE. WILL YOU COME WITH ME?
BACK TO OUR MOTEL ROOM?

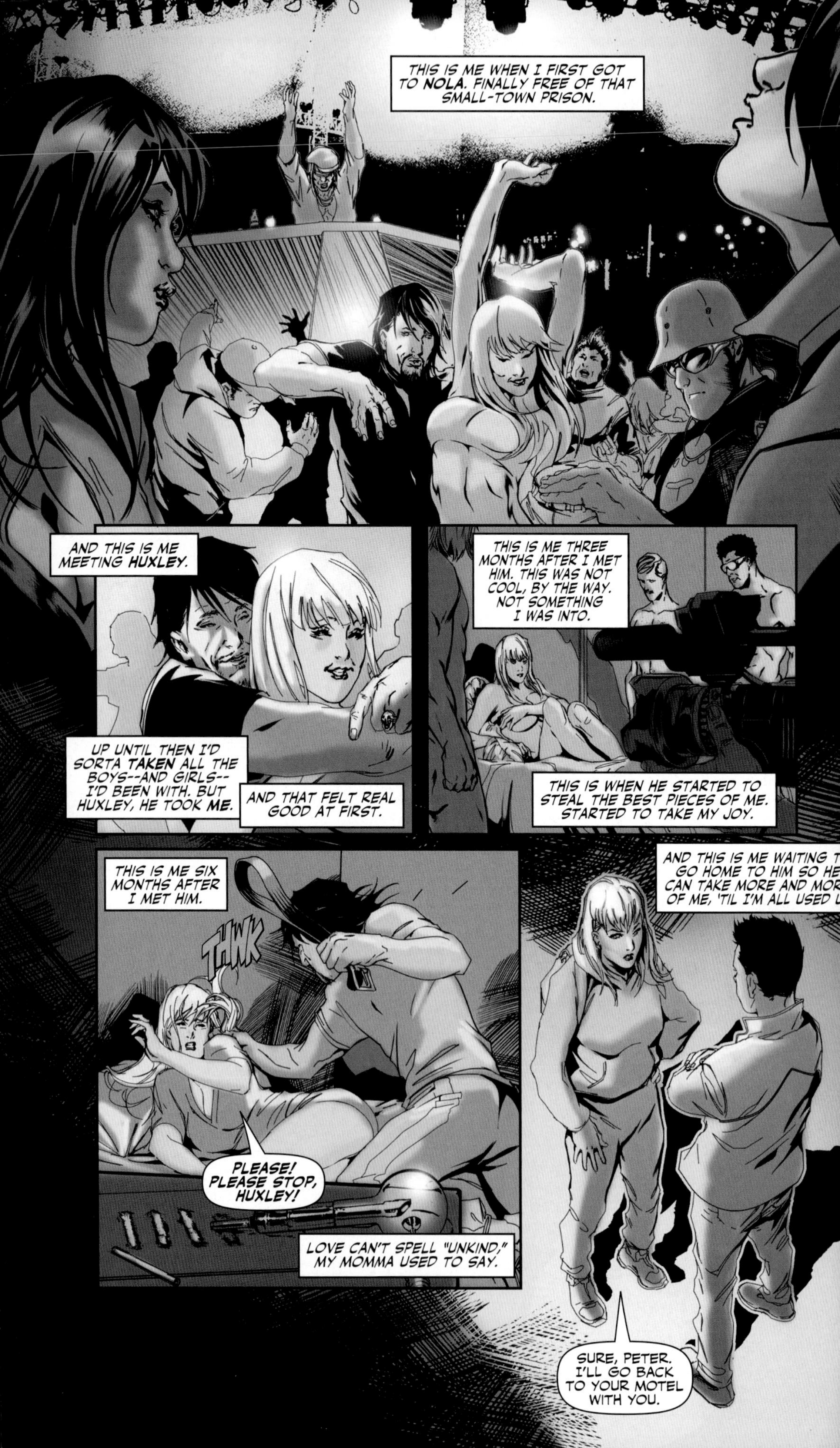
THIS IS ME WHEN I FIRST GOT TO NOLA. FINALLY FREE OF THAT SMALL-TOWN PRISON.
AND THIS IS ME MEETING HUXLEY.
UP UNTIL THEN I'D SORTA TAKEN ALL THE BOYS--AND GIRLS--I'D BEEN WITH. BUT HUXLEY, HE TOOK ME.
AND THAT FELT REAL GOOD AT FIRST.
THIS IS ME THREE MONTHS AFTER I MET HIM. THIS WAS NOT COOL, BY THE WAY. NOT SOMETHING I WAS INTO.
THIS IS WHEN HE STARTED TO STEAL THE BEST PIECES OF ME. STARTED TO TAKE MY JOY.
THIS IS ME SIX MONTHS AFTER I MET HIM.
THWK
PLEASE! PLEASE STOP, HUXLEY!
LOVE CAN'T SPELL "UNKIND," MY MOMMA USED TO SAY.
AND THIS IS ME WAITING T GO HOME TO HIM SO HE CAN TAKE MORE AND MOR OF ME, 'TIL I'M ALL USED U
SURE, PETER. I'LL GO BACK TO YOUR MOTEL WITH YOU.

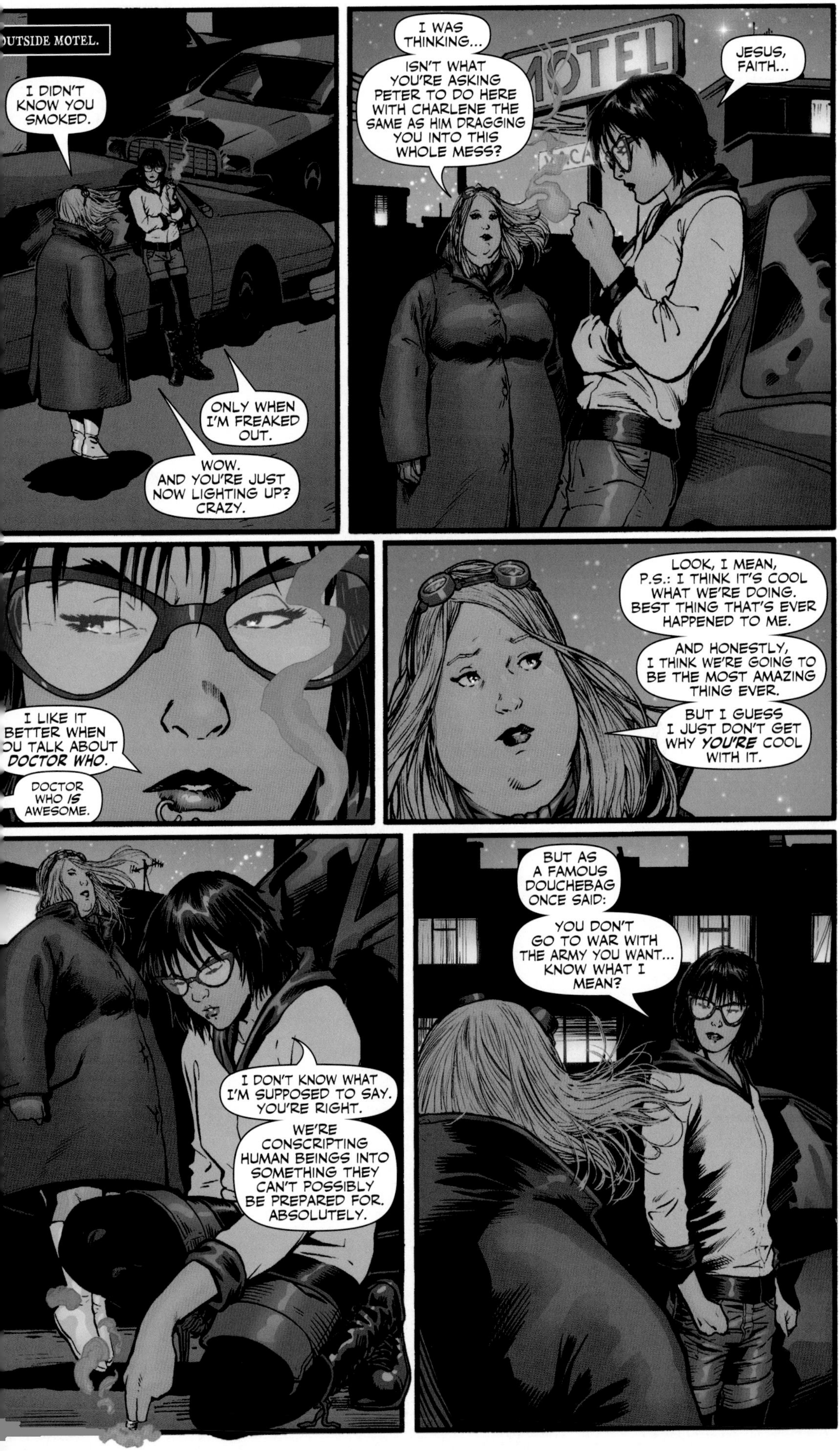

OUTSIDE MOTEL.
I DIDN'T KNOW YOU SMOKED.
ONLY WHEN I'M FREAKED OUT.
WOW. AND YOU'RE JUST NOW LIGHTING UP? CRAZY.
I WAS THINKING...
ISN'T WHAT YOU'RE ASKING PETER TO DO HERE WITH CHARLENE THE SAME AS HIM DRAGGING YOU INTO THIS WHOLE MESS?
JESUS, FAITH...
MOTEL
I LIKE IT BETTER WHEN OU TALK ABOUT DOCTOR WHO.
DOCTOR WHO IS AWESOME.
LOOK, I MEAN, P.S.: I THINK IT'S COOL WHAT WE'RE DOING. BEST THING THAT'S EVER HAPPENED TO ME.
AND HONESTLY, I THINK WE'RE GOING TO BE THE MOST AMAZING THING EVER.
BUT I GUESS I JUST DON'T GET WHY YOU'RE COOL WITH IT.
I DON'T KNOW WHAT I'M SUPPOSED TO SAY. YOU'RE RIGHT.
WE'RE CONSCRIPTING HUMAN BEINGS INTO SOMETHING THEY CAN'T POSSIBLY BE PREPARED FOR. ABSOLUTELY.
BUT AS A FAMOUS DOUCHEBAG ONCE SAID:
YOU DON'T GO TO WAR WITH THE ARMY YOU WANT... KNOW WHAT I MEAN?

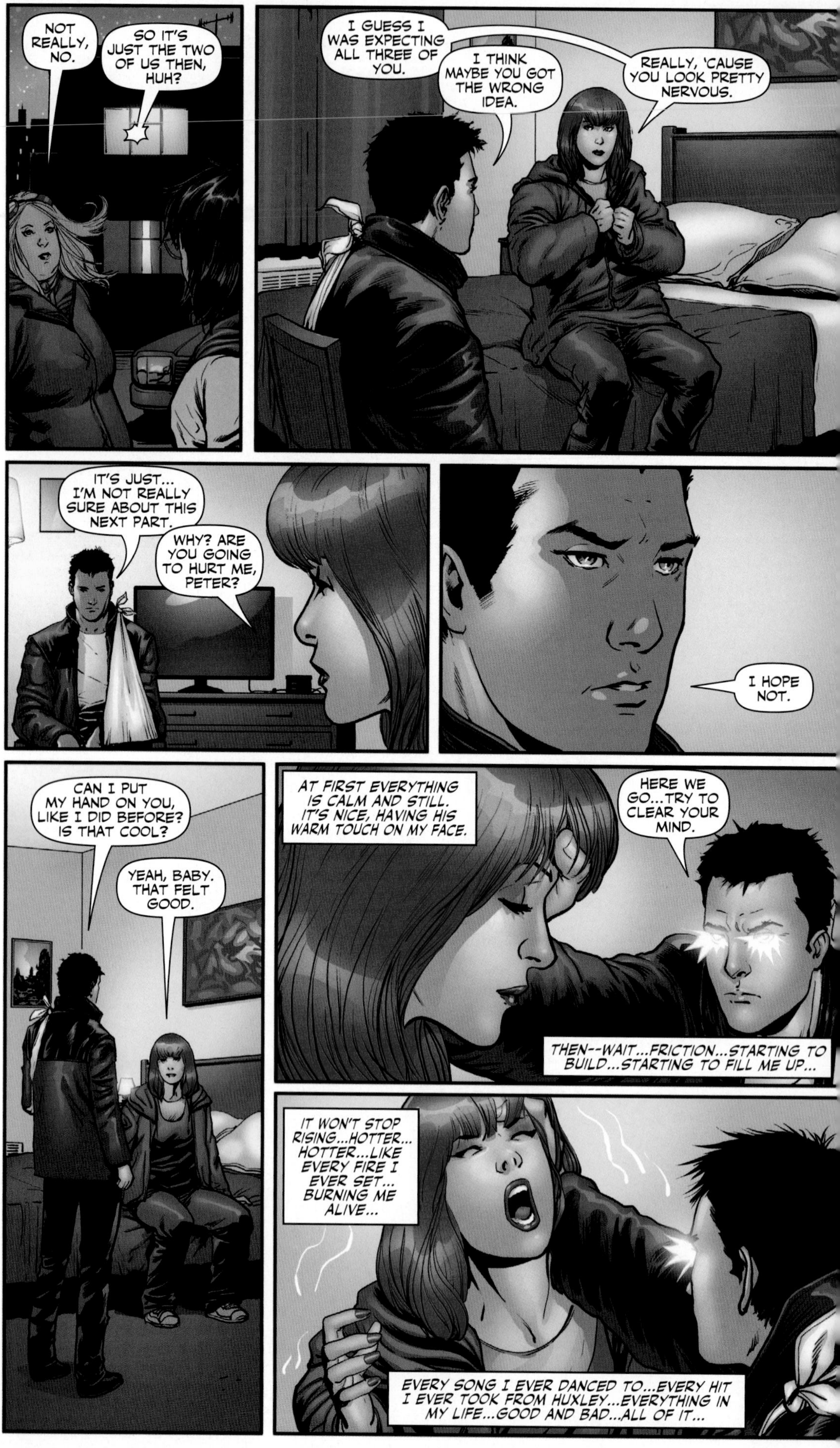
NOT REALLY, NO.
SO IT'S JUST THE TWO OF US THEN, HUH?
I GUESS I WAS EXPECTING ALL THREE OF YOU.
I THINK MAYBE YOU GOT THE WRONG IDEA.
REALLY, 'CAUSE YOU LOOK PRETTY NERVOUS.
IT'S JUST... I'M NOT REALLY SURE ABOUT THIS NEXT PART.
WHY? ARE YOU GOING TO HURT ME, PETER?
I HOPE NOT.
CAN I PUT MY HAND ON YOU, LIKE I DID BEFORE? IS THAT COOL?
YEAH, BABY. THAT FELT GOOD.
AT FIRST EVERYTHING IS CALM AND STILL. IT'S NICE, HAVING HIS WARM TOUCH ON MY FACE.
HERE WE GO...TRY TO CLEAR YOUR MIND.
THEN--WAIT...FRICTION...STARTING TO BUILD...STARTING TO FILL ME UP...
IT WON'T STOP RISING...HOTTER... HOTTER...LIKE EVERY FIRE I EVER SET... BURNING ME ALIVE...
EVERY SONG I EVER DANCED TO...EVERY HIT I EVER TOOK FROM HUXLEY...EVERYTHING IN MY LIFE...GOOD AND BAD...ALL OF IT...

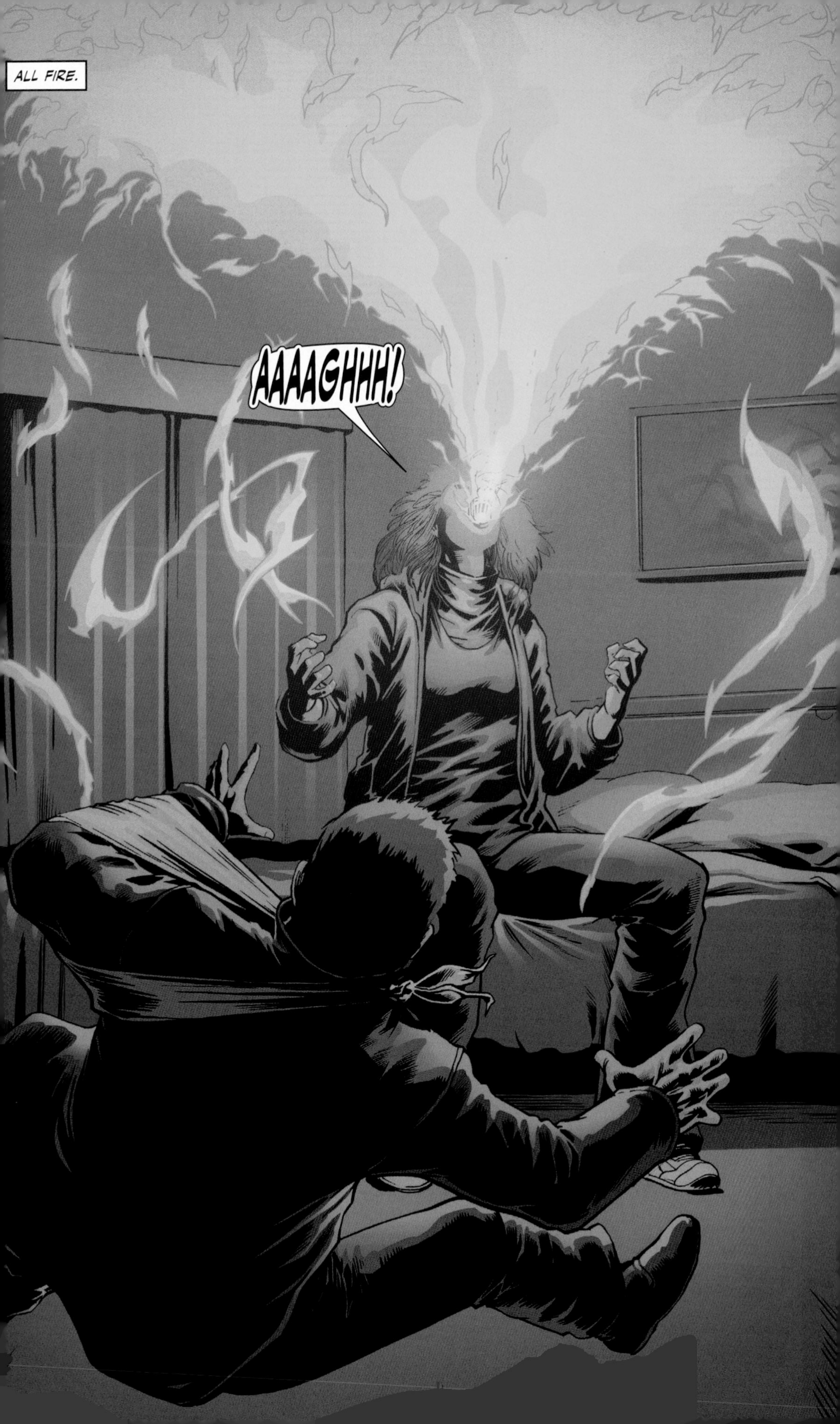
ALL FIRE.
AAAAGHHH!

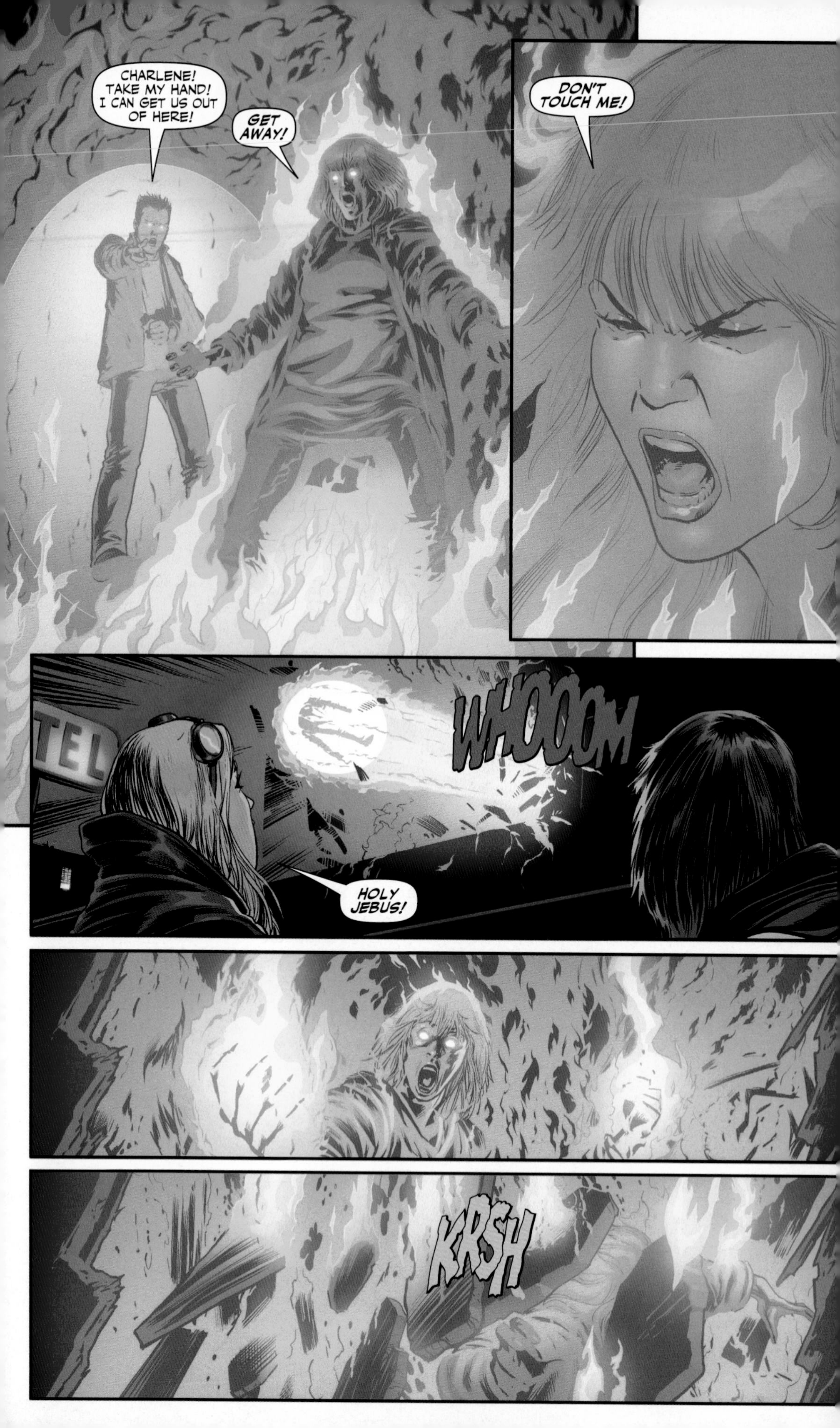
CHARLENE! TAKE MY HAND! I CAN GET US OUT OF HERE!
GET AWAY!
DON'T TOUCH ME!
WHOOOM
HOLY JEBUS!
KRSH

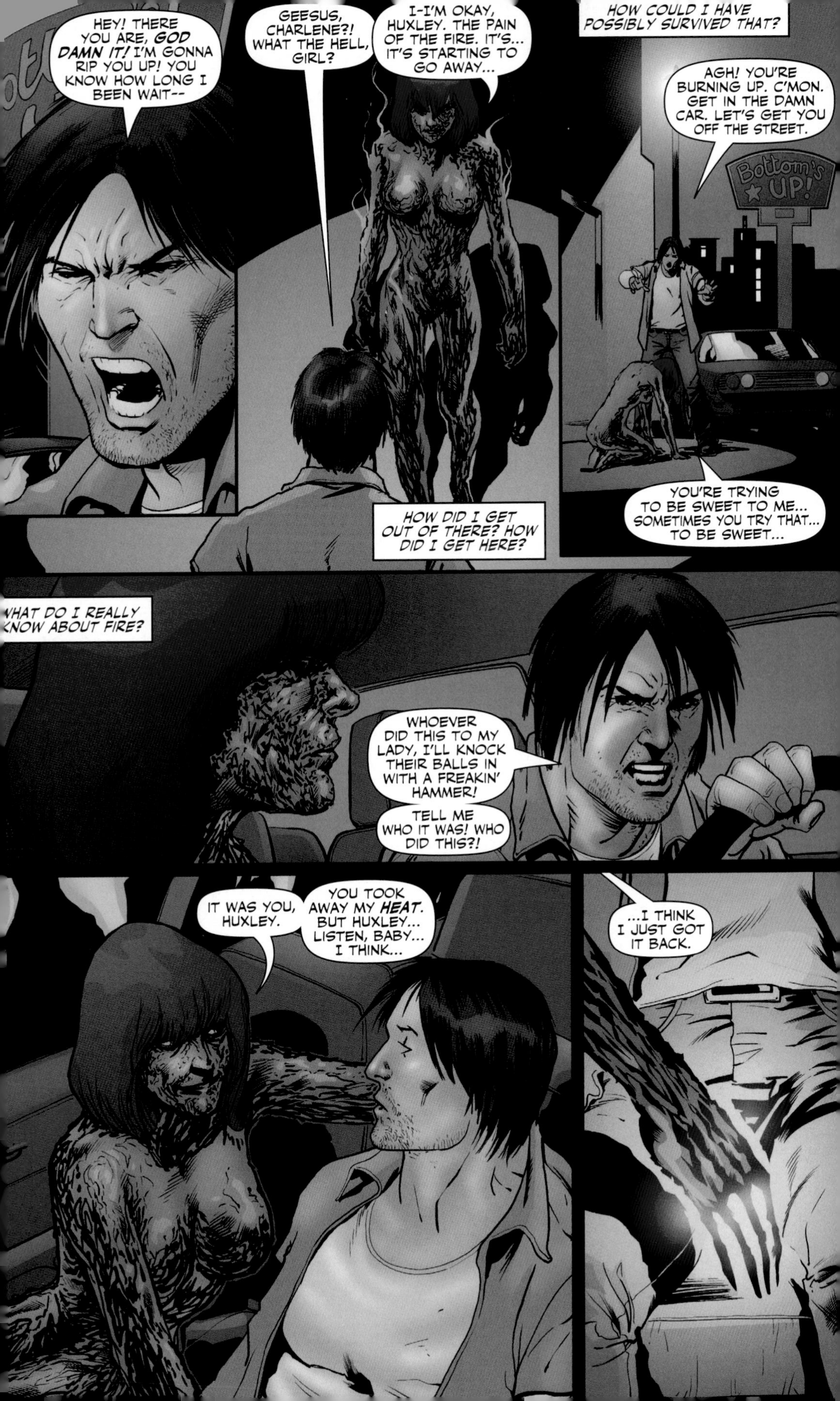

HEY! THERE YOU ARE, *GOD DAMN IT!* I'M GONNA RIP YOU UP! YOU KNOW HOW LONG I BEEN WAIT--
GEESUS, CHARLENE?! WHAT THE HELL, GIRL?
I-I'M OKAY, HUXLEY. THE PAIN OF THE FIRE. IT'S... IT'S STARTING TO GO AWAY...
*HOW DID I GET OUT OF THERE? HOW DID I GET HERE?*
*HOW COULD I HAVE POSSIBLY SURVIVED THAT?*
AGH! YOU'RE BURNING UP. C'MON. GET IN THE DAMN CAR. LET'S GET YOU OFF THE STREET.
Bottom's UP!
YOU'RE TRYING TO BE SWEET TO ME... SOMETIMES YOU TRY THAT... TO BE SWEET...
*WHAT DO I REALLY KNOW ABOUT FIRE?*
WHOEVER DID THIS TO MY LADY, I'LL KNOCK THEIR BALLS IN WITH A FREAKIN' HAMMER!
TELL ME WHO IT WAS! WHO DID THIS?!
IT WAS YOU, HUXLEY.
YOU TOOK AWAY MY *HEAT*. BUT HUXLEY... LISTEN, BABY... I THINK...
...I THINK I JUST GOT IT BACK.

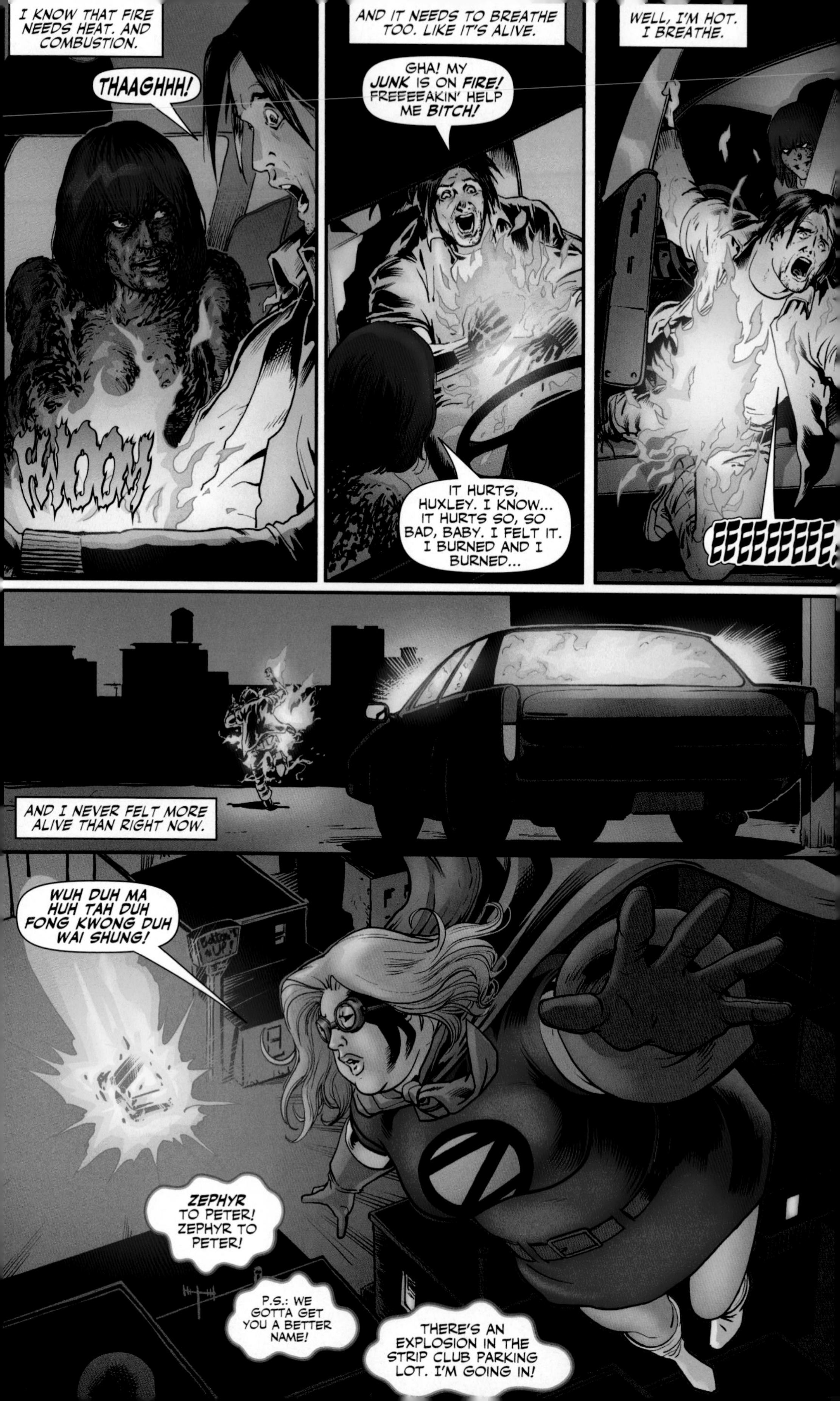
I KNOW THAT FIRE NEEDS HEAT. AND COMBUSTION.
THAAGHHH!
FWOOM
AND IT NEEDS TO BREATHE TOO. LIKE IT'S ALIVE.
GHA! MY JUNK IS ON FIRE! FREEEEAKIN' HELP ME BITCH!
IT HURTS, HUXLEY. I KNOW... IT HURTS SO, SO BAD, BABY. I FELT IT. I BURNED AND I BURNED...
WELL, I'M HOT. I BREATHE.
EEEEEEEEE
AND I NEVER FELT MORE ALIVE THAN RIGHT NOW.
WUH DUH MA HUH TAH DUH FONG KWONG DUH WAI SHUNG!
ZEPHYR TO PETER! ZEPHYR TO PETER!
P.S.: WE GOTTA GET YOU A BETTER NAME!
THERE'S AN EXPLOSION IN THE STRIP CLUB PARKING LOT. I'M GOING IN!

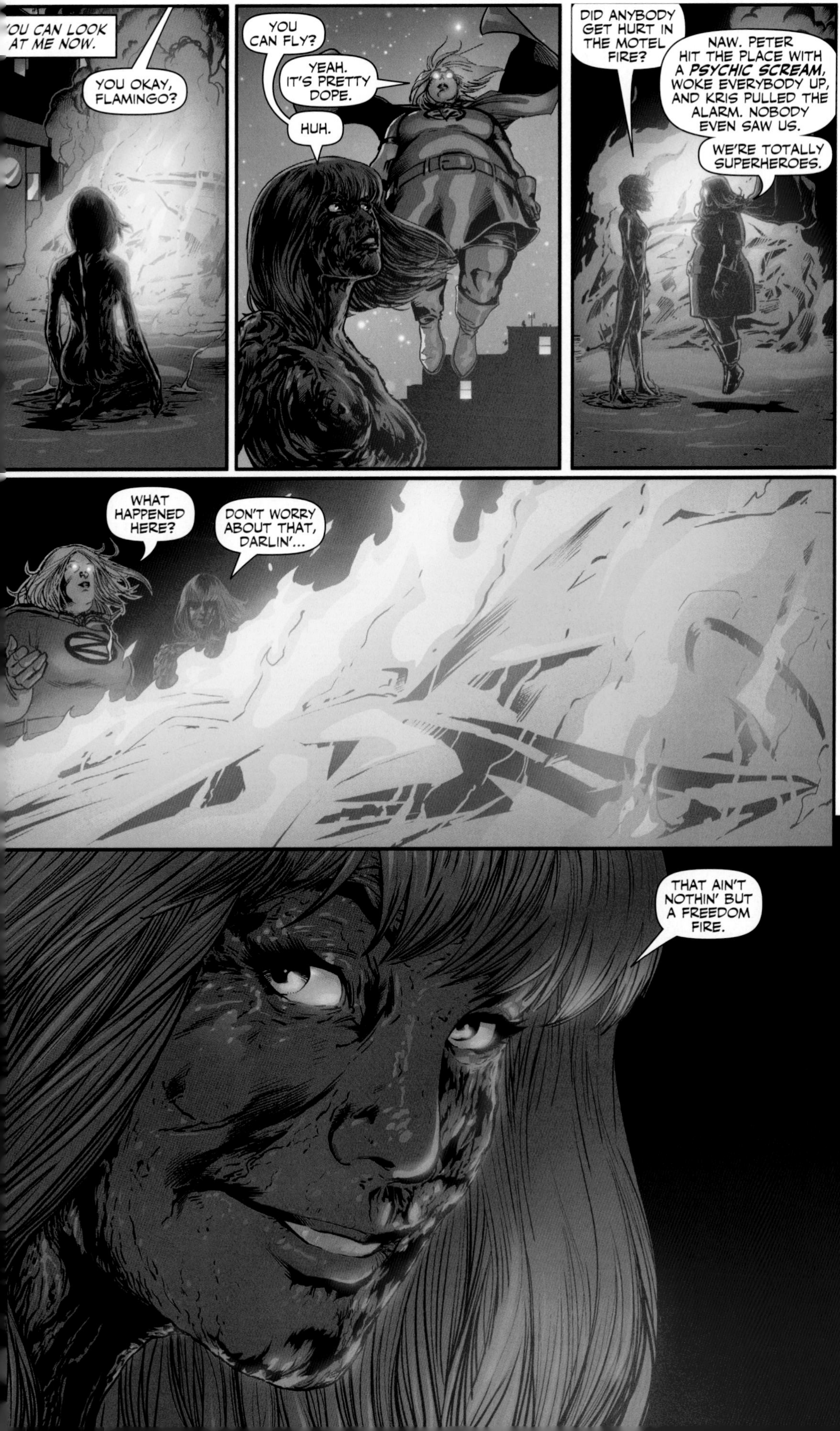

YOU CAN LOOK AT ME NOW.
YOU OKAY, FLAMINGO?
YOU CAN FLY?
YEAH. IT'S PRETTY DOPE.
HUH.
DID ANYBODY GET HURT IN THE MOTEL FIRE?
NAW. PETER HIT THE PLACE WITH A PSYCHIC SCREAM, WOKE EVERYBODY UP, AND KRIS PULLED THE ALARM. NOBODY EVEN SAW US.
WE'RE TOTALLY SUPERHEROES.
WHAT HAPPENED HERE?
DON'T WORRY ABOUT THAT, DARLIN'...
THAT AIN'T NOTHIN' BUT A FREEDOM FIRE.

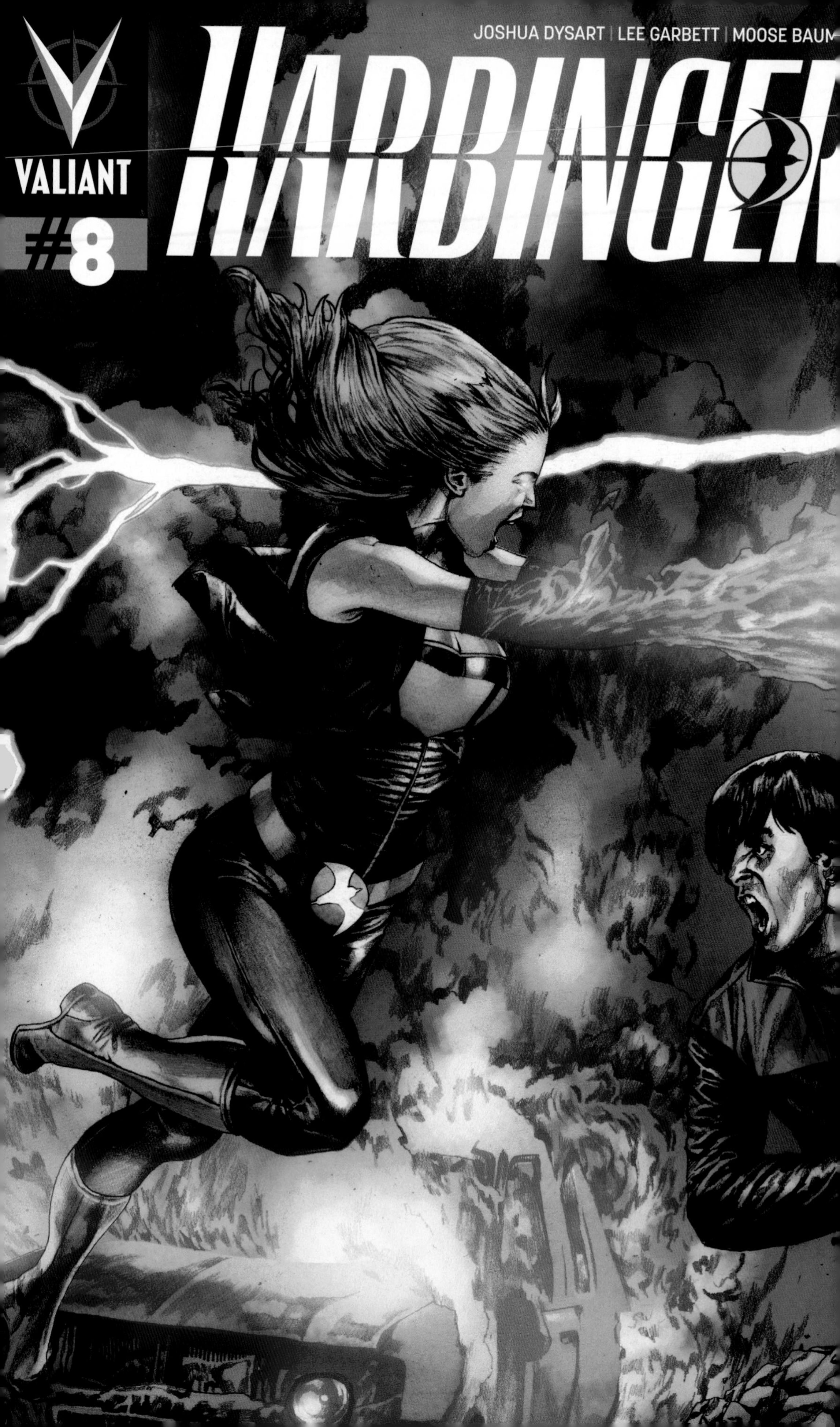
VALIANT
#8
JOSHUA DYSART | LEE GARBETT | MOOSE BAUM
HARBINGER

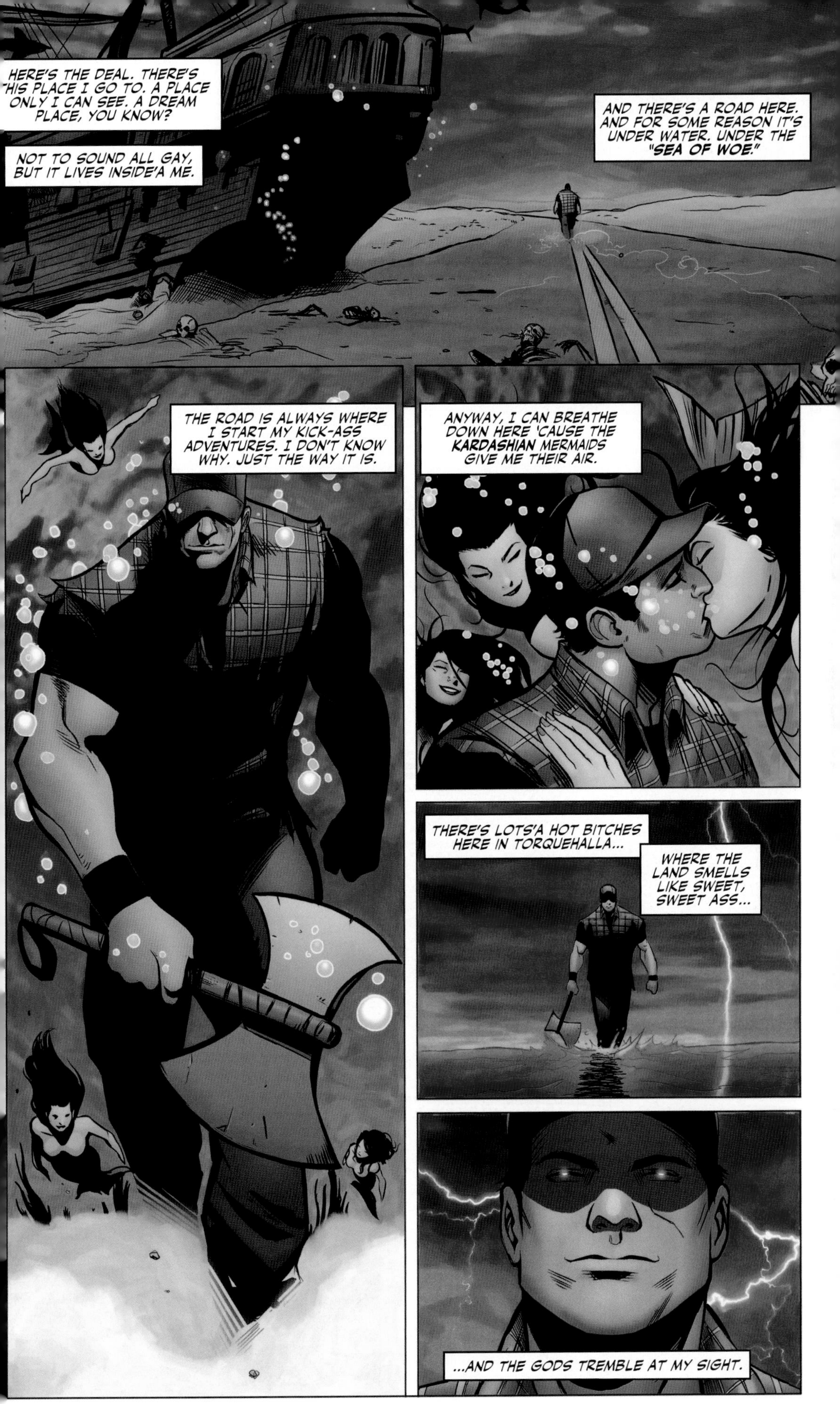
HERE'S THE DEAL. THERE'S THIS PLACE I GO TO. A PLACE ONLY I CAN SEE. A DREAM PLACE, YOU KNOW?
NOT TO SOUND ALL GAY, BUT IT LIVES INSIDE'A ME.
AND THERE'S A ROAD HERE. AND FOR SOME REASON IT'S UNDER WATER. UNDER THE "SEA OF WOE."
THE ROAD IS ALWAYS WHERE I START MY KICK-ASS ADVENTURES. I DON'T KNOW WHY. JUST THE WAY IT IS.
ANYWAY, I CAN BREATHE DOWN HERE 'CAUSE THE KARDASHIAN MERMAIDS GIVE ME THEIR AIR.
THERE'S LOTS'A HOT BITCHES HERE IN TORQUEHALLA...
WHERE THE LAND SMELLS LIKE SWEET, SWEET ASS...
...AND THE GODS TREMBLE AT MY SIGHT.

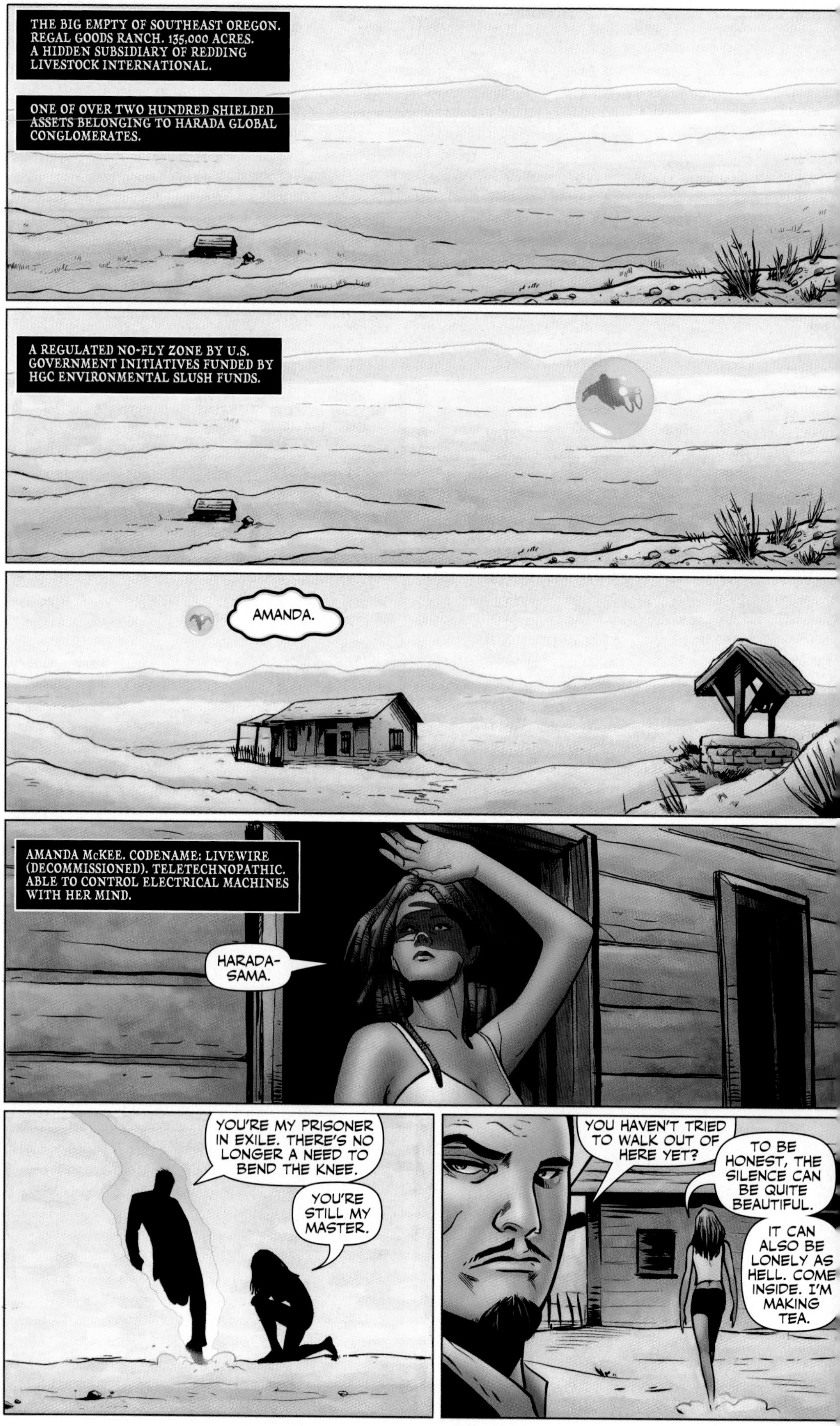
THE BIG EMPTY OF SOUTHEAST OREGON. REGAL GOODS RANCH. 135,000 ACRES. A HIDDEN SUBSIDIARY OF REDDING LIVESTOCK INTERNATIONAL.
ONE OF OVER TWO HUNDRED SHIELDED ASSETS BELONGING TO HARADA GLOBAL CONGLOMERATES.
A REGULATED NO-FLY ZONE BY U.S. GOVERNMENT INITIATIVES FUNDED BY HGC ENVIRONMENTAL SLUSH FUNDS.
AMANDA.
AMANDA McKEE. CODENAME: LIVEWIRE (DECOMMISSIONED). TELETECHNOPATHIC. ABLE TO CONTROL ELECTRICAL MACHINES WITH HER MIND.
HARADA-SAMA.
YOU'RE MY PRISONER IN EXILE. THERE'S NO LONGER A NEED TO BEND THE KNEE.
YOU'RE STILL MY MASTER.
YOU HAVEN'T TRIED TO WALK OUT OF HERE YET?
TO BE HONEST, THE SILENCE CAN BE QUITE BEAUTIFUL.
IT CAN ALSO BE LONELY AS HELL. COME INSIDE. I'M MAKING TEA.

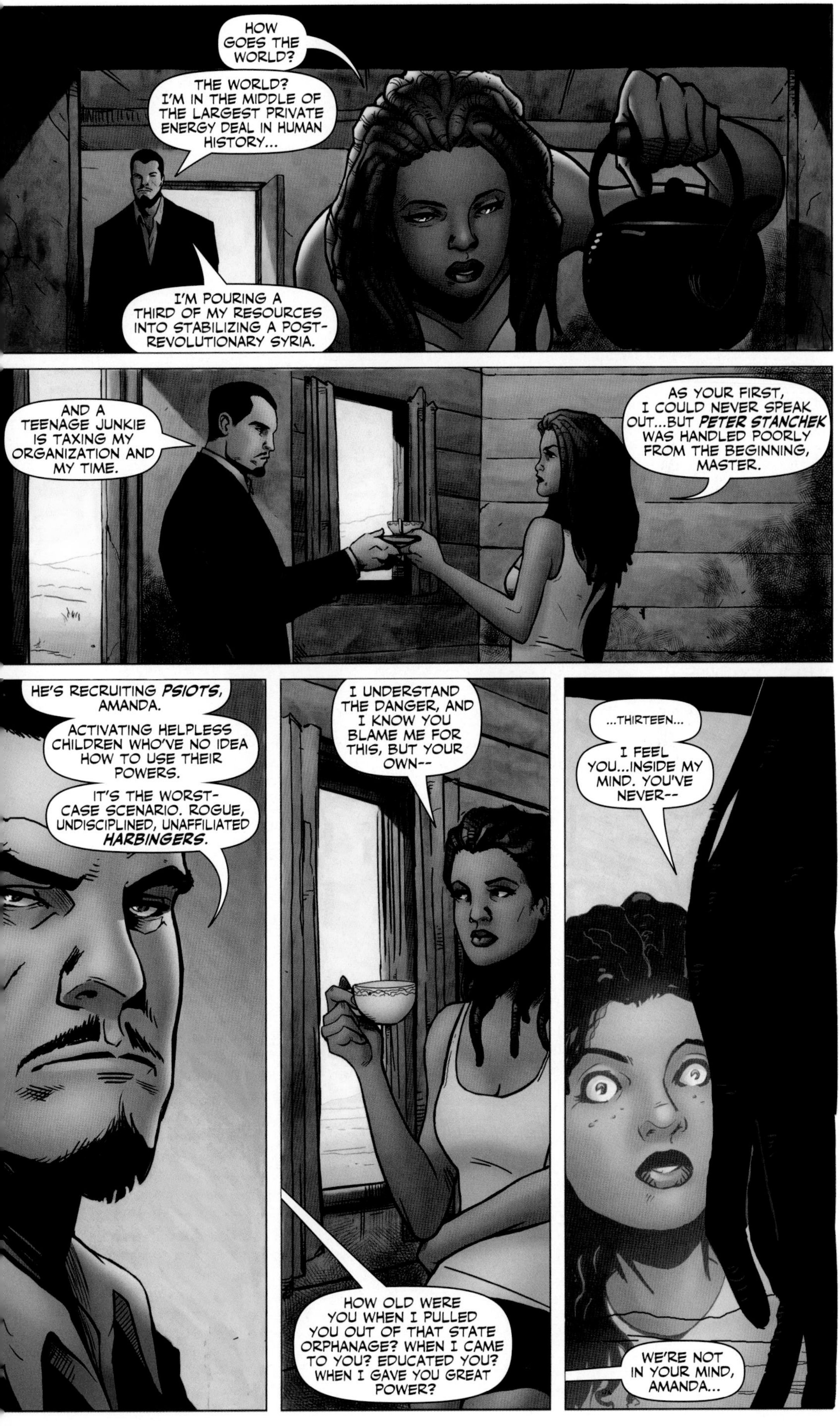
HOW GOES THE WORLD?
THE WORLD? I'M IN THE MIDDLE OF THE LARGEST PRIVATE ENERGY DEAL IN HUMAN HISTORY...
I'M POURING A THIRD OF MY RESOURCES INTO STABILIZING A POST-REVOLUTIONARY SYRIA.
AND A TEENAGE JUNKIE IS TAXING MY ORGANIZATION AND MY TIME.
AS YOUR FIRST, I COULD NEVER SPEAK OUT...BUT PETER STANCHEK WAS HANDLED POORLY FROM THE BEGINNING, MASTER.
HE'S RECRUITING PSIOTS, AMANDA.
ACTIVATING HELPLESS CHILDREN WHO'VE NO IDEA HOW TO USE THEIR POWERS.
IT'S THE WORST-CASE SCENARIO. ROGUE, UNDISCIPLINED, UNAFFILIATED HARBINGERS.
I UNDERSTAND THE DANGER, AND I KNOW YOU BLAME ME FOR THIS, BUT YOUR OWN--
HOW OLD WERE YOU WHEN I PULLED YOU OUT OF THAT STATE ORPHANAGE? WHEN I CAME TO YOU? EDUCATED YOU? WHEN I GAVE YOU GREAT POWER?
...THIRTEEN...
I FEEL YOU...INSIDE MY MIND. YOU'VE NEVER--
WE'RE NOT IN YOUR MIND, AMANDA...

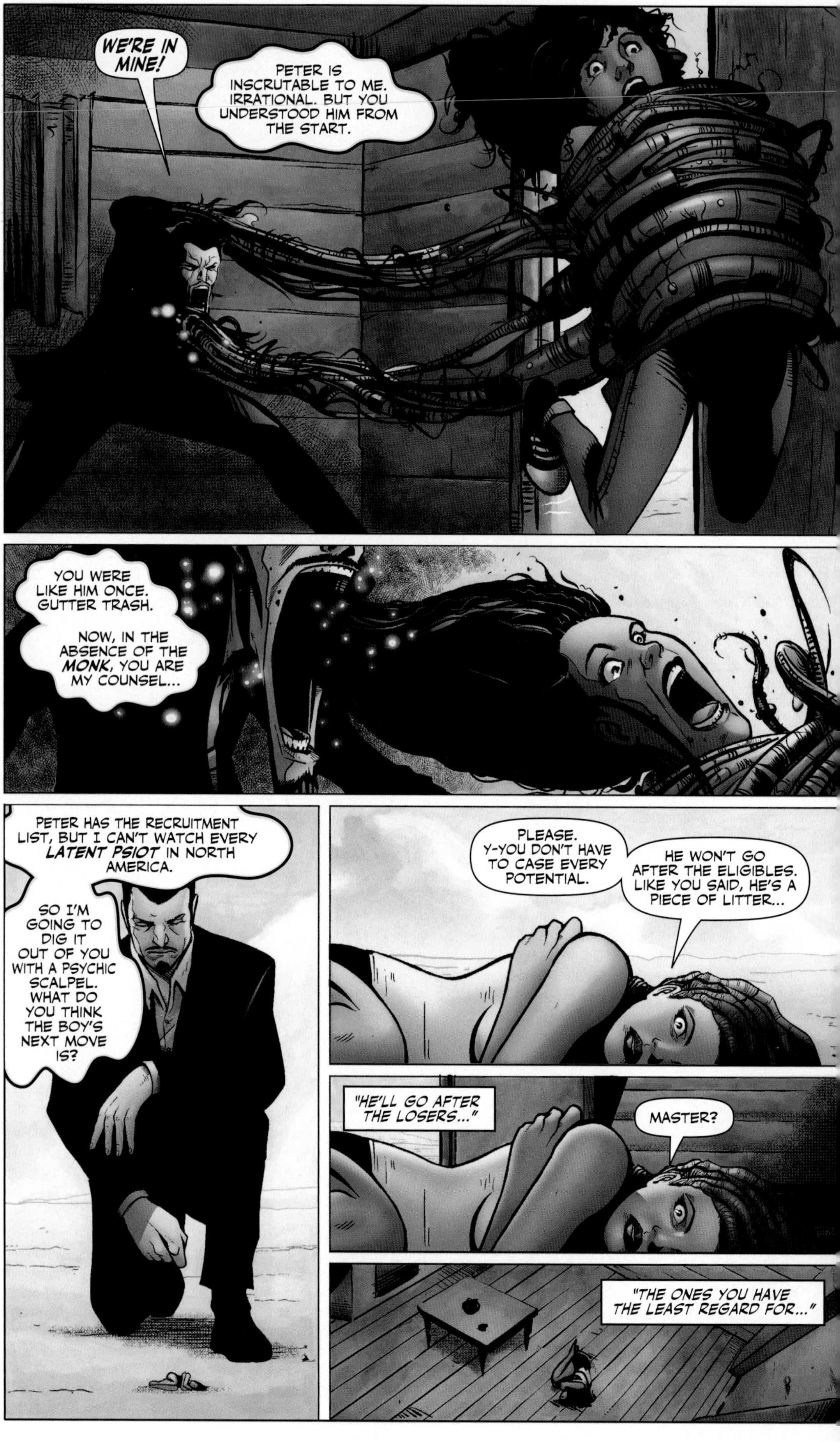
WE'RE IN MINE!
PETER IS INSCRUTABLE TO ME. IRRATIONAL. BUT YOU UNDERSTOOD HIM FROM THE START.
YOU WERE LIKE HIM ONCE. GUTTER TRASH.
NOW, IN THE ABSENCE OF THE MONK, YOU ARE MY COUNSEL...
PETER HAS THE RECRUITMENT LIST, BUT I CAN'T WATCH EVERY LATENT PSIOT IN NORTH AMERICA.
SO I'M GOING TO DIG IT OUT OF YOU WITH A PSYCHIC SCALPEL. WHAT DO YOU THINK THE BOY'S NEXT MOVE IS?
PLEASE. Y-YOU DON'T HAVE TO CASE EVERY POTENTIAL.
HE WON'T GO AFTER THE ELIGIBLES. LIKE YOU SAID, HE'S A PIECE OF LITTER...
"HE'LL GO AFTER THE LOSERS..."
MASTER?
"THE ONES YOU HAVE THE LEAST REGARD FOR..."

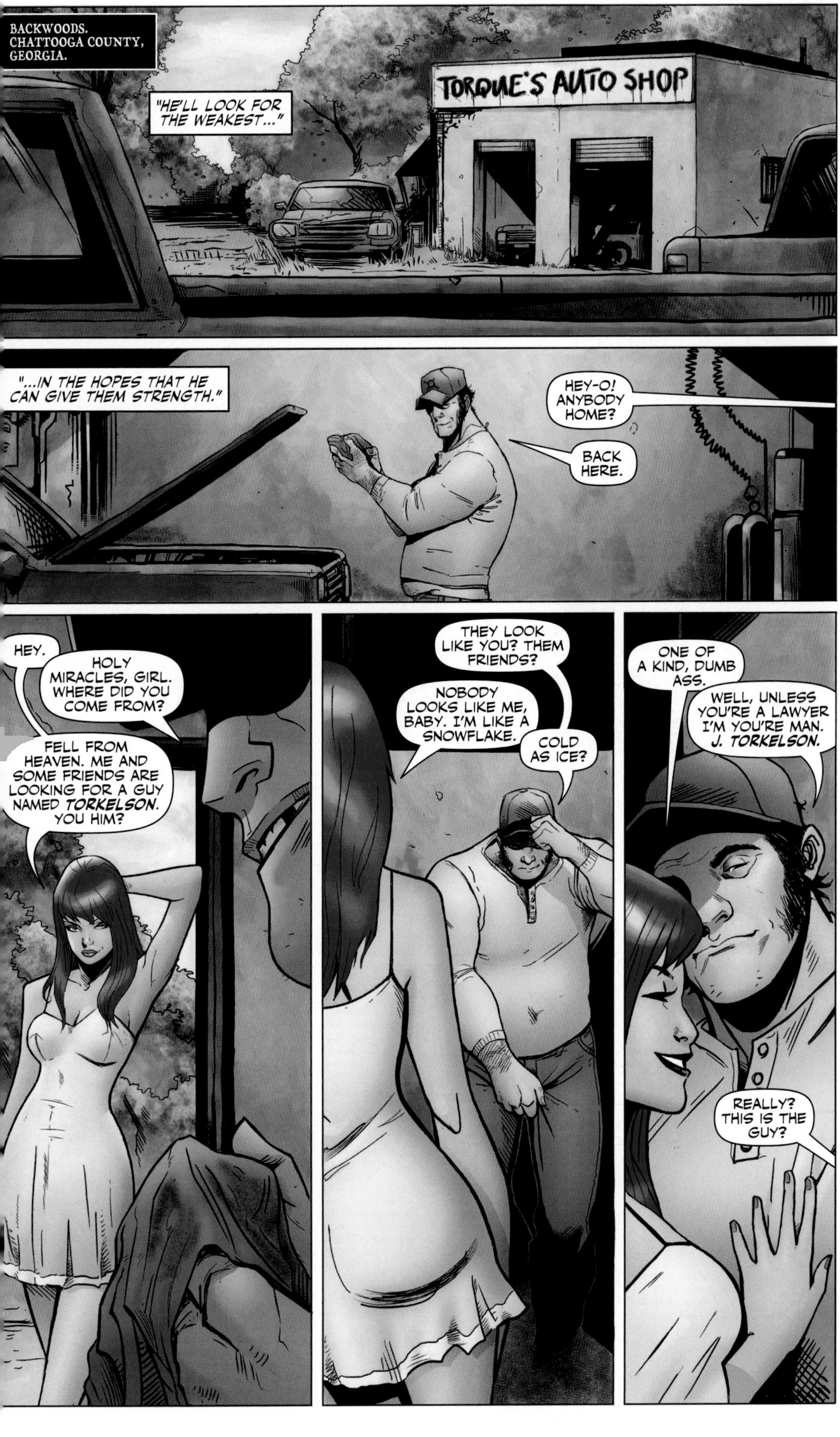
BACKWOODS. CHATTOOGA COUNTY, GEORGIA.
TORQUE'S AUTO SHOP
"HE'LL LOOK FOR THE WEAKEST..."
"...IN THE HOPES THAT HE CAN GIVE THEM STRENGTH."
HEY-O! ANYBODY HOME?
BACK HERE.
HEY.
HOLY MIRACLES, GIRL. WHERE DID YOU COME FROM?
FELL FROM HEAVEN. ME AND SOME FRIENDS ARE LOOKING FOR A GUY NAMED TORKELSON. YOU HIM?
THEY LOOK LIKE YOU? THEM FRIENDS?
NOBODY LOOKS LIKE ME, BABY. I'M LIKE A SNOWFLAKE.
COLD AS ICE?
ONE OF A KIND, DUMB ASS.
WELL, UNLESS YOU'RE A LAWYER I'M YOU'RE MAN. J. TORKELSON.
REALLY? THIS IS THE GUY?

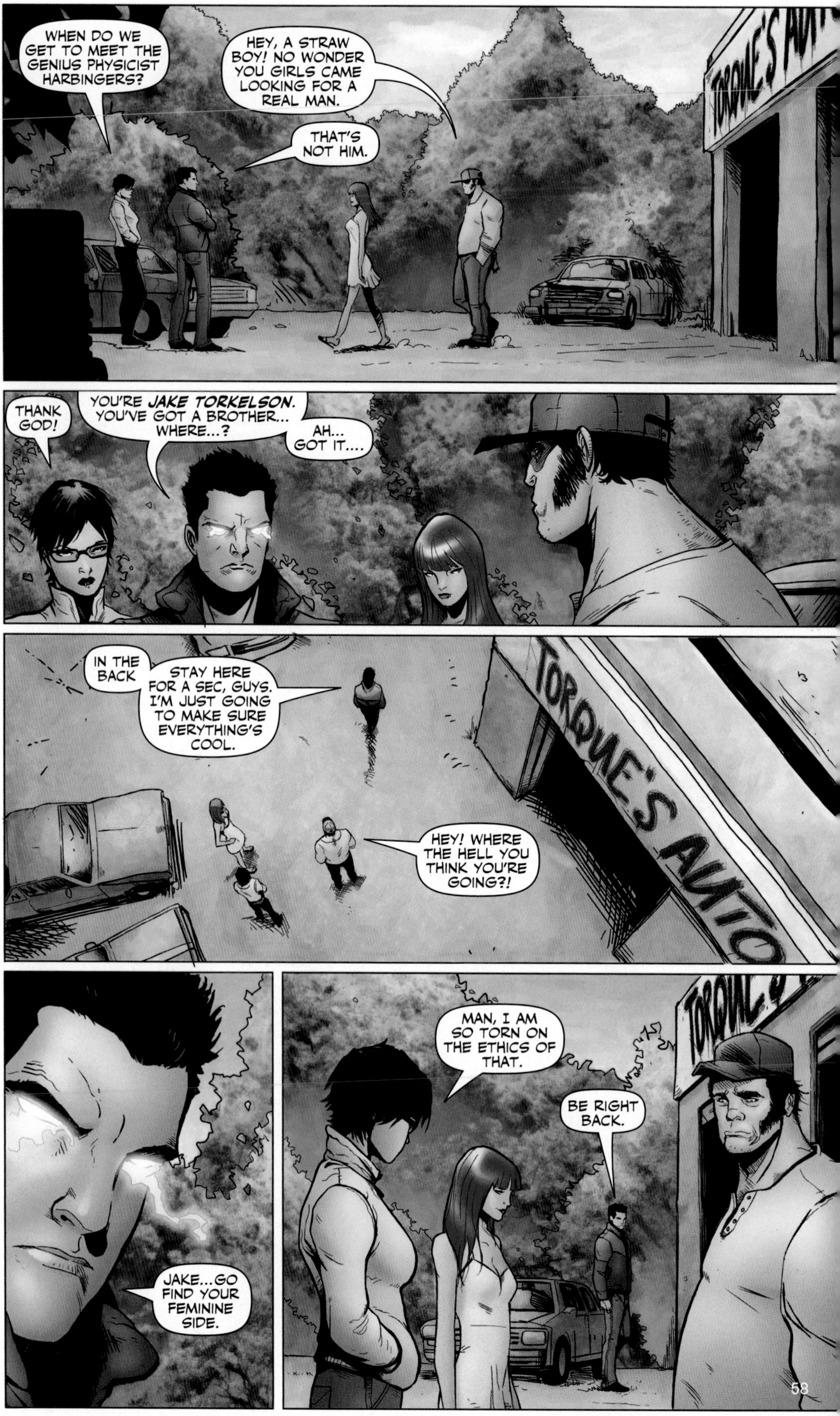
WHEN DO WE GET TO MEET THE GENIUS PHYSICIST HARBINGERS?
HEY, A STRAW BOY! NO WONDER YOU GIRLS CAME LOOKING FOR A REAL MAN.
THAT'S NOT HIM.
TORQUE'S AUTO
THANK GOD!
YOU'RE JAKE TORKELSON. YOU'VE GOT A BROTHER... WHERE...?
AH... GOT IT....
IN THE BACK
STAY HERE FOR A SEC, GUYS. I'M JUST GOING TO MAKE SURE EVERYTHING'S COOL.
TORQUE'S AUTO
HEY! WHERE THE HELL YOU THINK YOU'RE GOING?!
JAKE...GO FIND YOUR FEMININE SIDE.
MAN, I AM SO TORN ON THE ETHICS OF THAT.
BE RIGHT BACK.

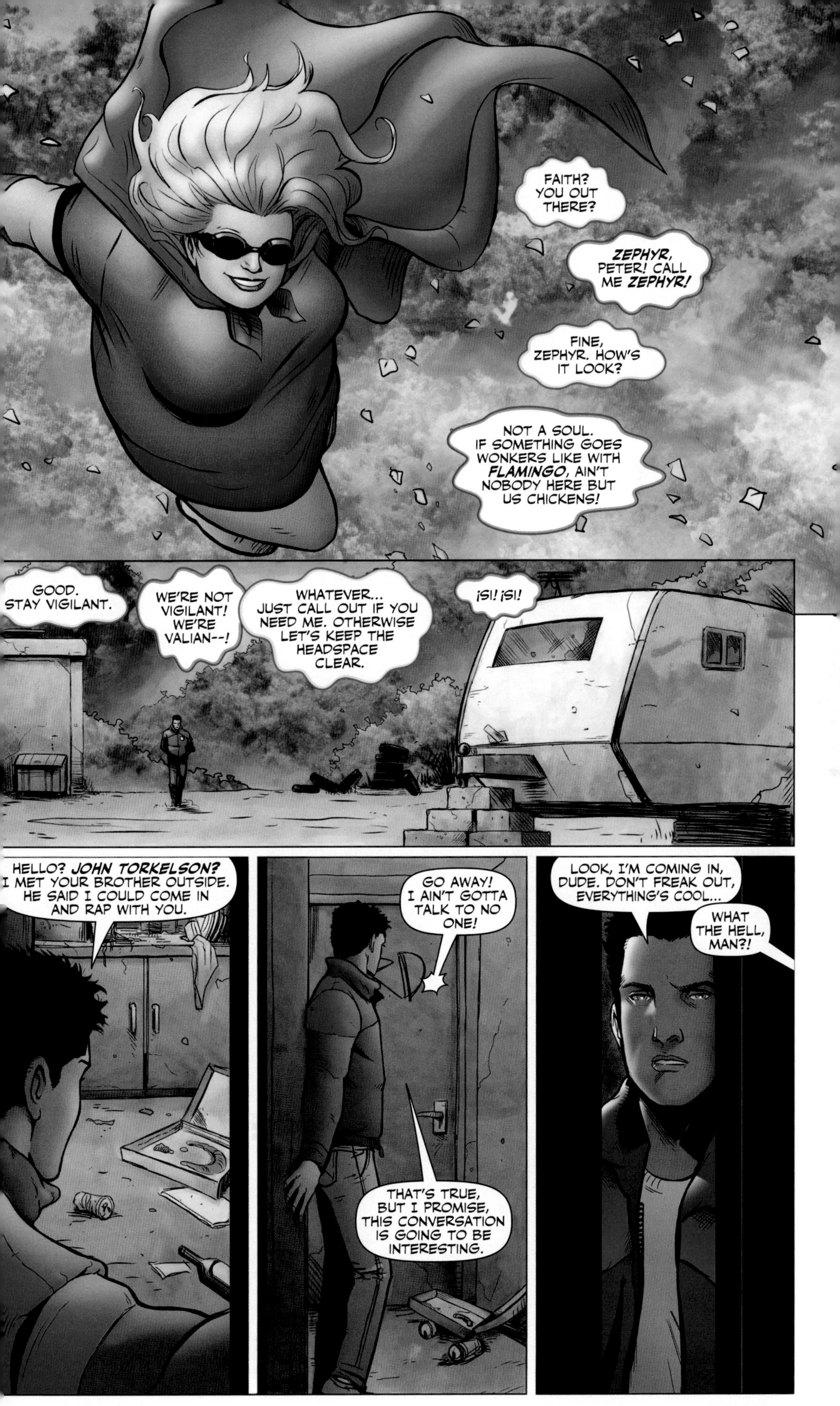
FAITH? YOU OUT THERE?
*ZEPHYR*, PETER! CALL ME *ZEPHYR!*
FINE, ZEPHYR. HOW'S IT LOOK?
NOT A SOUL. IF SOMETHING GOES WONKERS LIKE WITH *FLAMINGO*, AIN'T NOBODY HERE BUT US CHICKENS!
GOOD. STAY VIGILANT.
WE'RE NOT VIGILANT! WE'RE VALIAN--!
WHATEVER... JUST CALL OUT IF YOU NEED ME. OTHERWISE LET'S KEEP THE HEADSPACE CLEAR.
¡SI! ¡SI!
HELLO? *JOHN TORKELSON?* I MET YOUR BROTHER OUTSIDE. HE SAID I COULD COME IN AND RAP WITH YOU.
GO AWAY! I AIN'T GOTTA TALK TO NO ONE!
THAT'S TRUE, BUT I PROMISE, THIS CONVERSATION IS GOING TO BE INTERESTING.
LOOK, I'M COMING IN, DUDE. DON'T FREAK OUT, EVERYTHING'S COOL...
WHAT THE HELL, MAN?!

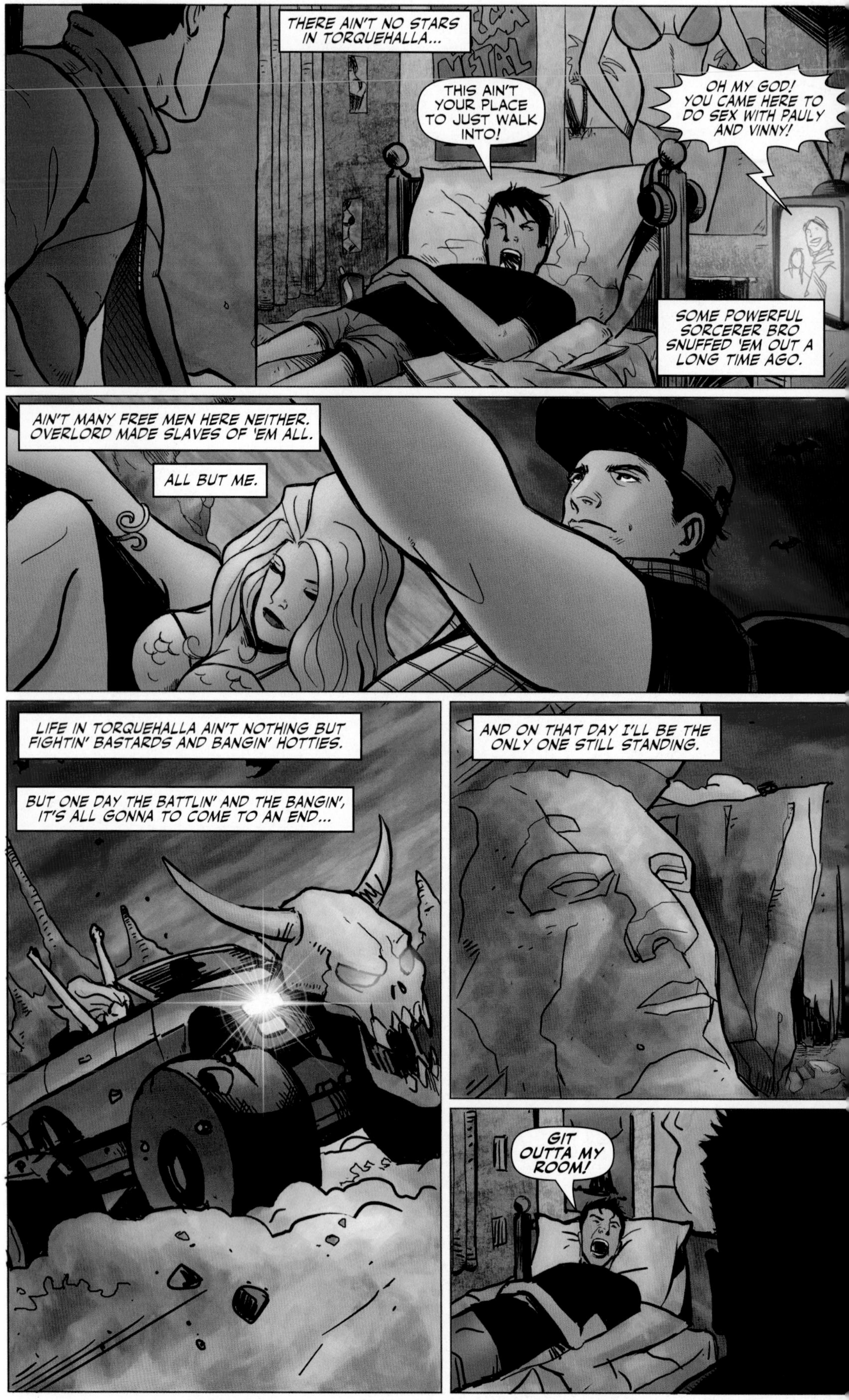

THERE AIN'T NO STARS IN TORQUEHALLA...
THIS AIN'T YOUR PLACE TO JUST WALK INTO!
OH MY GOD! YOU CAME HERE TO DO SEX WITH PAULY AND VINNY!
SOME POWERFUL SORCERER BRO SNUFFED 'EM OUT A LONG TIME AGO.
AIN'T MANY FREE MEN HERE NEITHER. OVERLORD MADE SLAVES OF 'EM ALL.
ALL BUT ME.
LIFE IN TORQUEHALLA AIN'T NOTHING BUT FIGHTIN' BASTARDS AND BANGIN' HOTTIES.
BUT ONE DAY THE BATTLIN' AND THE BANGIN', IT'S ALL GONNA TO COME TO AN END...
AND ON THAT DAY I'LL BE THE ONLY ONE STILL STANDING.
GIT OUTTA MY ROOM!

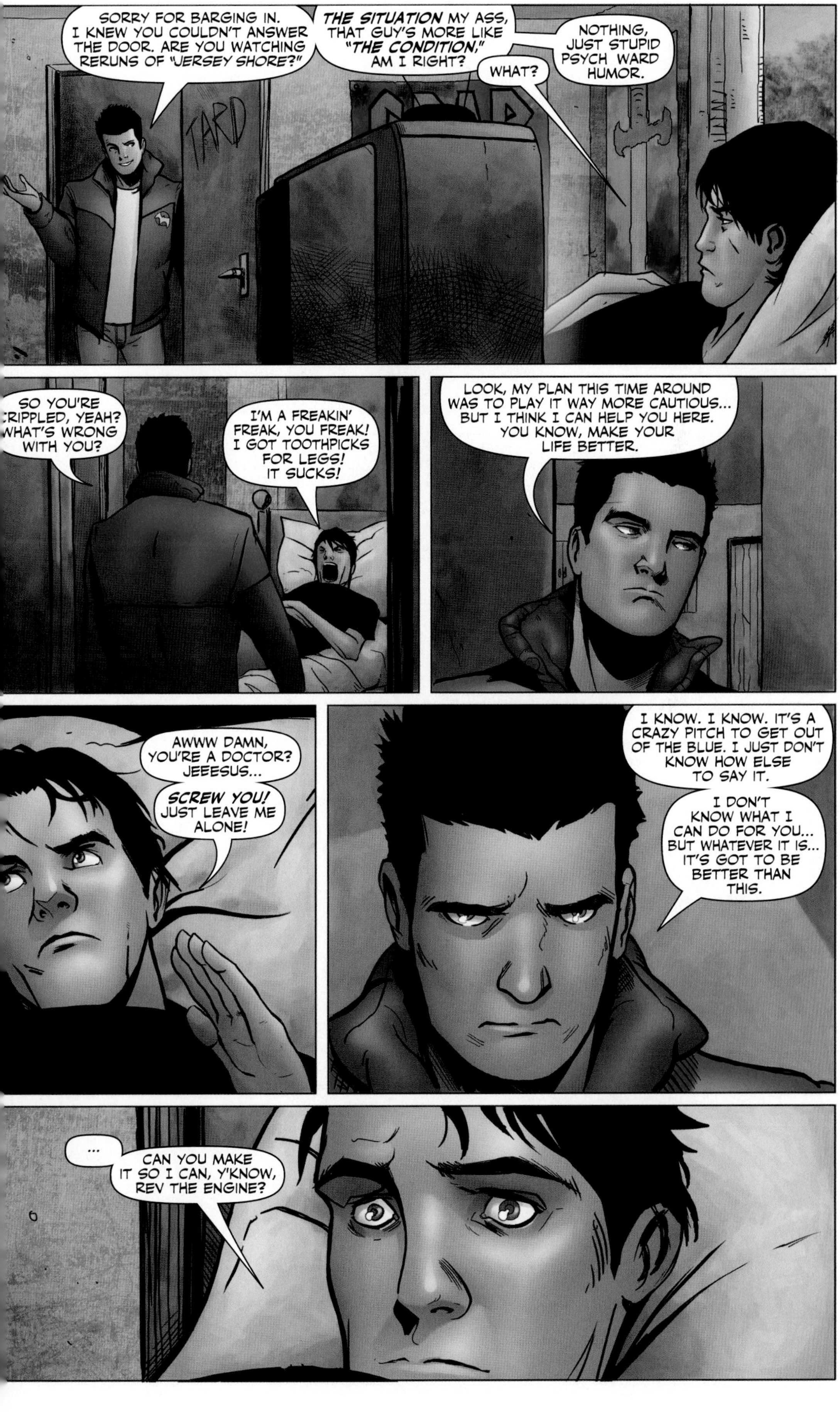
SORRY FOR BARGING IN. I KNEW YOU COULDN'T ANSWER THE DOOR. ARE YOU WATCHING RERUNS OF "JERSEY SHORE?"
THE SITUATION MY ASS, THAT GUY'S MORE LIKE "THE CONDITION," AM I RIGHT?
WHAT?
NOTHING, JUST STUPID PSYCH WARD HUMOR.
TARD
SO YOU'RE CRIPPLED, YEAH? WHAT'S WRONG WITH YOU?
I'M A FREAKIN' FREAK, YOU FREAK! I GOT TOOTHPICKS FOR LEGS! IT SUCKS!
LOOK, MY PLAN THIS TIME AROUND WAS TO PLAY IT WAY MORE CAUTIOUS... BUT I THINK I CAN HELP YOU HERE. YOU KNOW, MAKE YOUR LIFE BETTER.
AWWW DAMN, YOU'RE A DOCTOR? JEEESUS...
SCREW YOU! JUST LEAVE ME ALONE!
I KNOW. I KNOW. IT'S A CRAZY PITCH TO GET OUT OF THE BLUE. I JUST DON'T KNOW HOW ELSE TO SAY IT.
I DON'T KNOW WHAT I CAN DO FOR YOU... BUT WHATEVER IT IS... IT'S GOT TO BE BETTER THAN THIS.
...
CAN YOU MAKE IT SO I CAN, Y'KNOW, REV THE ENGINE?

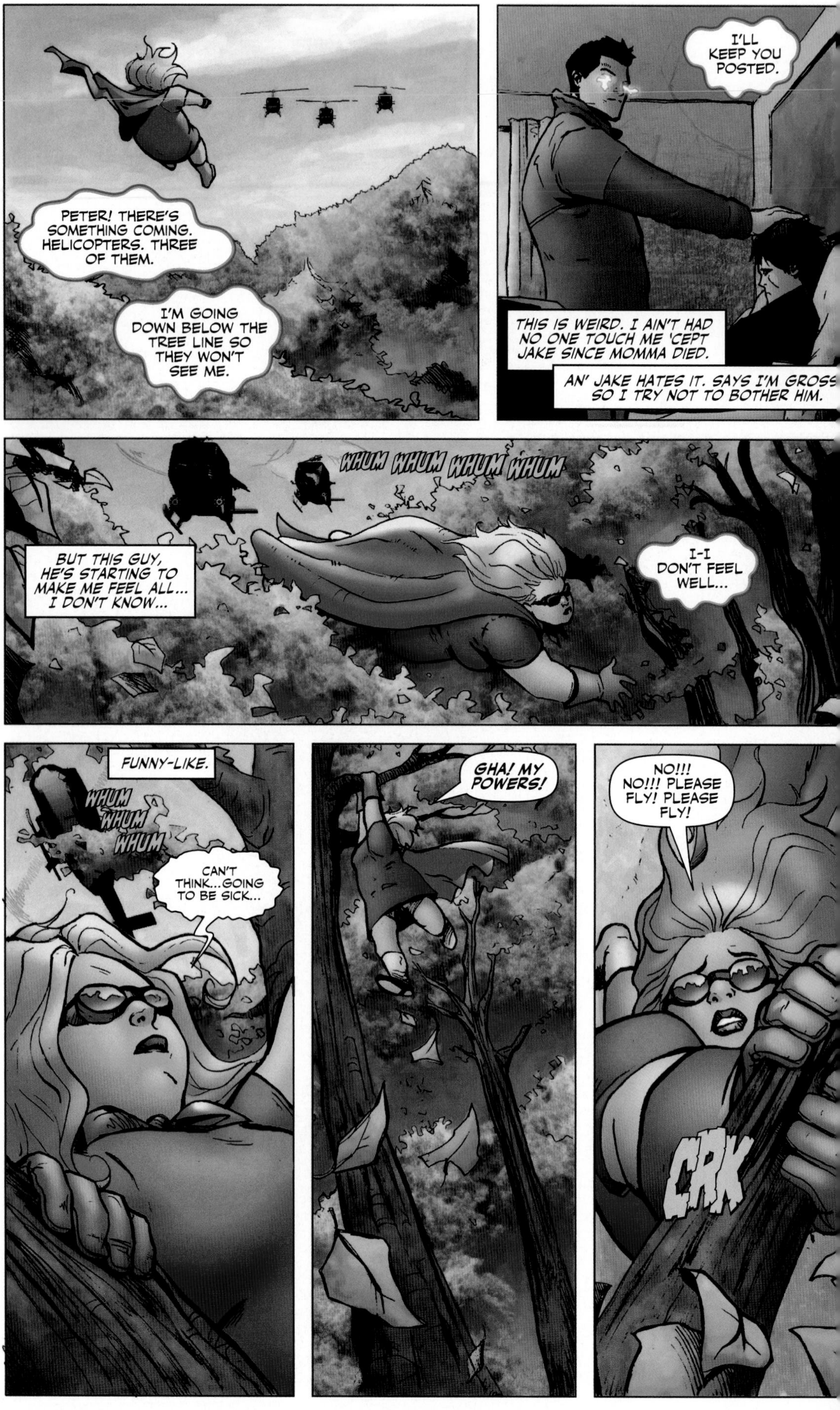
PETER! THERE'S SOMETHING COMING. HELICOPTERS. THREE OF THEM.
I'M GOING DOWN BELOW THE TREE LINE SO THEY WON'T SEE ME.
I'LL KEEP YOU POSTED.
THIS IS WEIRD. I AIN'T HAD NO ONE TOUCH ME 'CEPT JAKE SINCE MOMMA DIED.
AN' JAKE HATES IT. SAYS I'M GROSS SO I TRY NOT TO BOTHER HIM.
WHUM WHUM WHUM WHUM
BUT THIS GUY, HE'S STARTING TO MAKE ME FEEL ALL... I DON'T KNOW...
I-I DON'T FEEL WELL...
FUNNY-LIKE.
WHUM WHUM WHUM
CAN'T THINK...GOING TO BE SICK...
GHA! MY POWERS!
NO!!! NO!!! PLEASE FLY! PLEASE FLY!
CRK

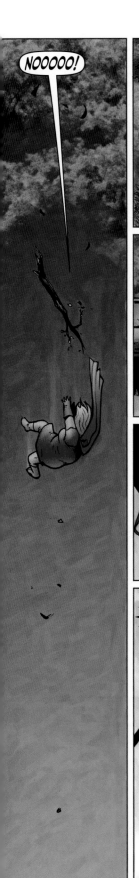

NOOOOO!

YOU HEAR THAT?

HELICOPT... UGH...ERS?

AGHH! WHAAA--

SOMETHING'S WRONG. MY HEAD... OH NO...

THEY FOUND US!

GRAY LEADER. WE HAVE A VISUAL ON HATHAWAY.

RELEASING SYNAPTIC BOMBS NOW.

ROGER THAT, AIR ONE.

FIRST FIELD TEST FOR NEW TECH IS ALWAYS A THRILL.

AGHHH!!!

FWOOSHH

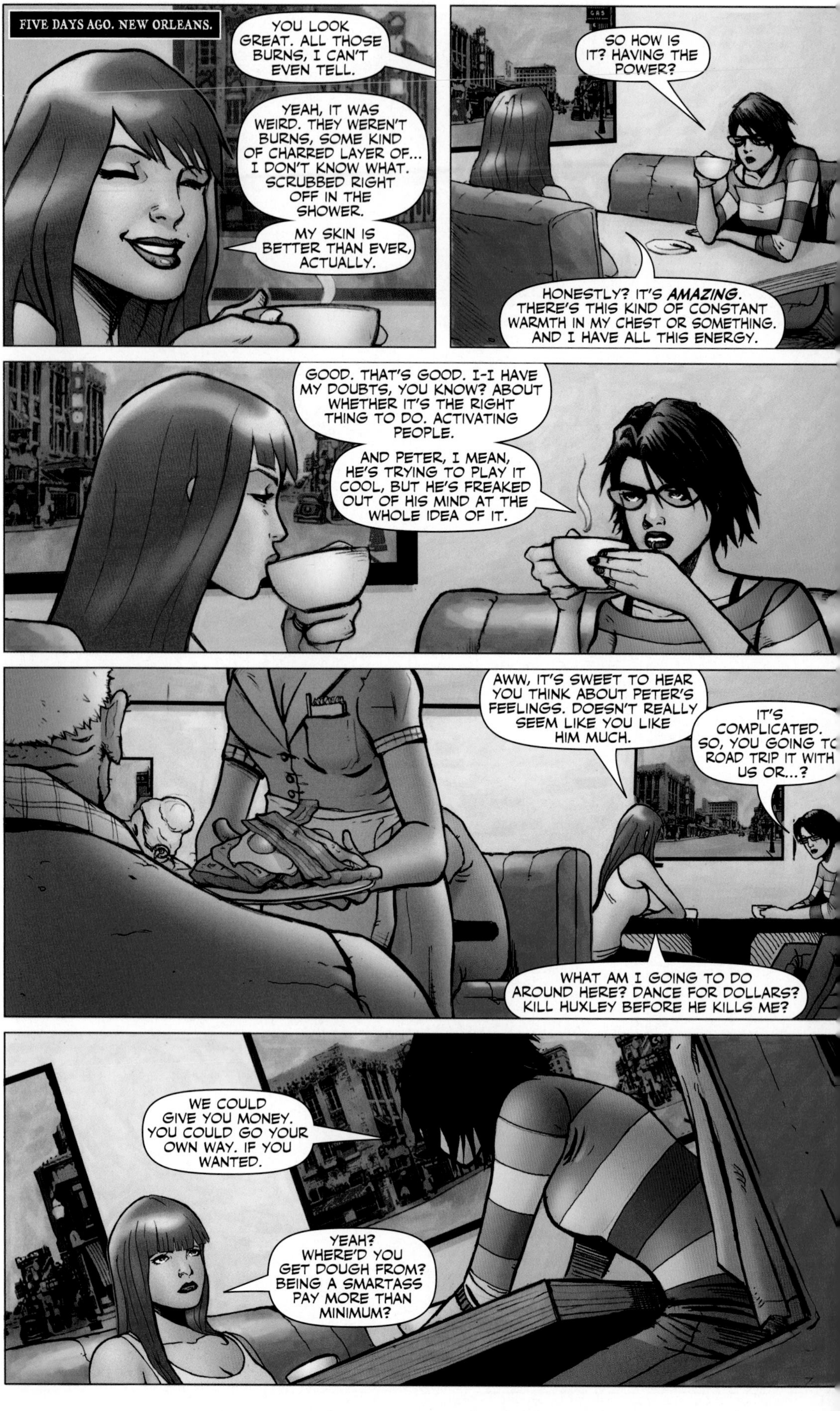
FIVE DAYS AGO. NEW ORLEANS.
YOU LOOK GREAT. ALL THOSE BURNS, I CAN'T EVEN TELL.
YEAH, IT WAS WEIRD. THEY WEREN'T BURNS, SOME KIND OF CHARRED LAYER OF... I DON'T KNOW WHAT. SCRUBBED RIGHT OFF IN THE SHOWER.
MY SKIN IS BETTER THAN EVER, ACTUALLY.
SO HOW IS IT? HAVING THE POWER?
HONESTLY? IT'S *AMAZING*. THERE'S THIS KIND OF CONSTANT WARMTH IN MY CHEST OR SOMETHING. AND I HAVE ALL THIS ENERGY.
GOOD. THAT'S GOOD. I-I HAVE MY DOUBTS, YOU KNOW? ABOUT WHETHER IT'S THE RIGHT THING TO DO. ACTIVATING PEOPLE.
AND PETER, I MEAN, HE'S TRYING TO PLAY IT COOL, BUT HE'S FREAKED OUT OF HIS MIND AT THE WHOLE IDEA OF IT.
AWW, IT'S SWEET TO HEAR YOU THINK ABOUT PETER'S FEELINGS. DOESN'T REALLY SEEM LIKE YOU LIKE HIM MUCH.
IT'S COMPLICATED. SO, YOU GOING TO ROAD TRIP IT WITH US OR...?
WHAT AM I GOING TO DO AROUND HERE? DANCE FOR DOLLARS? KILL HUXLEY BEFORE HE KILLS ME?
WE COULD GIVE YOU MONEY. YOU COULD GO YOUR OWN WAY. IF YOU WANTED.
YEAH? WHERE'D YOU GET DOUGH FROM? BEING A SMARTASS PAY MORE THAN MINIMUM?

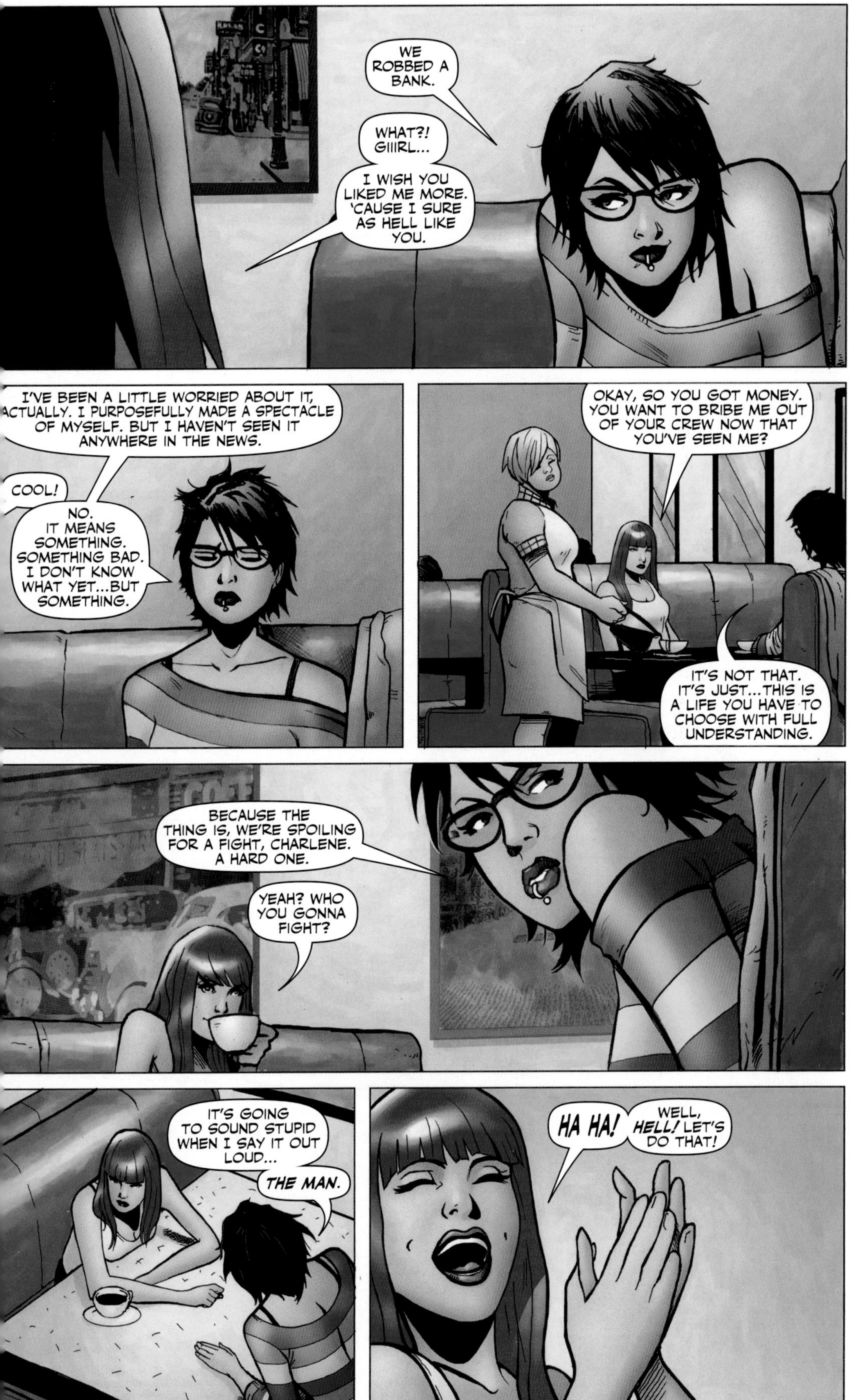

WE ROBBED A BANK.
WHAT?! GIIIRL...
I WISH YOU LIKED ME MORE. 'CAUSE I SURE AS HELL LIKE YOU.
I'VE BEEN A LITTLE WORRIED ABOUT IT, ACTUALLY. I PURPOSEFULLY MADE A SPECTACLE OF MYSELF. BUT I HAVEN'T SEEN IT ANYWHERE IN THE NEWS.
COOL!
NO. IT MEANS SOMETHING. SOMETHING BAD. I DON'T KNOW WHAT YET...BUT SOMETHING.
OKAY, SO YOU GOT MONEY. YOU WANT TO BRIBE ME OUT OF YOUR CREW NOW THAT YOU'VE SEEN ME?
IT'S NOT THAT. IT'S JUST...THIS IS A LIFE YOU HAVE TO CHOOSE WITH FULL UNDERSTANDING.
BECAUSE THE THING IS, WE'RE SPOILING FOR A FIGHT, CHARLENE. A HARD ONE.
YEAH? WHO YOU GONNA FIGHT?
IT'S GOING TO SOUND STUPID WHEN I SAY IT OUT LOUD...
THE MAN.
HA HA!
WELL, HELL! LET'S DO THAT!

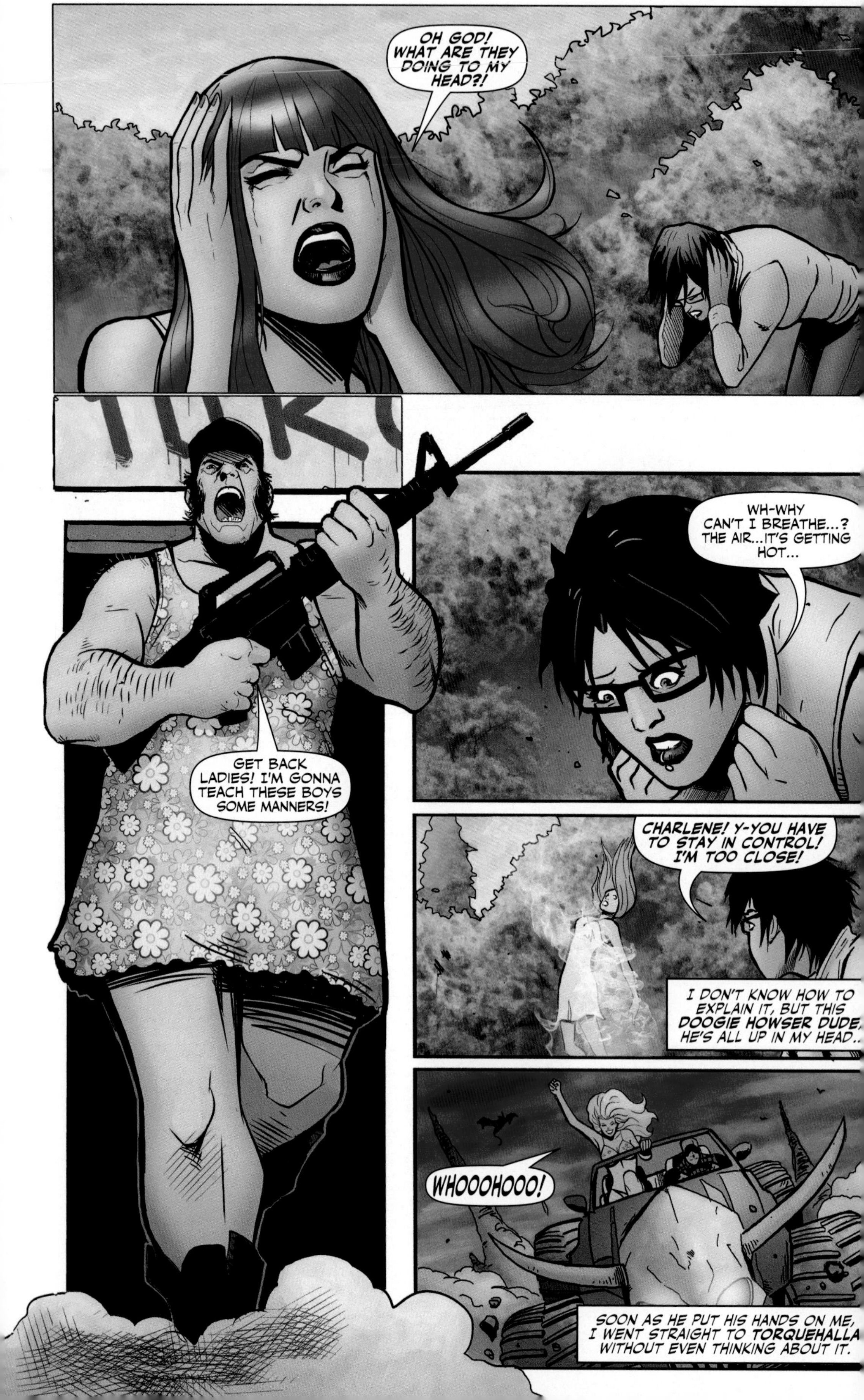

OH GOD! WHAT ARE THEY DOING TO MY HEAD?!
GET BACK LADIES! I'M GONNA TEACH THESE BOYS SOME MANNERS!
WH-WHY CAN'T I BREATHE...? THE AIR...IT'S GETTING HOT...
CHARLENE! Y-YOU HAVE TO STAY IN CONTROL! I'M TOO CLOSE!
I DON'T KNOW HOW TO EXPLAIN IT, BUT THIS DOOGIE HOWSER DUDE, HE'S ALL UP IN MY HEAD...
WHOOOHOOO!
SOON AS HE PUT HIS HANDS ON ME, I WENT STRAIGHT TO TORQUEHALLA WITHOUT EVEN THINKING ABOUT IT.

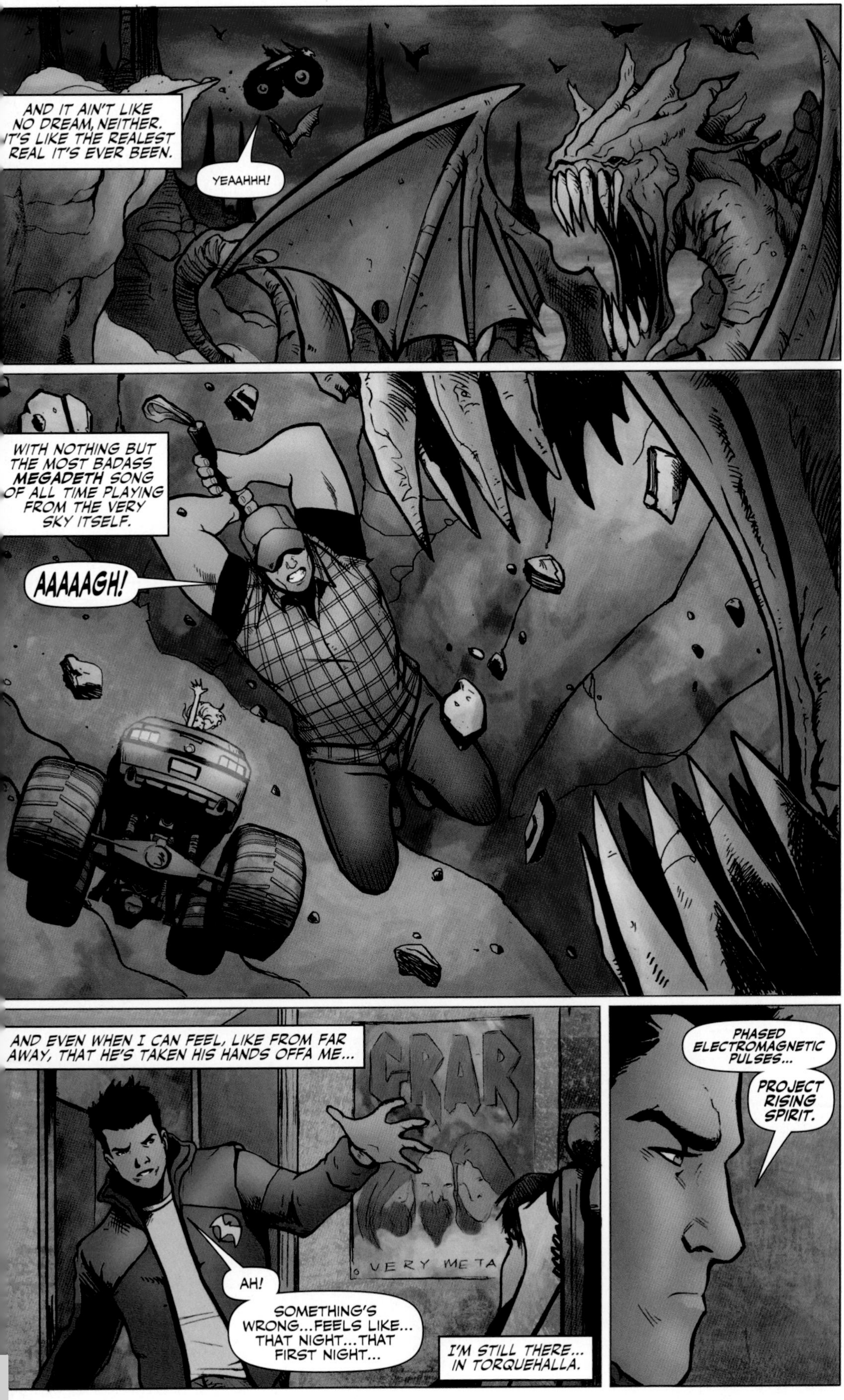
AND IT AIN'T LIKE NO DREAM, NEITHER. IT'S LIKE THE REALEST REAL IT'S EVER BEEN.
YEAAHHH!
WITH NOTHING BUT THE MOST BADASS MEGADETH SONG OF ALL TIME PLAYING FROM THE VERY SKY ITSELF.
AAAAAGH!
AND EVEN WHEN I CAN FEEL, LIKE FROM FAR AWAY, THAT HE'S TAKEN HIS HANDS OFFA ME...
CRAR
VERY META
AH!
SOMETHING'S WRONG...FEELS LIKE... THAT NIGHT...THAT FIRST NIGHT...
I'M STILL THERE... IN TORQUEHALLA.
PHASED ELECTROMAGNETIC PULSES...
PROJECT RISING SPIRIT.

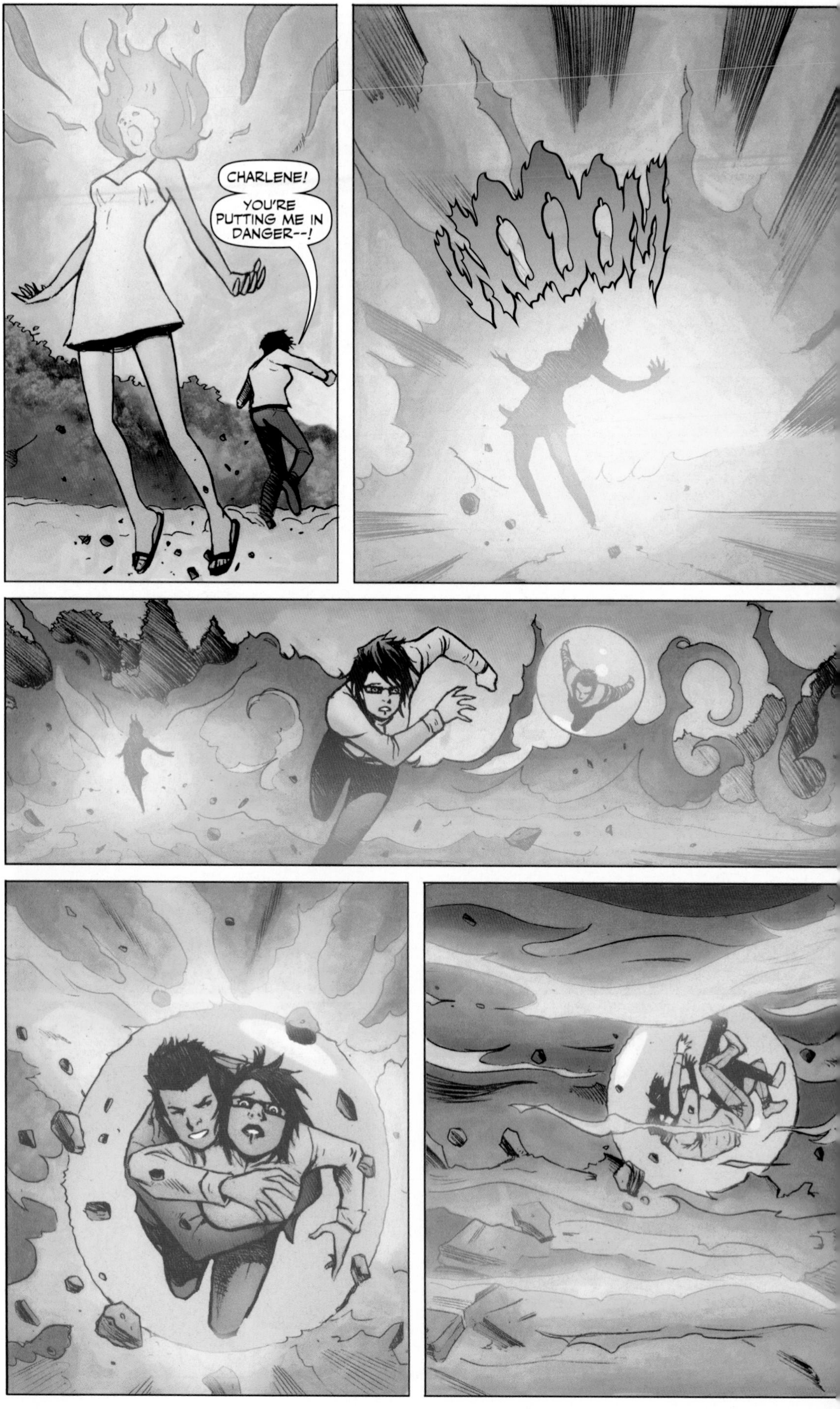
CHARLENE!
YOU'RE PUTTING ME IN DANGER--!

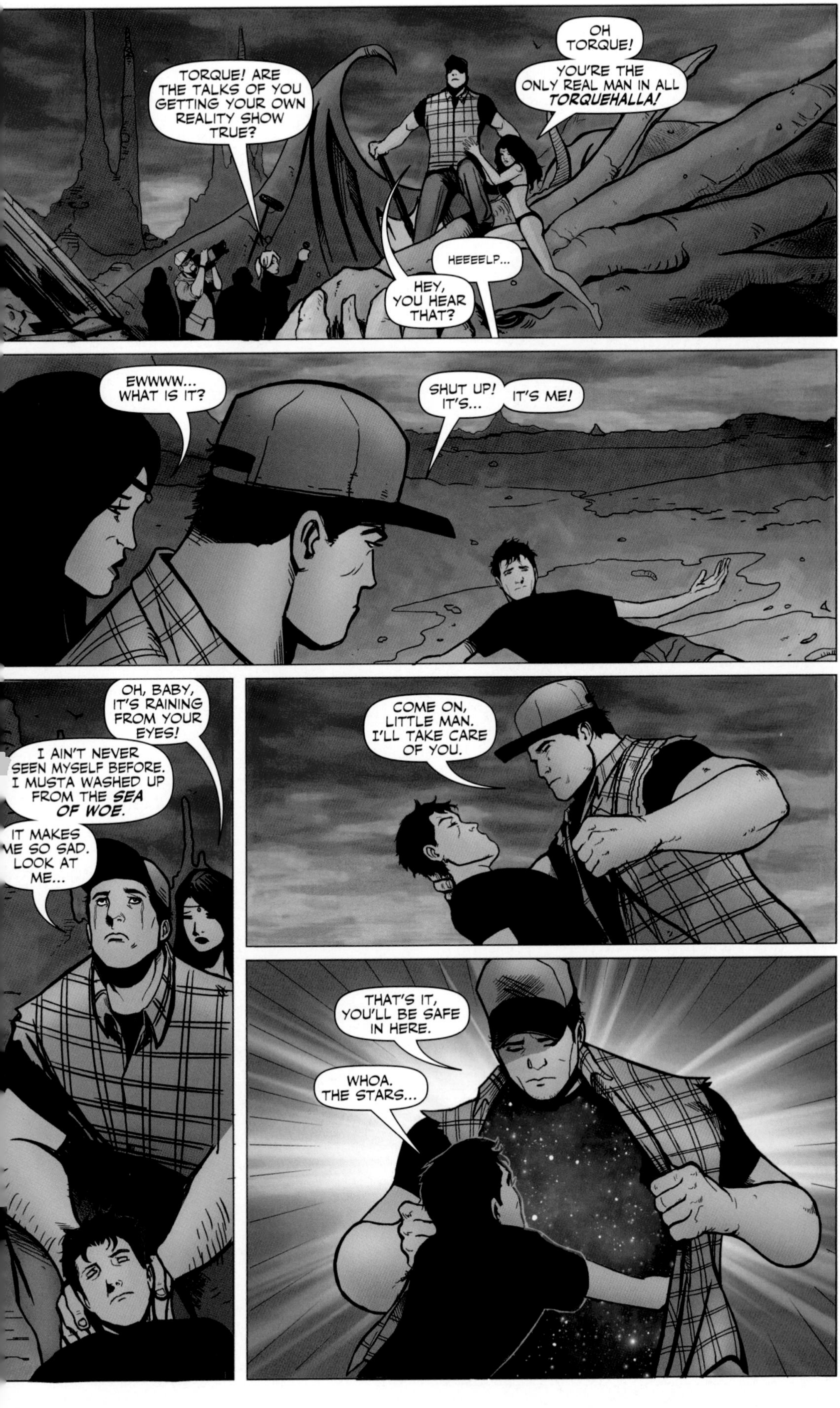
TORQUE! ARE THE TALKS OF YOU GETTING YOUR OWN REALITY SHOW TRUE?
OH TORQUE! YOU'RE THE ONLY REAL MAN IN ALL TORQUEHALLA!
HEEEELP...
HEY, YOU HEAR THAT?
EWWWW... WHAT IS IT?
SHUT UP! IT'S...
IT'S ME!
OH, BABY, IT'S RAINING FROM YOUR EYES!
I AIN'T NEVER SEEN MYSELF BEFORE. I MUSTA WASHED UP FROM THE SEA OF WOE.
IT MAKES ME SO SAD. LOOK AT ME...
COME ON, LITTLE MAN. I'LL TAKE CARE OF YOU.
THAT'S IT, YOU'LL BE SAFE IN HERE.
WHOA. THE STARS...

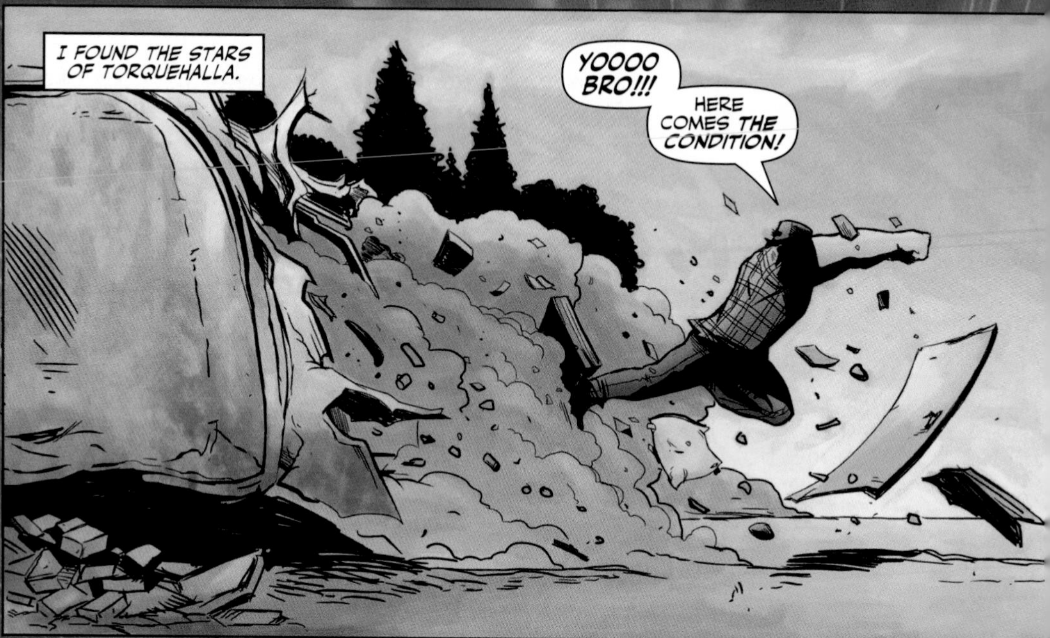
I FOUND THE STARS OF TORQUEHALLA.
YOOOO BRO!!!
HERE COMES THE CONDITION!

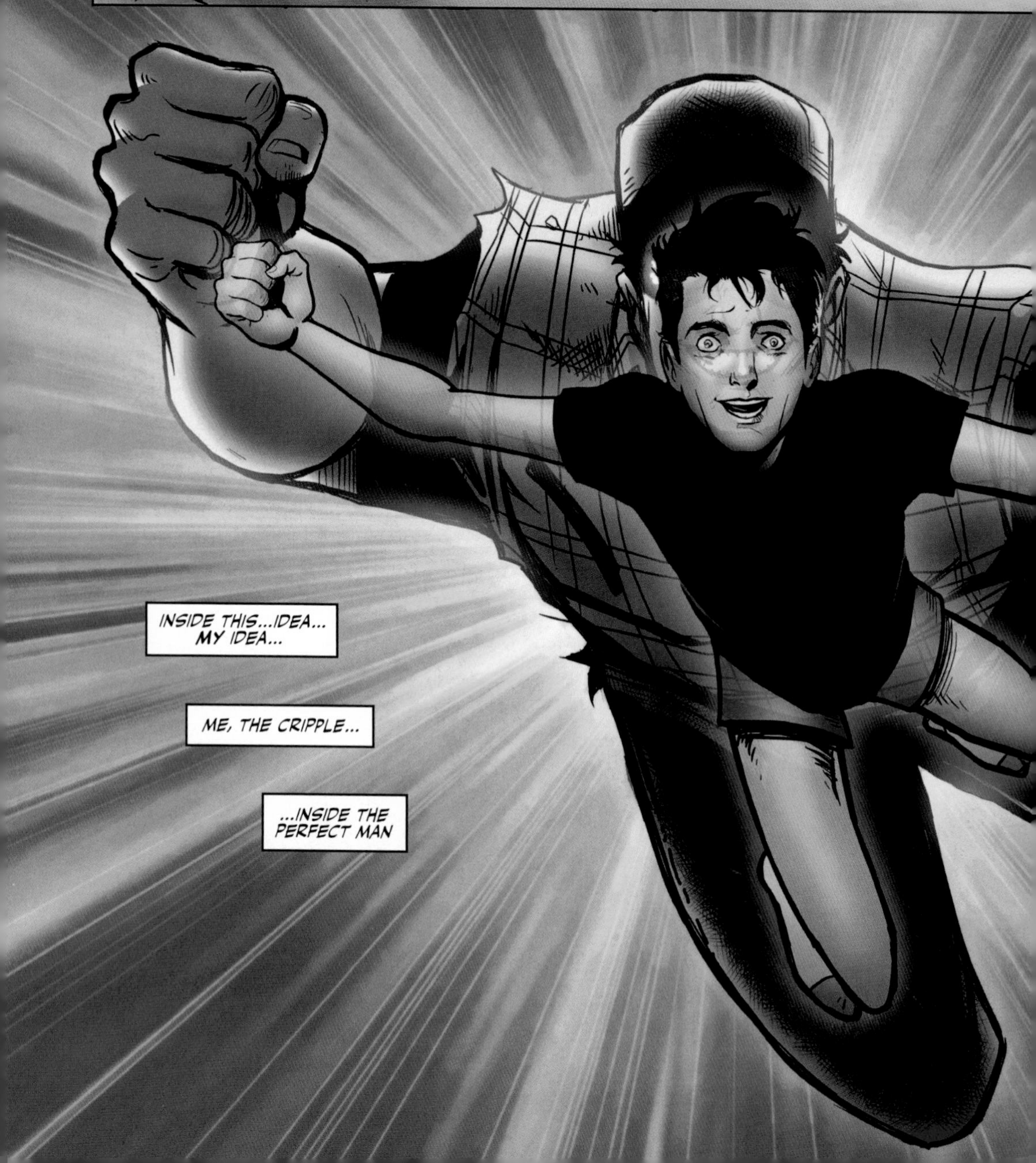
INSIDE THIS...IDEA... MY IDEA...
ME, THE CRIPPLE...
...INSIDE THE PERFECT MAN

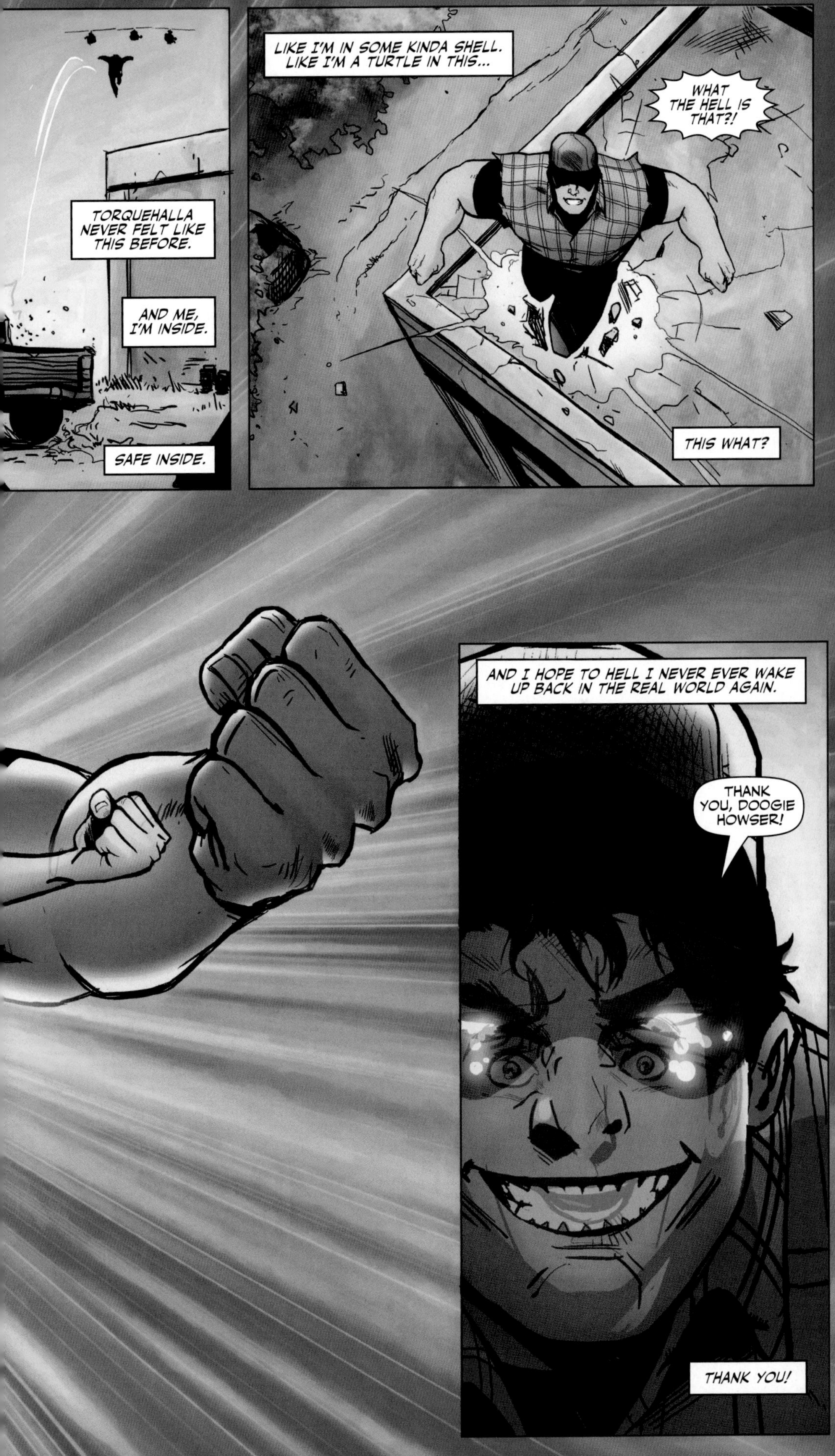
TORQUEHALLA NEVER FELT LIKE THIS BEFORE.
AND ME, I'M INSIDE.
SAFE INSIDE.
LIKE I'M IN SOME KINDA SHELL. LIKE I'M A TURTLE IN THIS...
WHAT THE HELL IS THAT?!
THIS WHAT?
AND I HOPE TO HELL I NEVER EVER WAKE UP BACK IN THE REAL WORLD AGAIN.
THANK YOU, DOOGIE HOWSER!
THANK YOU!

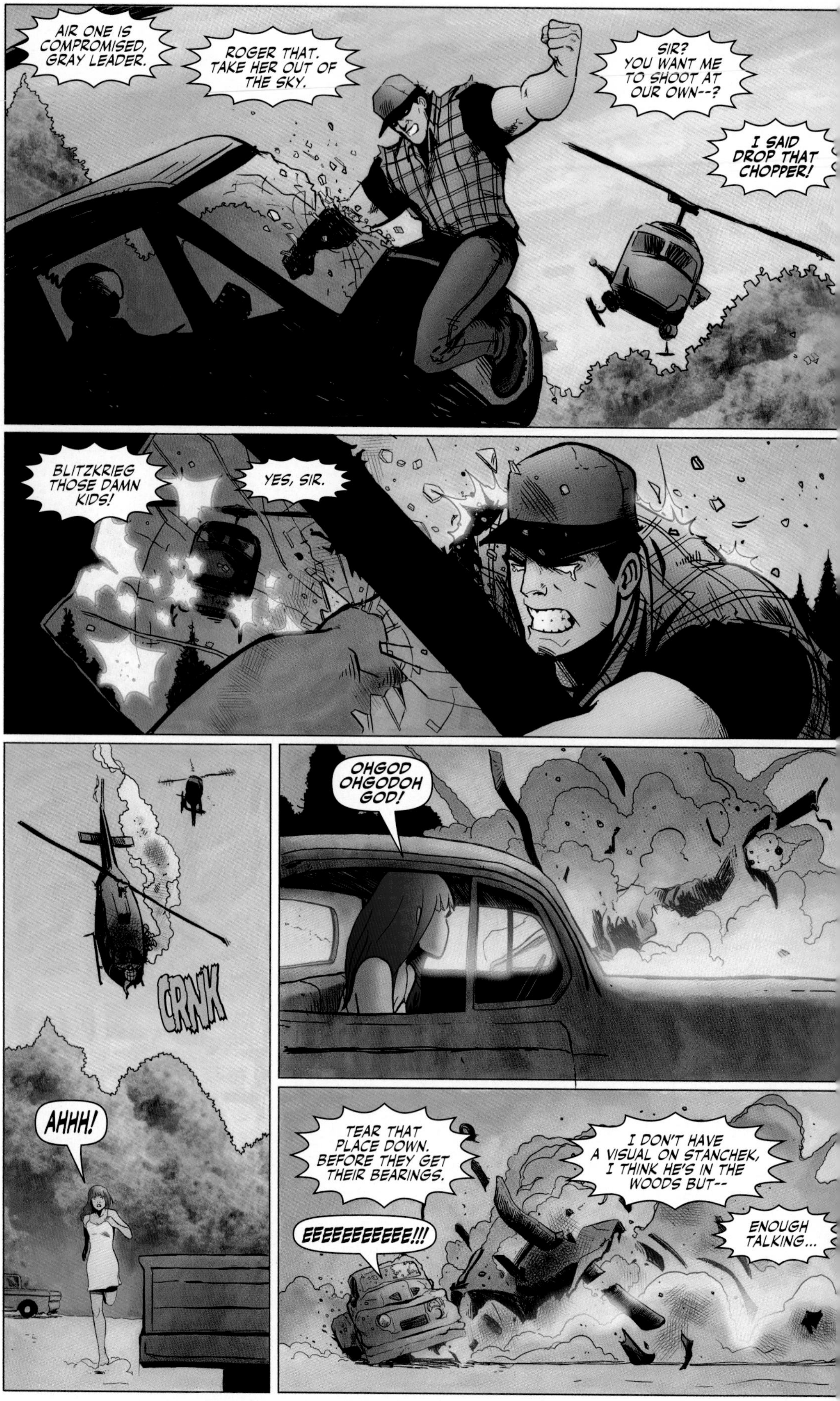
AIR ONE IS COMPROMISED, GRAY LEADER.
ROGER THAT. TAKE HER OUT OF THE SKY.
SIR? YOU WANT ME TO SHOOT AT OUR OWN--?
I SAID DROP THAT CHOPPER!
BLITZKRIEG THOSE DAMN KIDS!
YES, SIR.
CRNK
AHHH!
OHGOD OHGODOH GOD!
TEAR THAT PLACE DOWN. BEFORE THEY GET THEIR BEARINGS.
I DON'T HAVE A VISUAL ON STANCHEK, I THINK HE'S IN THE WOODS BUT--
EEEEEEEEEEE!!!
ENOUGH TALKING...

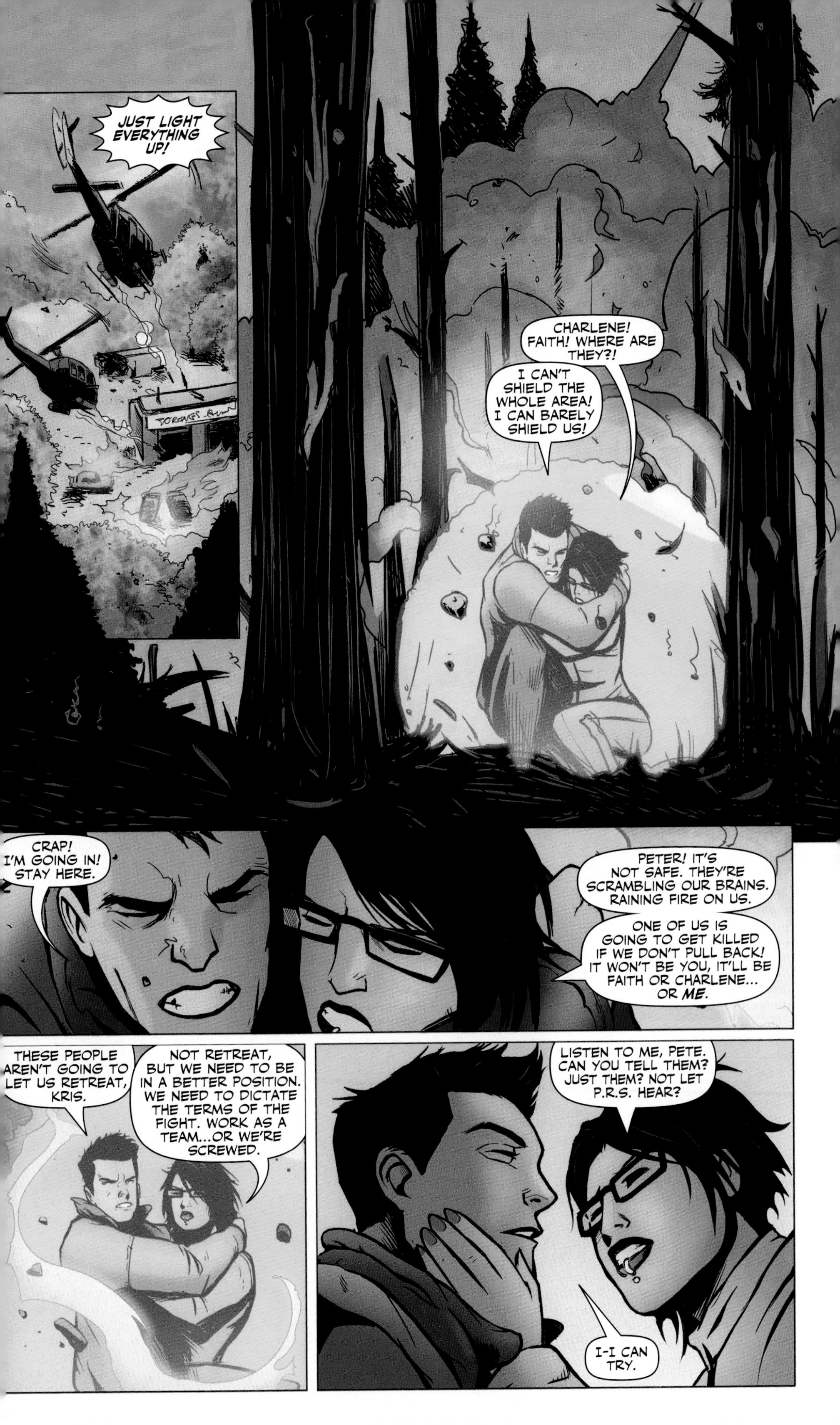
JUST LIGHT EVERYTHING UP!
CHARLENE! FAITH! WHERE ARE THEY?!
I CAN'T SHIELD THE WHOLE AREA! I CAN BARELY SHIELD US!
CRAP! I'M GOING IN! STAY HERE.
PETER! IT'S NOT SAFE. THEY'RE SCRAMBLING OUR BRAINS. RAINING FIRE ON US.
ONE OF US IS GOING TO GET KILLED IF WE DON'T PULL BACK! IT WON'T BE YOU, IT'LL BE FAITH OR CHARLENE... OR *ME*.
THESE PEOPLE AREN'T GOING TO LET US RETREAT, KRIS.
NOT RETREAT, BUT WE NEED TO BE IN A BETTER POSITION. WE NEED TO DICTATE THE TERMS OF THE FIGHT. WORK AS A TEAM...OR WE'RE SCREWED.
LISTEN TO ME, PETE. CAN YOU TELL THEM? JUST THEM? NOT LET P.R.S. HEAR?
I-I CAN TRY.

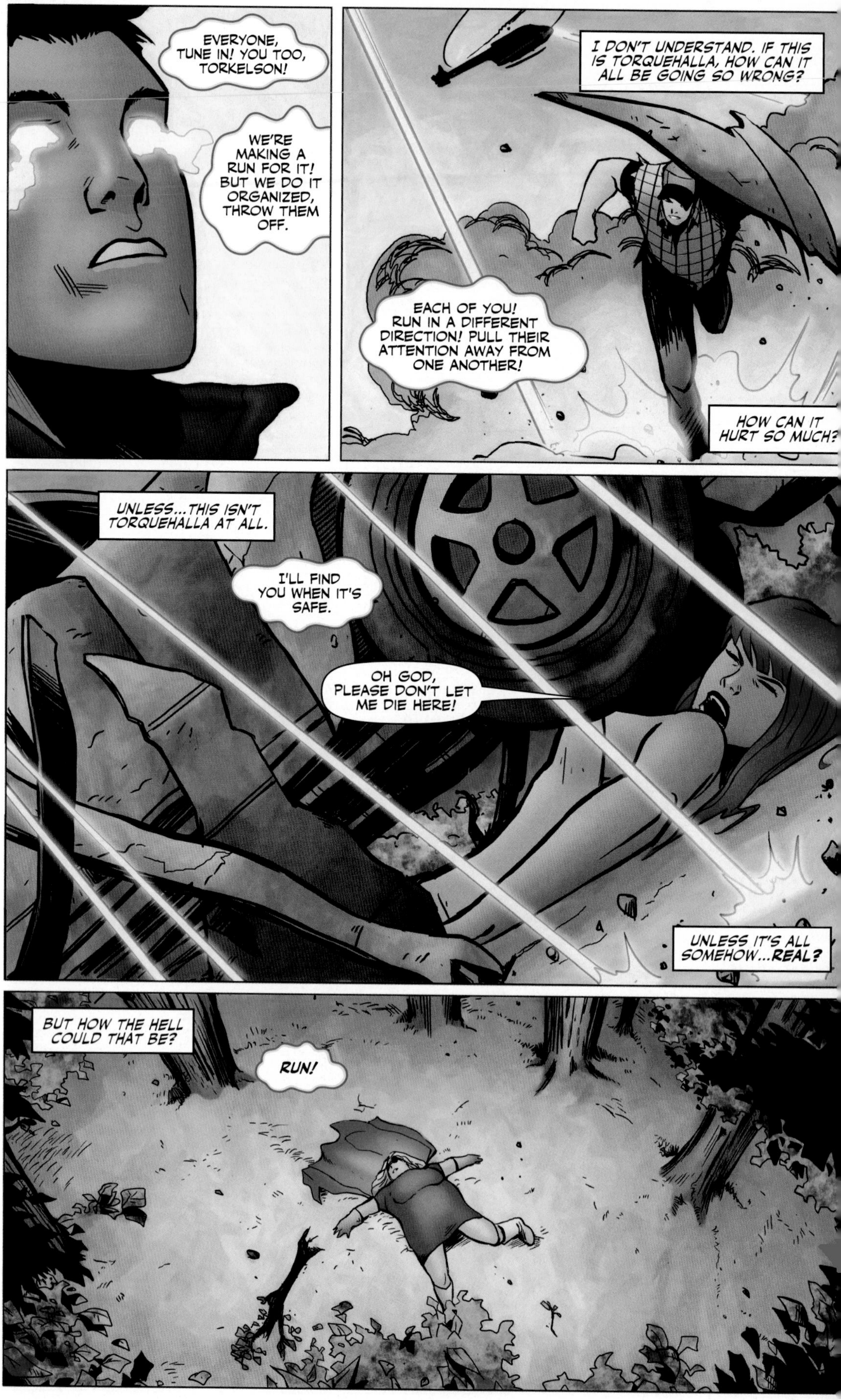
EVERYONE, TUNE IN! YOU TOO, TORKELSON!
WE'RE MAKING A RUN FOR IT! BUT WE DO IT ORGANIZED, THROW THEM OFF.
I DON'T UNDERSTAND. IF THIS IS TORQUEHALLA, HOW CAN IT ALL BE GOING SO WRONG?
EACH OF YOU! RUN IN A DIFFERENT DIRECTION! PULL THEIR ATTENTION AWAY FROM ONE ANOTHER!
HOW CAN IT HURT SO MUCH?
UNLESS...THIS ISN'T TORQUEHALLA AT ALL.
I'LL FIND YOU WHEN IT'S SAFE.
OH GOD, PLEASE DON'T LET ME DIE HERE!
UNLESS IT'S ALL SOMEHOW...**REAL?**
BUT HOW THE HELL COULD THAT BE?
RUN!

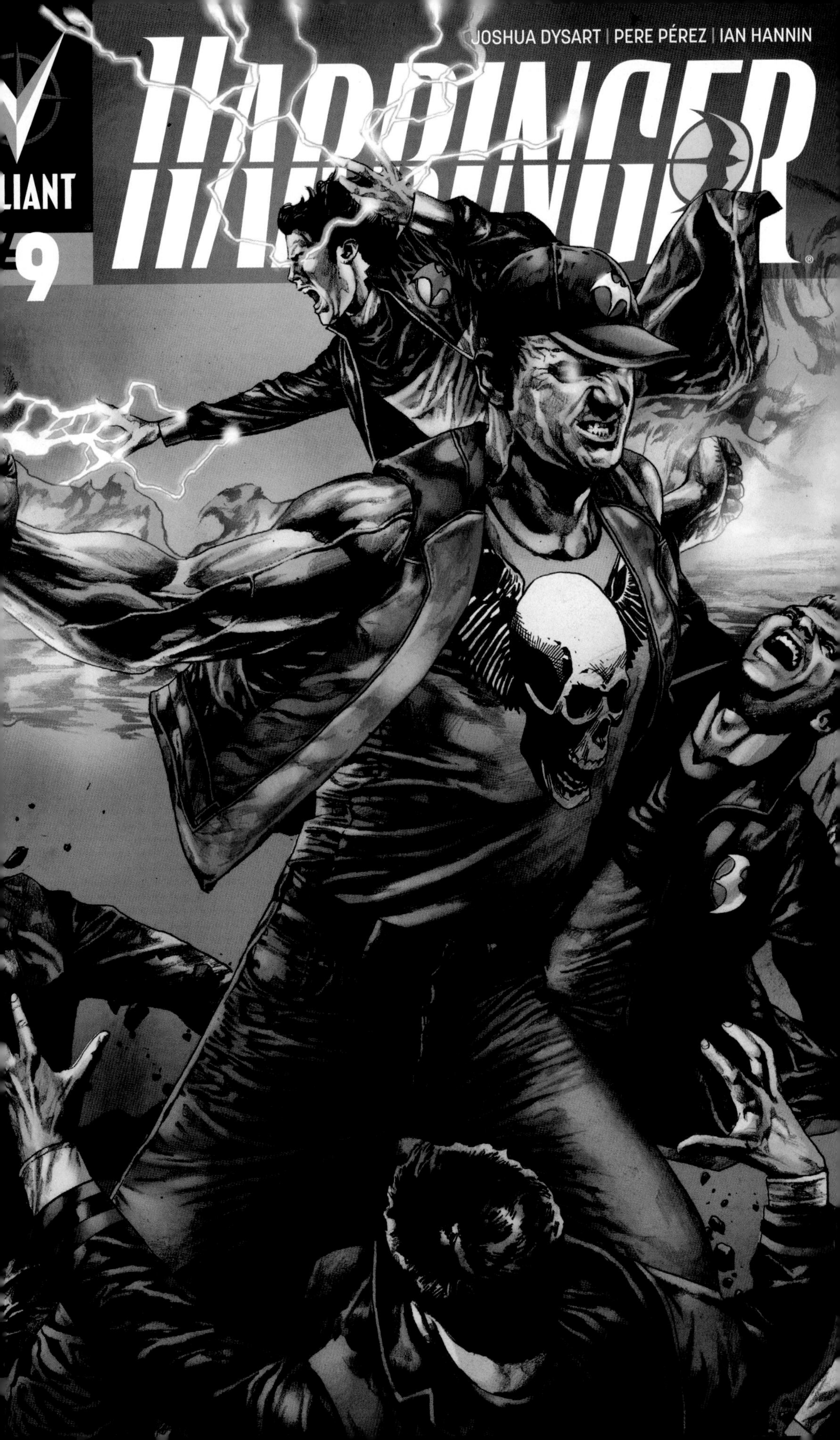
JOSHUA DYSART | PERE PÉREZ | IAN HANNIN
HARBINGER
VALIANT
9

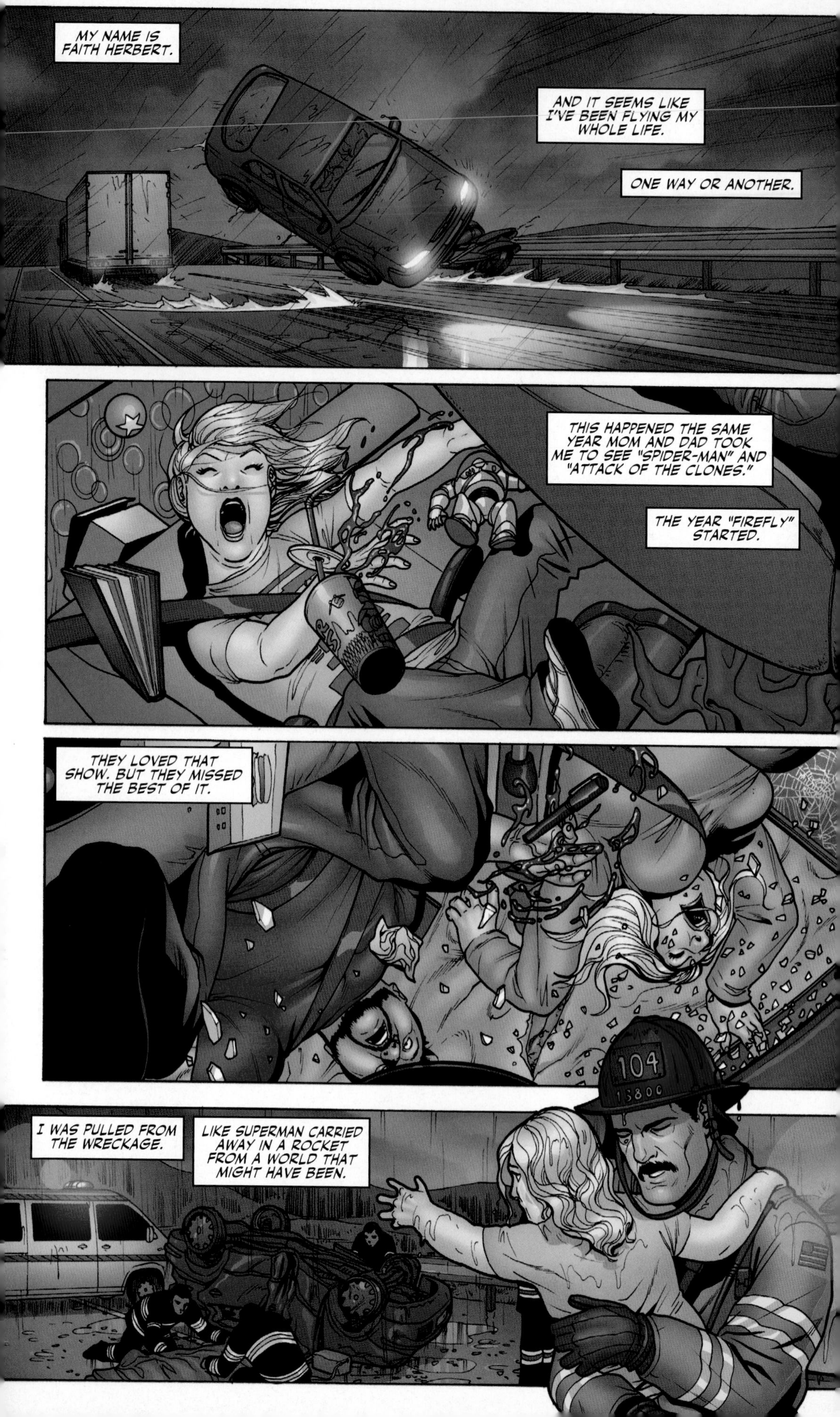
MY NAME IS FAITH HERBERT.
AND IT SEEMS LIKE I'VE BEEN FLYING MY WHOLE LIFE.
ONE WAY OR ANOTHER.
THIS HAPPENED THE SAME YEAR MOM AND DAD TOOK ME TO SEE "SPIDER-MAN" AND "ATTACK OF THE CLONES."
THE YEAR "FIREFLY" STARTED.
THEY LOVED THAT SHOW. BUT THEY MISSED THE BEST OF IT.
104
I WAS PULLED FROM THE WRECKAGE.
LIKE SUPERMAN CARRIED AWAY IN A ROCKET FROM A WORLD THAT MIGHT HAVE BEEN.

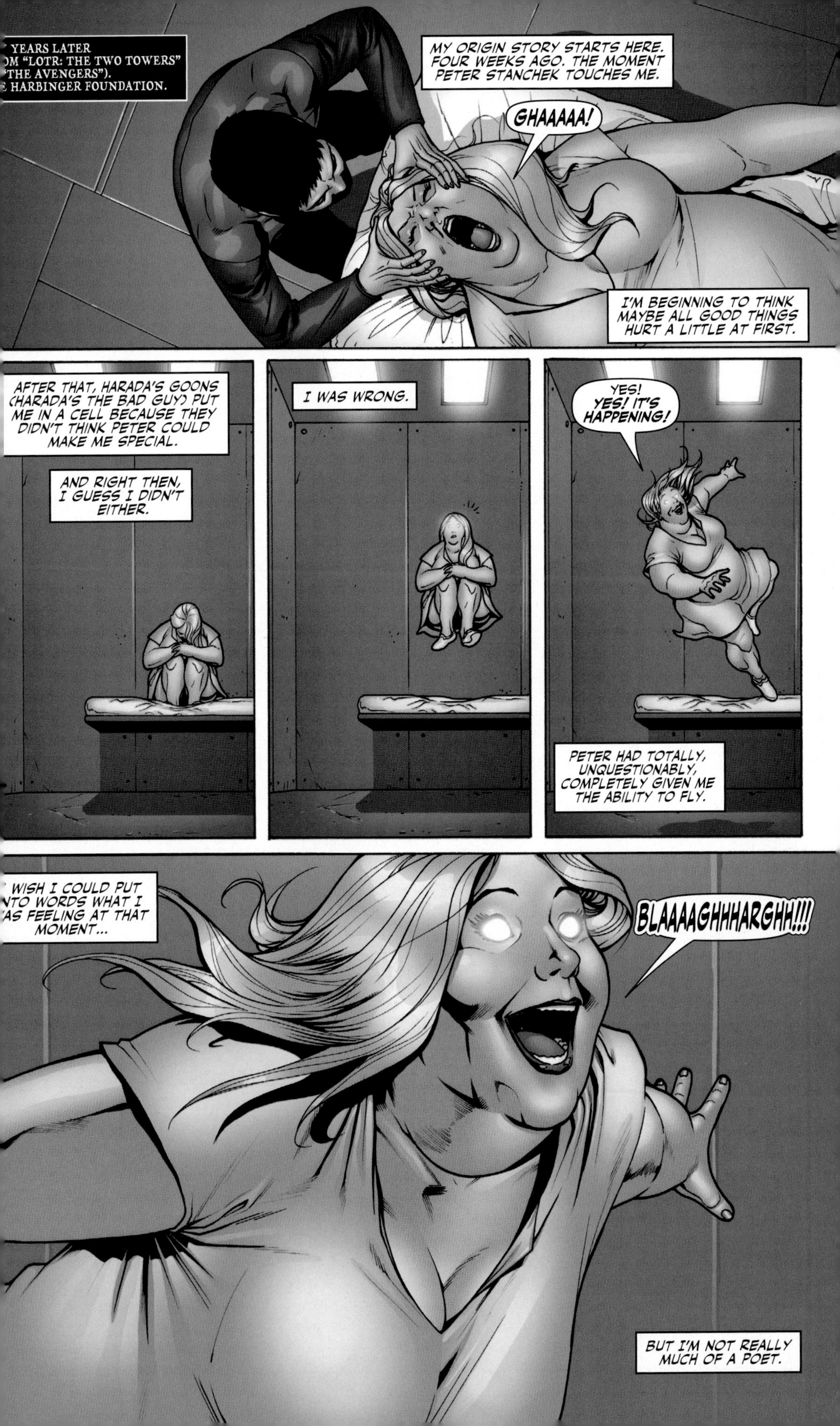
YEARS LATER
OM "LOTR: THE TWO TOWERS"
"THE AVENGERS").
E HARBINGER FOUNDATION.
MY ORIGIN STORY STARTS HERE. FOUR WEEKS AGO. THE MOMENT PETER STANCHEK TOUCHES ME.
GHAAAAA!
I'M BEGINNING TO THINK MAYBE ALL GOOD THINGS HURT A LITTLE AT FIRST.
AFTER THAT, HARADA'S GOONS (HARADA'S THE BAD GUY) PUT ME IN A CELL BECAUSE THEY DIDN'T THINK PETER COULD MAKE ME SPECIAL.
AND RIGHT THEN, I GUESS I DIDN'T EITHER.
I WAS WRONG.
YES! YES! IT'S HAPPENING!
PETER HAD TOTALLY, UNQUESTIONABLY, COMPLETELY GIVEN ME THE ABILITY TO FLY.
WISH I COULD PUT NTO WORDS WHAT I AS FEELING AT THAT MOMENT...
BLAAAAGHHHARGHH!!!
BUT I'M NOT REALLY MUCH OF A POET.

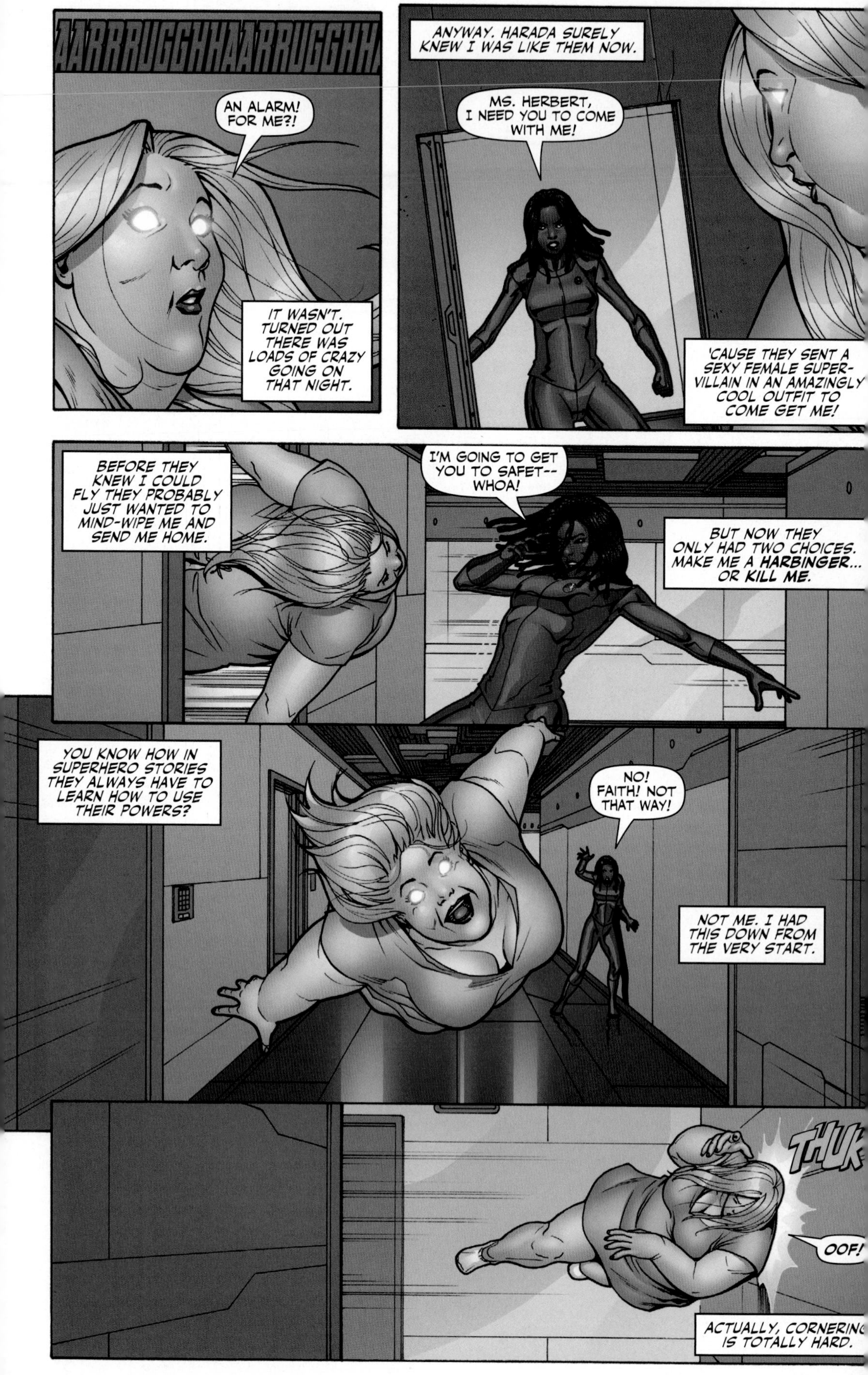
AARRUGGHHAARRUGGHHA
AN ALARM! FOR ME?!
IT WASN'T. TURNED OUT THERE WAS LOADS OF CRAZY GOING ON THAT NIGHT.
ANYWAY. HARADA SURELY KNEW I WAS LIKE THEM NOW.
MS. HERBERT, I NEED YOU TO COME WITH ME!
'CAUSE THEY SENT A SEXY FEMALE SUPER-VILLAIN IN AN AMAZINGLY COOL OUTFIT TO COME GET ME!
BEFORE THEY KNEW I COULD FLY THEY PROBABLY JUST WANTED TO MIND-WIPE ME AND SEND ME HOME.
I'M GOING TO GET YOU TO SAFET-- WHOA!
BUT NOW THEY ONLY HAD TWO CHOICES. MAKE ME A **HARBINGER**... OR **KILL ME**.
YOU KNOW HOW IN SUPERHERO STORIES THEY ALWAYS HAVE TO LEARN HOW TO USE THEIR POWERS?
NO! FAITH! NOT THAT WAY!
NOT ME. I HAD THIS DOWN FROM THE VERY START.
THUK
OOF!
ACTUALLY, CORNERING IS TOTALLY HARD.

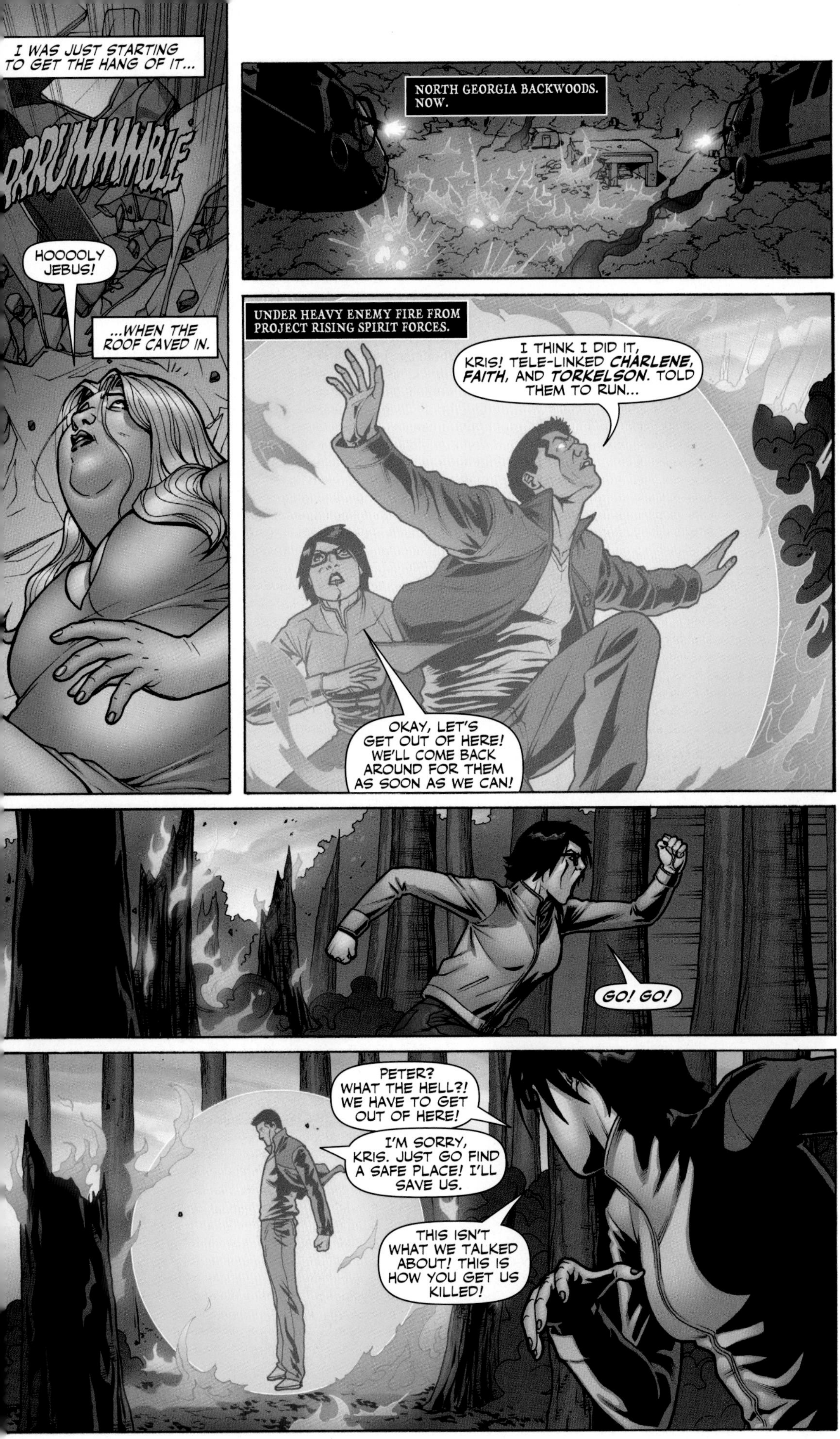

I WAS JUST STARTING TO GET THE HANG OF IT...
RRRUMMMBLE
HOOOOLY JEBUS!
...WHEN THE ROOF CAVED IN.
NORTH GEORGIA BACKWOODS. NOW.
UNDER HEAVY ENEMY FIRE FROM PROJECT RISING SPIRIT FORCES.
I THINK I DID IT, KRIS! TELE-LINKED CHARLENE, FAITH, AND TORKELSON. TOLD THEM TO RUN...
OKAY, LET'S GET OUT OF HERE! WE'LL COME BACK AROUND FOR THEM AS SOON AS WE CAN!
GO! GO!
PETER? WHAT THE HELL?! WE HAVE TO GET OUT OF HERE!
I'M SORRY, KRIS. JUST GO FIND A SAFE PLACE! I'LL SAVE US.
THIS ISN'T WHAT WE TALKED ABOUT! THIS IS HOW YOU GET US KILLED!

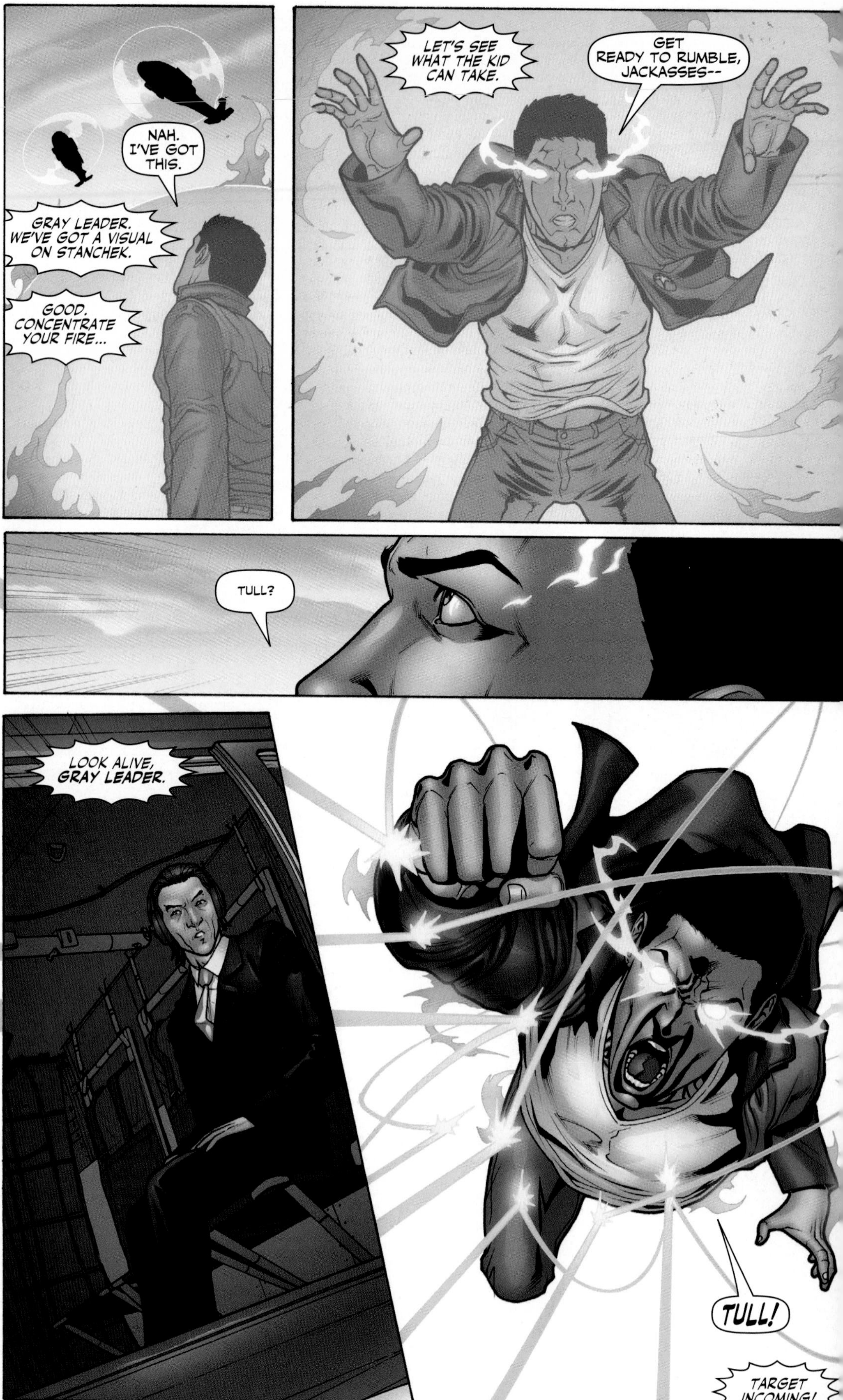
NAH. I'VE GOT THIS.
GRAY LEADER. WE'VE GOT A VISUAL ON STANCHEK.
GOOD. CONCENTRATE YOUR FIRE...
LET'S SEE WHAT THE KID CAN TAKE.
GET READY TO RUMBLE, JACKASSES--
TULL?
LOOK ALIVE, GRAY LEADER.
TULL!
TARGET INCOMING!

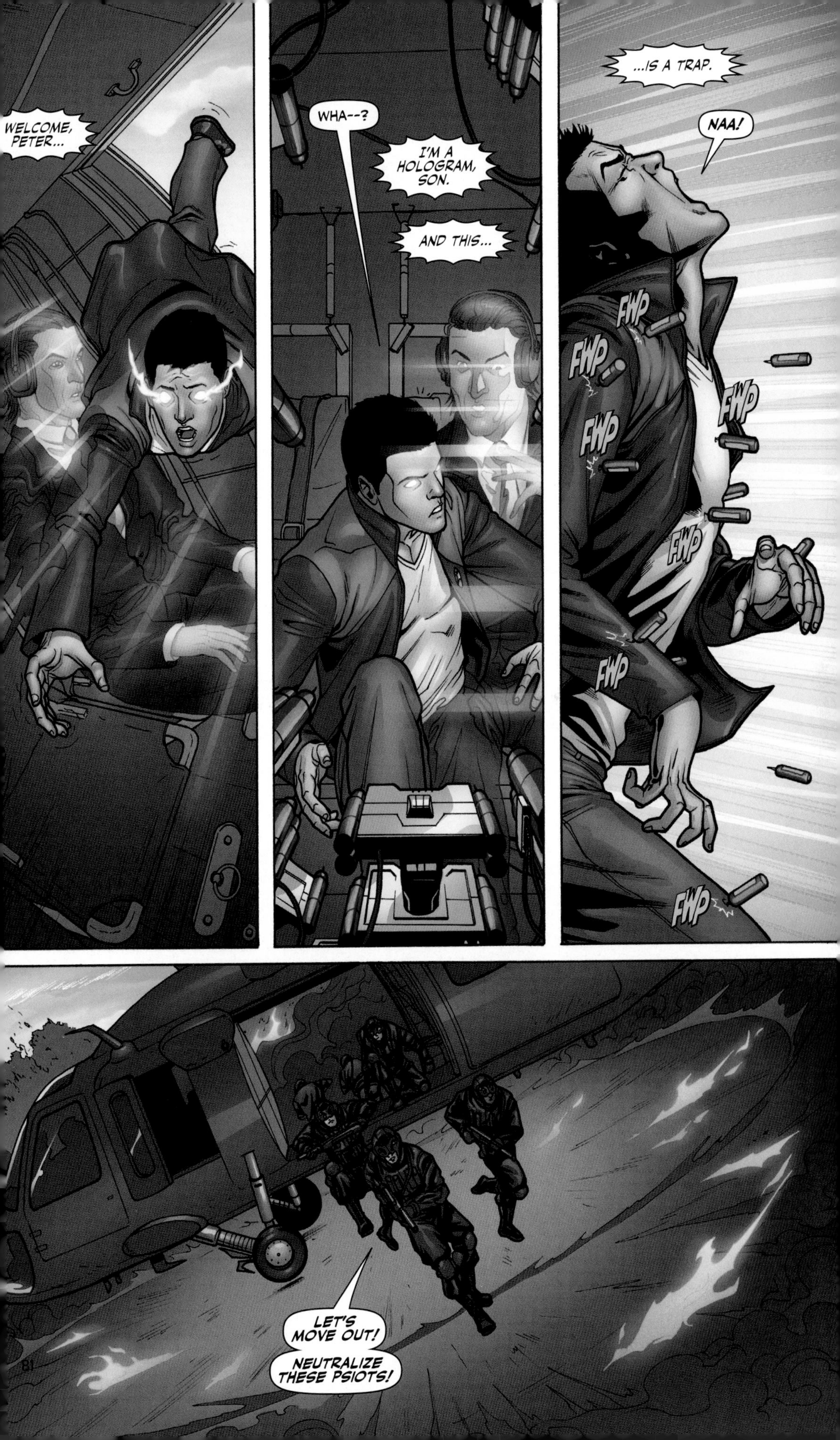
WELCOME, PETER...
WHA--?
I'M A HOLOGRAM, SON.
AND THIS...
...IS A TRAP.
NAA!
FWP
FWP
FWP
FWP
FWP
FWP
FWP
LET'S MOVE OUT!
NEUTRALIZE THESE PSIOTS!

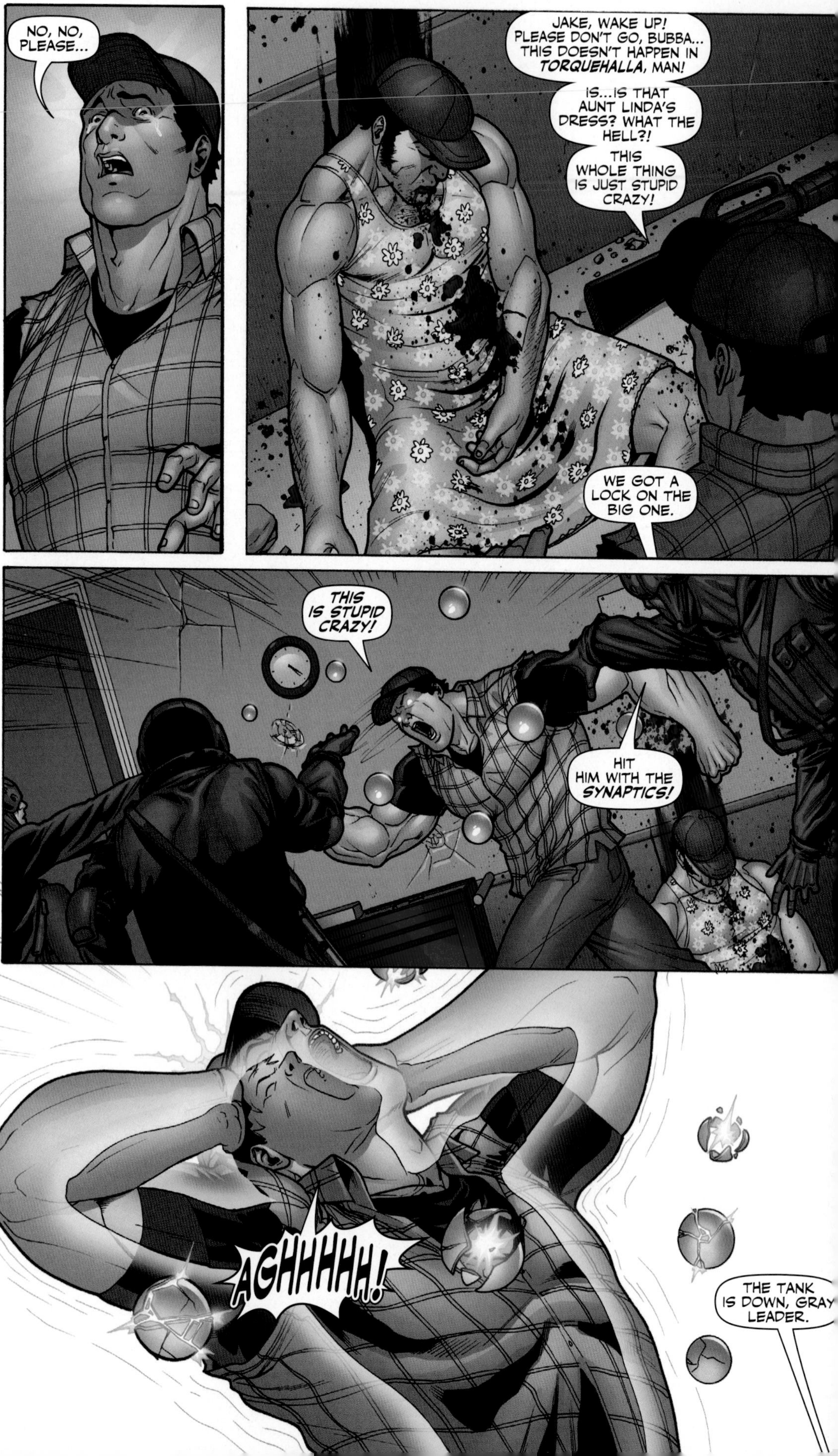
NO, NO, PLEASE...
JAKE, WAKE UP! PLEASE DON'T GO, BUBBA... THIS DOESN'T HAPPEN IN TORQUEHALLA, MAN!
IS...IS THAT AUNT LINDA'S DRESS? WHAT THE HELL?!
THIS WHOLE THING IS JUST STUPID CRAZY!
WE GOT A LOCK ON THE BIG ONE.
THIS IS STUPID CRAZY!
HIT HIM WITH THE SYNAPTICS!
AGHHHHH!
THE TANK IS DOWN, GRAY LEADER.

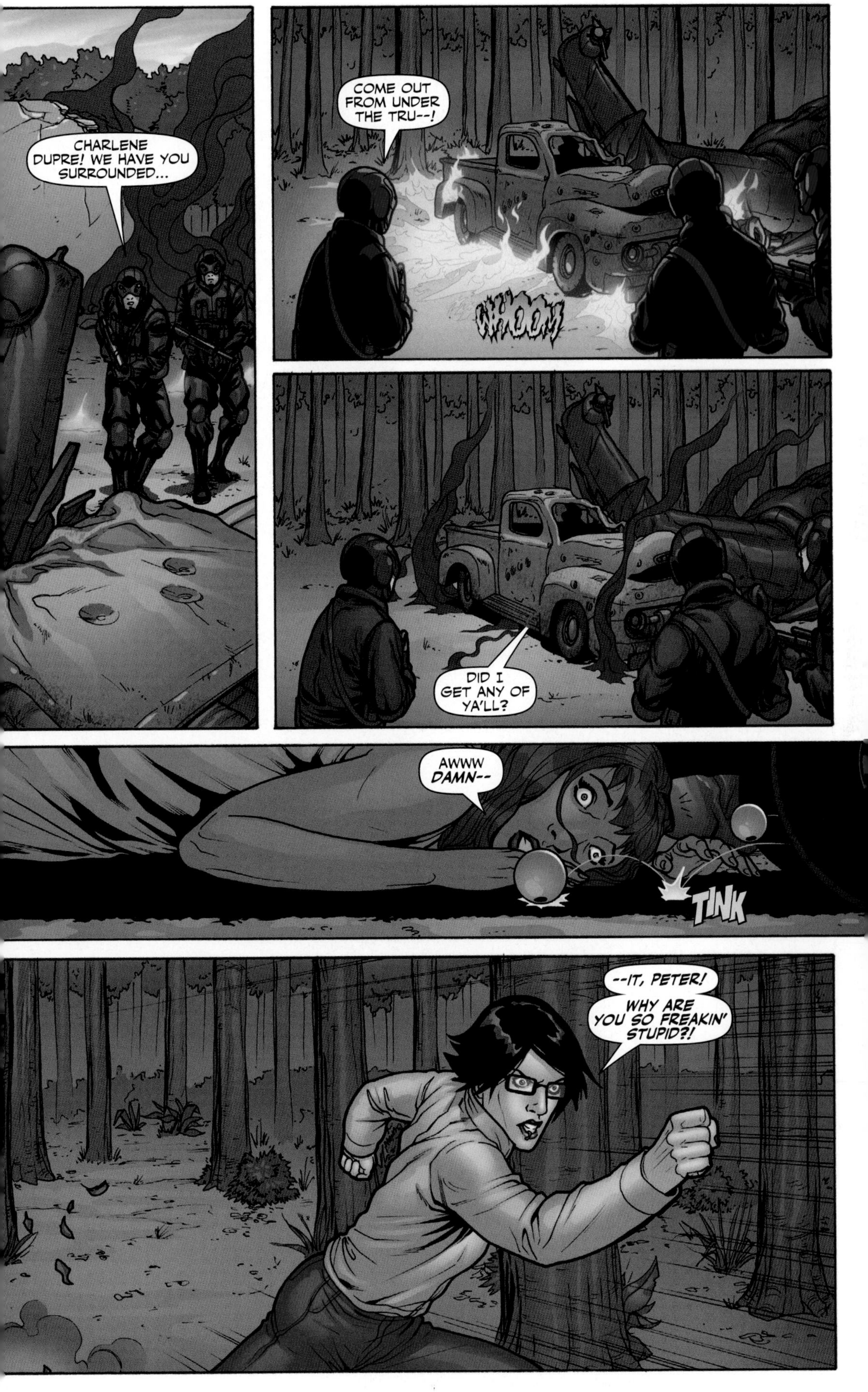
CHARLENE DUPRE! WE HAVE YOU SURROUNDED...
COME OUT FROM UNDER THE TRU--!
WHOOM
DID I GET ANY OF YA'LL?
AWWW DAMN--
TINK
--IT, PETER! WHY ARE YOU SO FREAKIN' STUPID?!

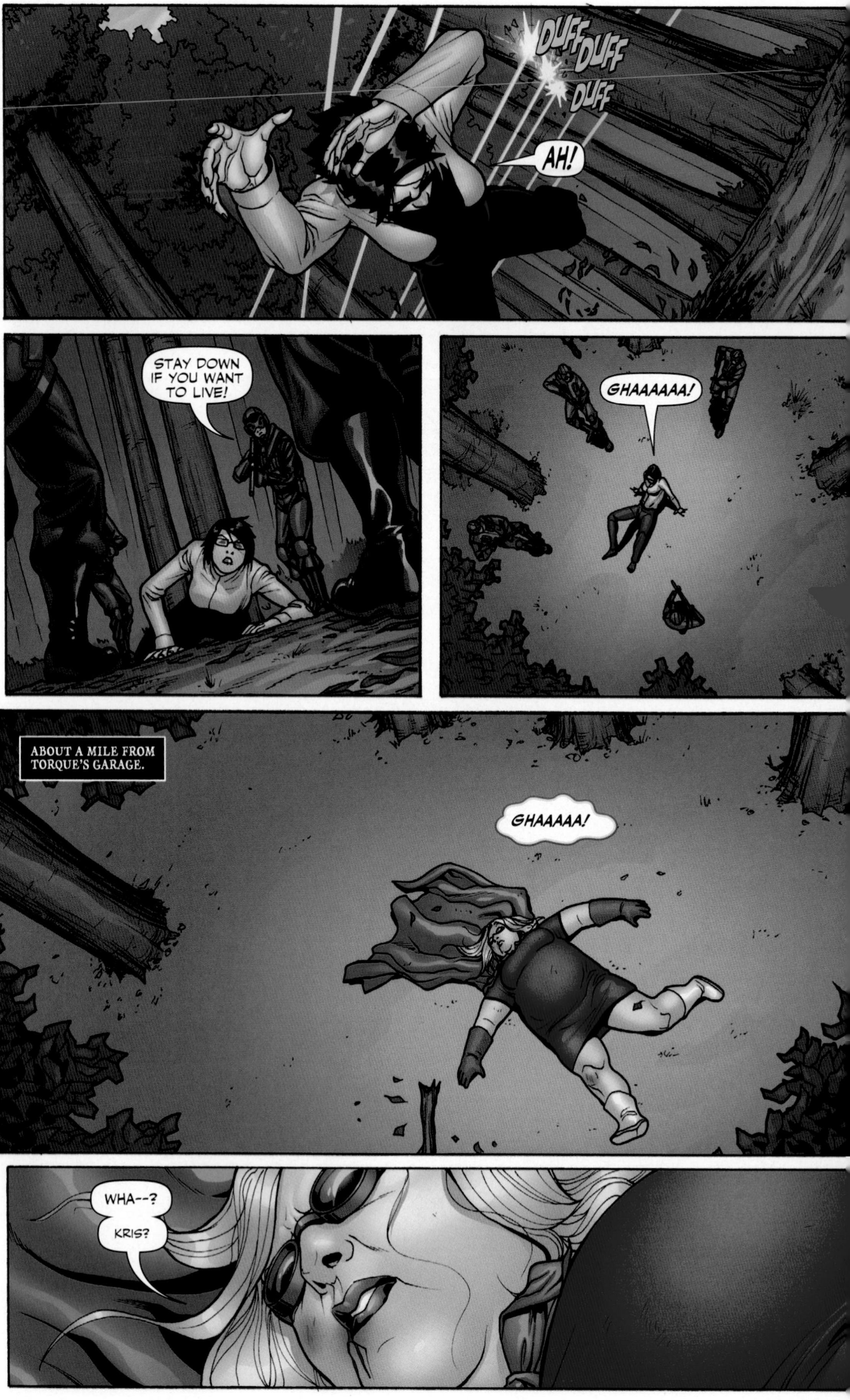
DUFF DUFF
DUFF
AH!
STAY DOWN IF YOU WANT TO LIVE!
GHAAAAAA!
ABOUT A MILE FROM TORQUE'S GARAGE.
GHAAAAA!
WHA--?
KRIS?

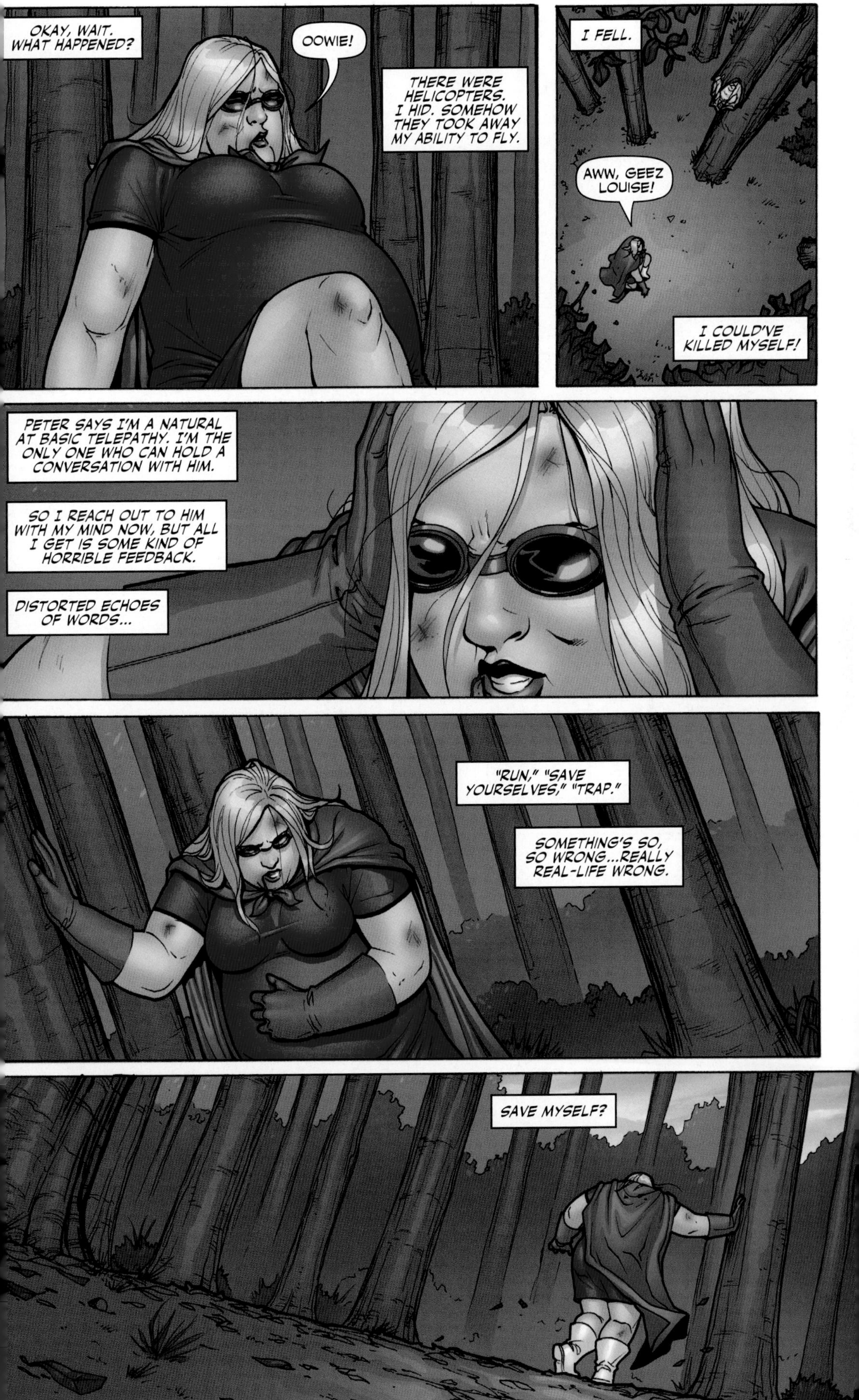
OKAY, WAIT. WHAT HAPPENED?
OOWIE!
THERE WERE HELICOPTERS. I HID. SOMEHOW THEY TOOK AWAY MY ABILITY TO FLY.
I FELL.
AWW, GEEZ LOUISE!
I COULD'VE KILLED MYSELF!
PETER SAYS I'M A NATURAL AT BASIC TELEPATHY. I'M THE ONLY ONE WHO CAN HOLD A CONVERSATION WITH HIM.
SO I REACH OUT TO HIM WITH MY MIND NOW, BUT ALL I GET IS SOME KIND OF HORRIBLE FEEDBACK.
DISTORTED ECHOES OF WORDS...
"RUN," "SAVE YOURSELVES," "TRAP."
SOMETHING'S SO, SO WRONG...REALLY REAL-LIFE WRONG.
SAVE MYSELF?

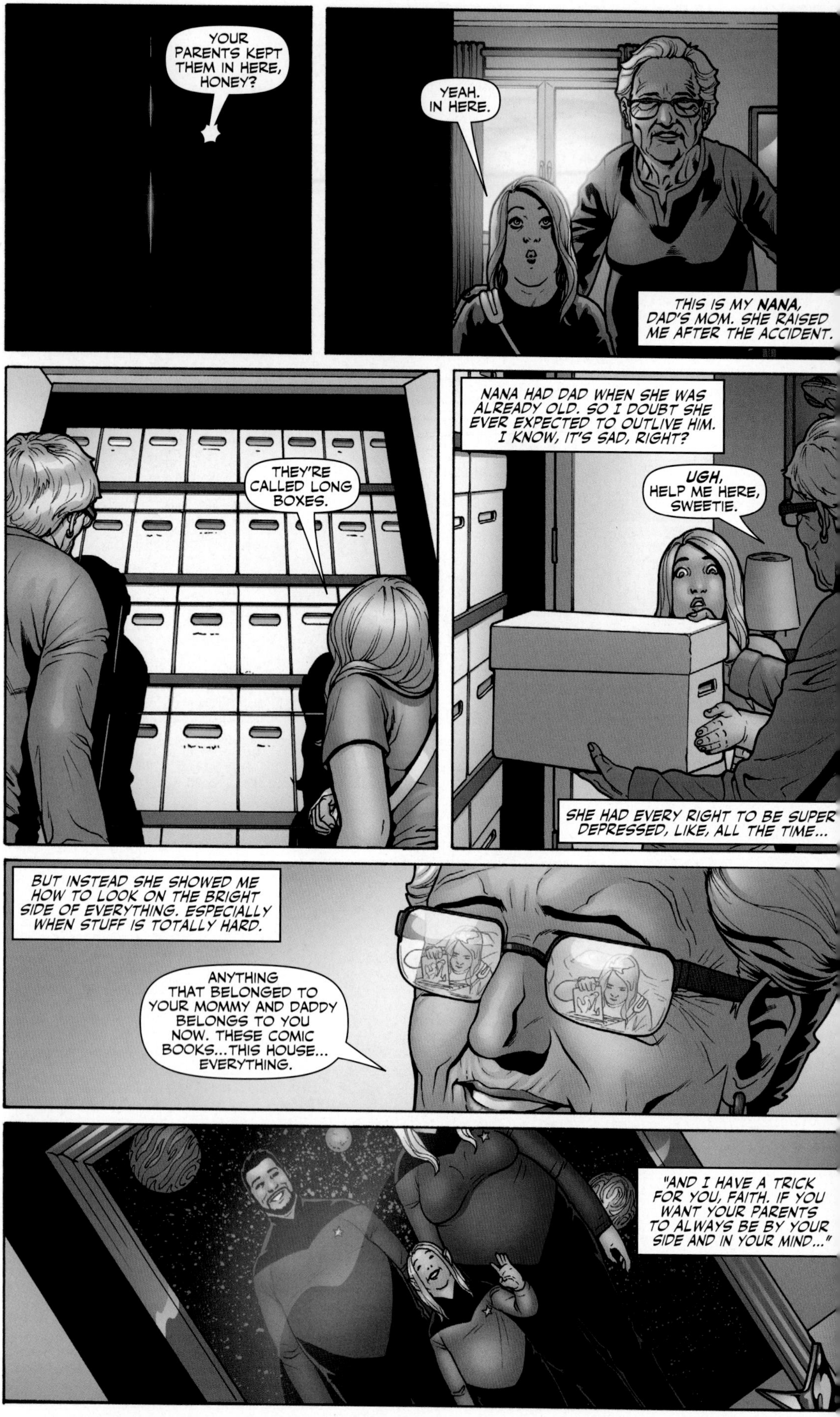
YOUR PARENTS KEPT THEM IN HERE, HONEY?
YEAH. IN HERE.
THIS IS MY NANA, DAD'S MOM. SHE RAISED ME AFTER THE ACCIDENT.
THEY'RE CALLED LONG BOXES.
NANA HAD DAD WHEN SHE WAS ALREADY OLD. SO I DOUBT SHE EVER EXPECTED TO OUTLIVE HIM. I KNOW, IT'S SAD, RIGHT?
UGH, HELP ME HERE, SWEETIE.
SHE HAD EVERY RIGHT TO BE SUPER DEPRESSED, LIKE, ALL THE TIME...
BUT INSTEAD SHE SHOWED ME HOW TO LOOK ON THE BRIGHT SIDE OF EVERYTHING. ESPECIALLY WHEN STUFF IS TOTALLY HARD.
ANYTHING THAT BELONGED TO YOUR MOMMY AND DADDY BELONGS TO YOU NOW. THESE COMIC BOOKS...THIS HOUSE... EVERYTHING.
"AND I HAVE A TRICK FOR YOU, FAITH. IF YOU WANT YOUR PARENTS TO ALWAYS BE BY YOUR SIDE AND IN YOUR MIND..."

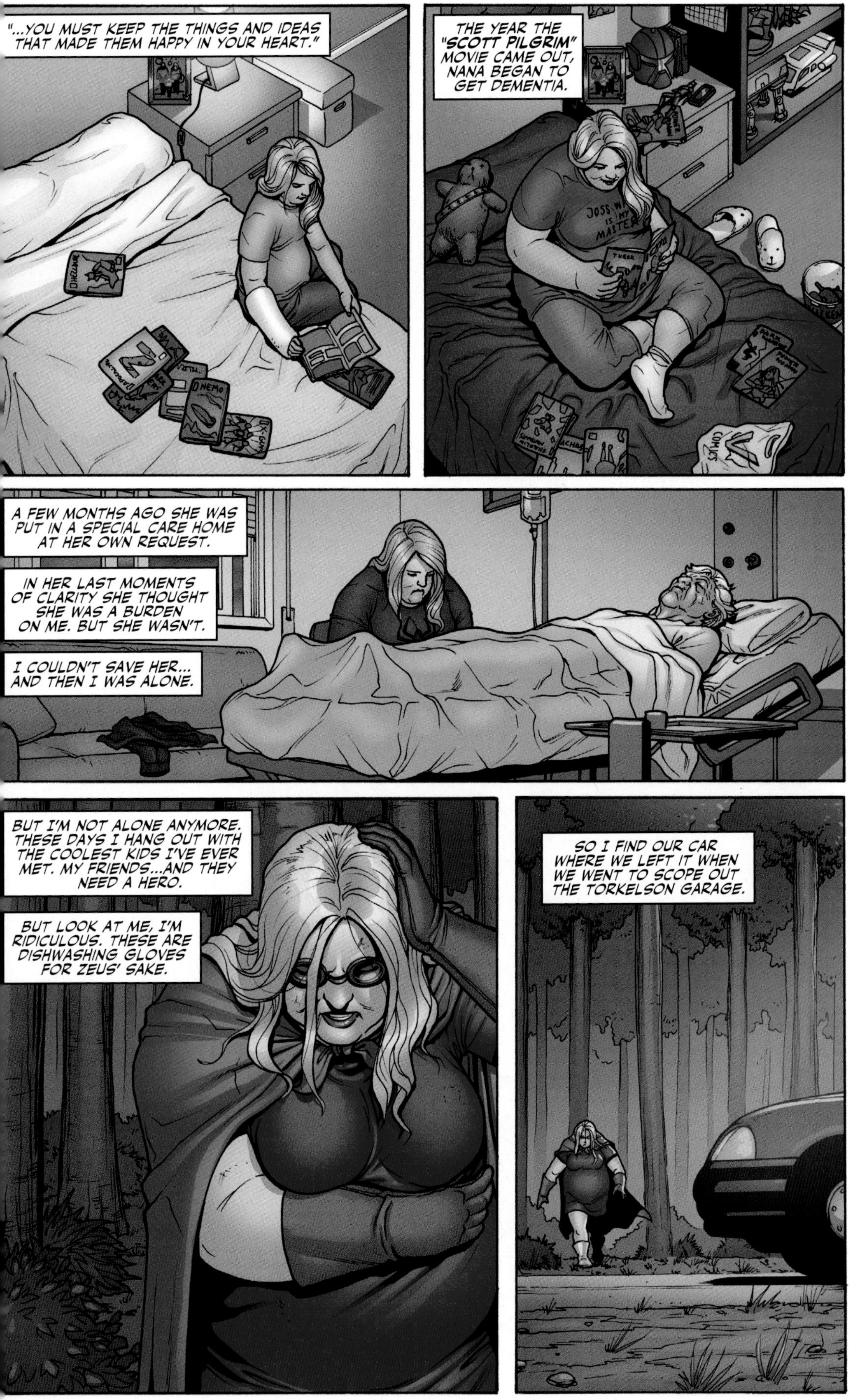
"...YOU MUST KEEP THE THINGS AND IDEAS THAT MADE THEM HAPPY IN YOUR HEART."
THE YEAR THE "SCOTT PILGRIM" MOVIE CAME OUT, NANA BEGAN TO GET DEMENTIA.
A FEW MONTHS AGO SHE WAS PUT IN A SPECIAL CARE HOME AT HER OWN REQUEST.
IN HER LAST MOMENTS OF CLARITY SHE THOUGHT SHE WAS A BURDEN ON ME. BUT SHE WASN'T.
I COULDN'T SAVE HER... AND THEN I WAS ALONE.
BUT I'M NOT ALONE ANYMORE. THESE DAYS I HANG OUT WITH THE COOLEST KIDS I'VE EVER MET. MY FRIENDS...AND THEY NEED A HERO.
BUT LOOK AT ME, I'M RIDICULOUS. THESE ARE DISHWASHING GLOVES FOR ZEUS' SAKE.
SO I FIND OUR CAR WHERE WE LEFT IT WHEN WE WENT TO SCOPE OUT THE TORKELSON GARAGE.

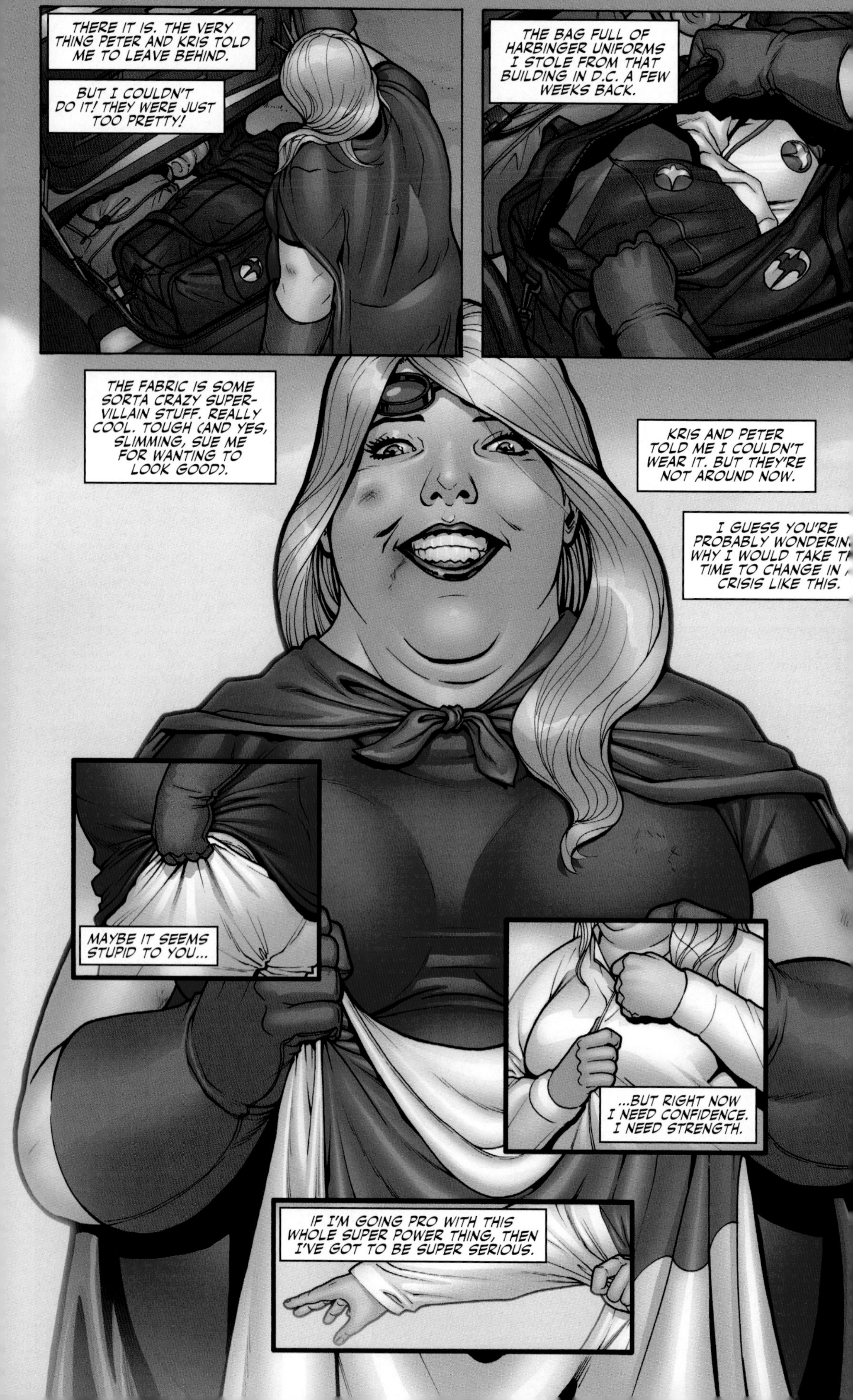
THERE IT IS. THE VERY THING PETER AND KRIS TOLD ME TO LEAVE BEHIND.
BUT I COULDN'T DO IT! THEY WERE JUST TOO PRETTY!
THE BAG FULL OF HARBINGER UNIFORMS I STOLE FROM THAT BUILDING IN D.C. A FEW WEEKS BACK.
THE FABRIC IS SOME SORTA CRAZY SUPER-VILLAIN STUFF. REALLY COOL. TOUGH (AND YES, SLIMMING, SUE ME FOR WANTING TO LOOK GOOD).
KRIS AND PETER TOLD ME I COULDN'T WEAR IT. BUT THEY'RE NOT AROUND NOW.
I GUESS YOU'RE PROBABLY WONDERIN WHY I WOULD TAKE T TIME TO CHANGE IN CRISIS LIKE THIS.
MAYBE IT SEEMS STUPID TO YOU...
...BUT RIGHT NOW I NEED CONFIDENCE. I NEED STRENGTH.
IF I'M GOING PRO WITH THIS WHOLE SUPER POWER THING, THEN I'VE GOT TO BE SUPER SERIOUS.

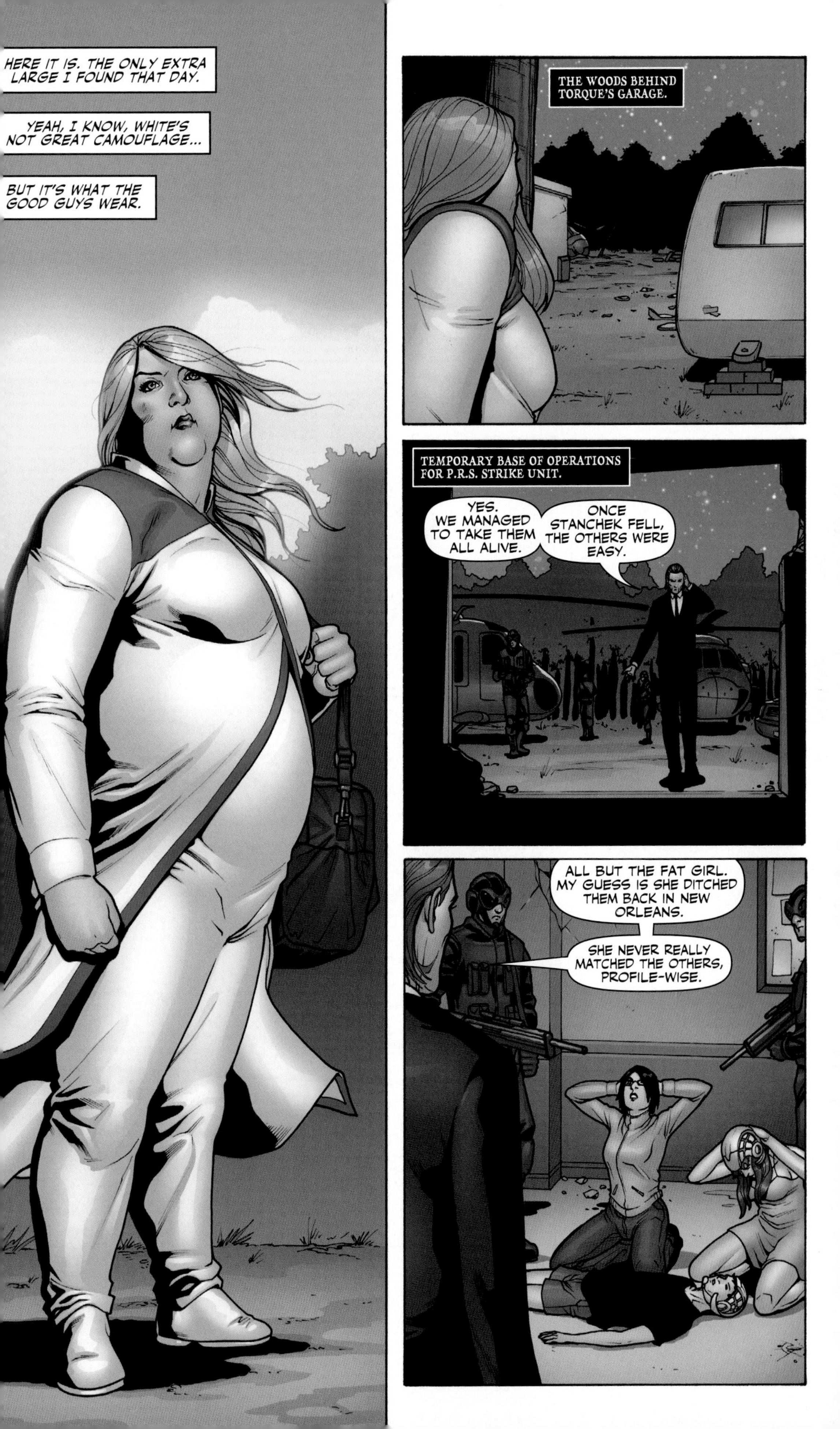
HERE IT IS. THE ONLY EXTRA LARGE I FOUND THAT DAY.
YEAH, I KNOW, WHITE'S NOT GREAT CAMOUFLAGE...
BUT IT'S WHAT THE GOOD GUYS WEAR.
THE WOODS BEHIND TORQUE'S GARAGE.
TEMPORARY BASE OF OPERATIONS FOR P.R.S. STRIKE UNIT.
YES. WE MANAGED TO TAKE THEM ALL ALIVE.
ONCE STANCHEK FELL, THE OTHERS WERE EASY.
ALL BUT THE FAT GIRL. MY GUESS IS SHE DITCHED THEM BACK IN NEW ORLEANS.
SHE NEVER REALLY MATCHED THE OTHERS, PROFILE-WISE.

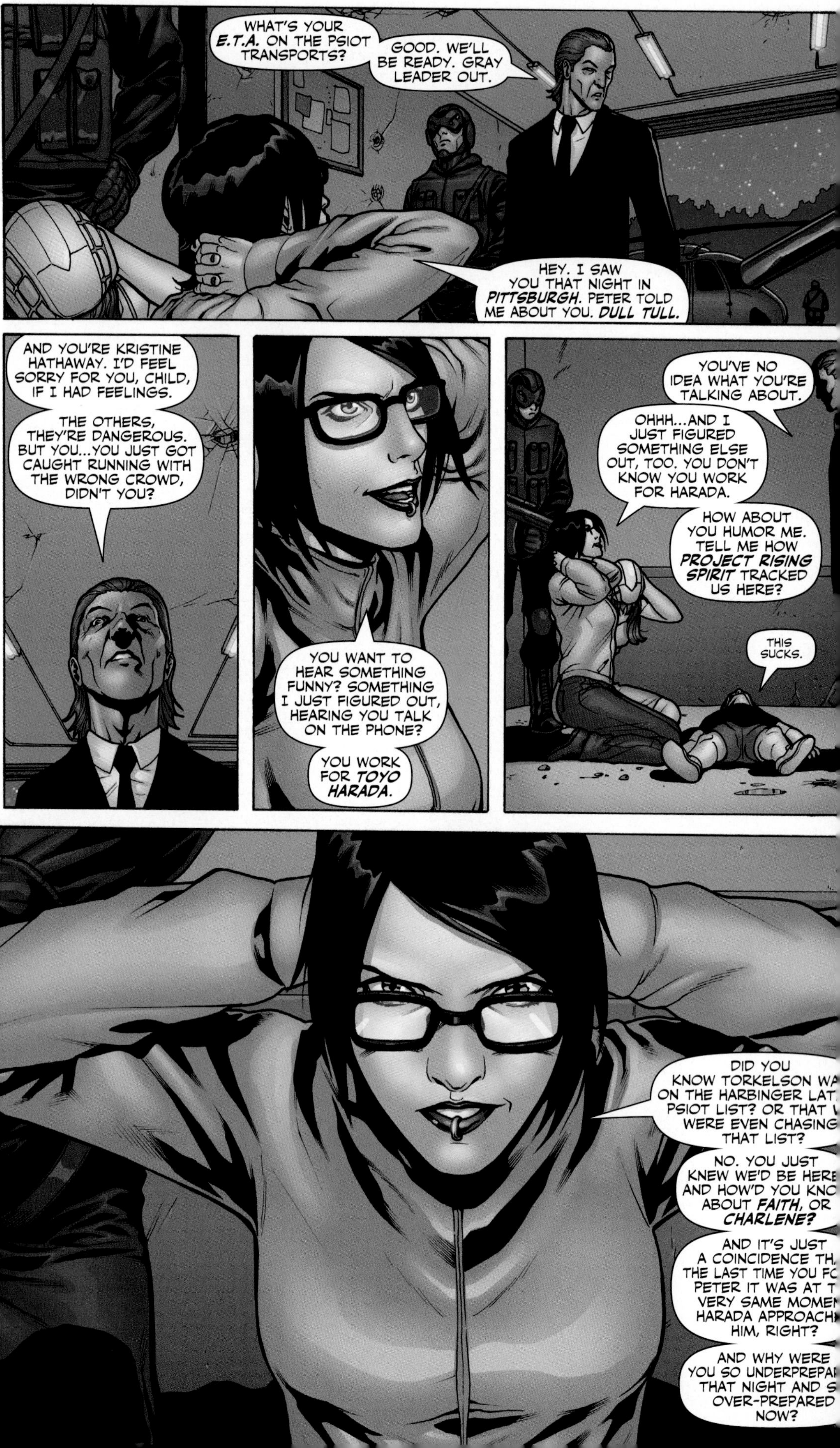
WHAT'S YOUR E.T.A. ON THE PSIOT TRANSPORTS?
GOOD. WE'LL BE READY. GRAY LEADER OUT.
HEY. I SAW YOU THAT NIGHT IN PITTSBURGH. PETER TOLD ME ABOUT YOU. DULL TULL.
AND YOU'RE KRISTINE HATHAWAY. I'D FEEL SORRY FOR YOU, CHILD, IF I HAD FEELINGS.
THE OTHERS, THEY'RE DANGEROUS. BUT YOU...YOU JUST GOT CAUGHT RUNNING WITH THE WRONG CROWD, DIDN'T YOU?
YOU WANT TO HEAR SOMETHING FUNNY? SOMETHING I JUST FIGURED OUT, HEARING YOU TALK ON THE PHONE?
YOU WORK FOR TOYO HARADA.
YOU'VE NO IDEA WHAT YOU'RE TALKING ABOUT.
OHHH...AND I JUST FIGURED SOMETHING ELSE OUT, TOO. YOU DON'T KNOW YOU WORK FOR HARADA.
HOW ABOUT YOU HUMOR ME. TELL ME HOW PROJECT RISING SPIRIT TRACKED US HERE?
THIS SUCKS.
DID YOU KNOW TORKELSON WA ON THE HARBINGER LAT PSIOT LIST? OR THAT WERE EVEN CHASING THAT LIST?
NO. YOU JUST KNEW WE'D BE HERE AND HOW'D YOU KNO ABOUT FAITH, OR CHARLENE?
AND IT'S JUST A COINCIDENCE TH THE LAST TIME YOU FO PETER IT WAS AT T VERY SAME MOMEN HARADA APPROACH HIM, RIGHT?
AND WHY WERE YOU SO UNDERPREPA THAT NIGHT AND S OVER-PREPARED NOW?

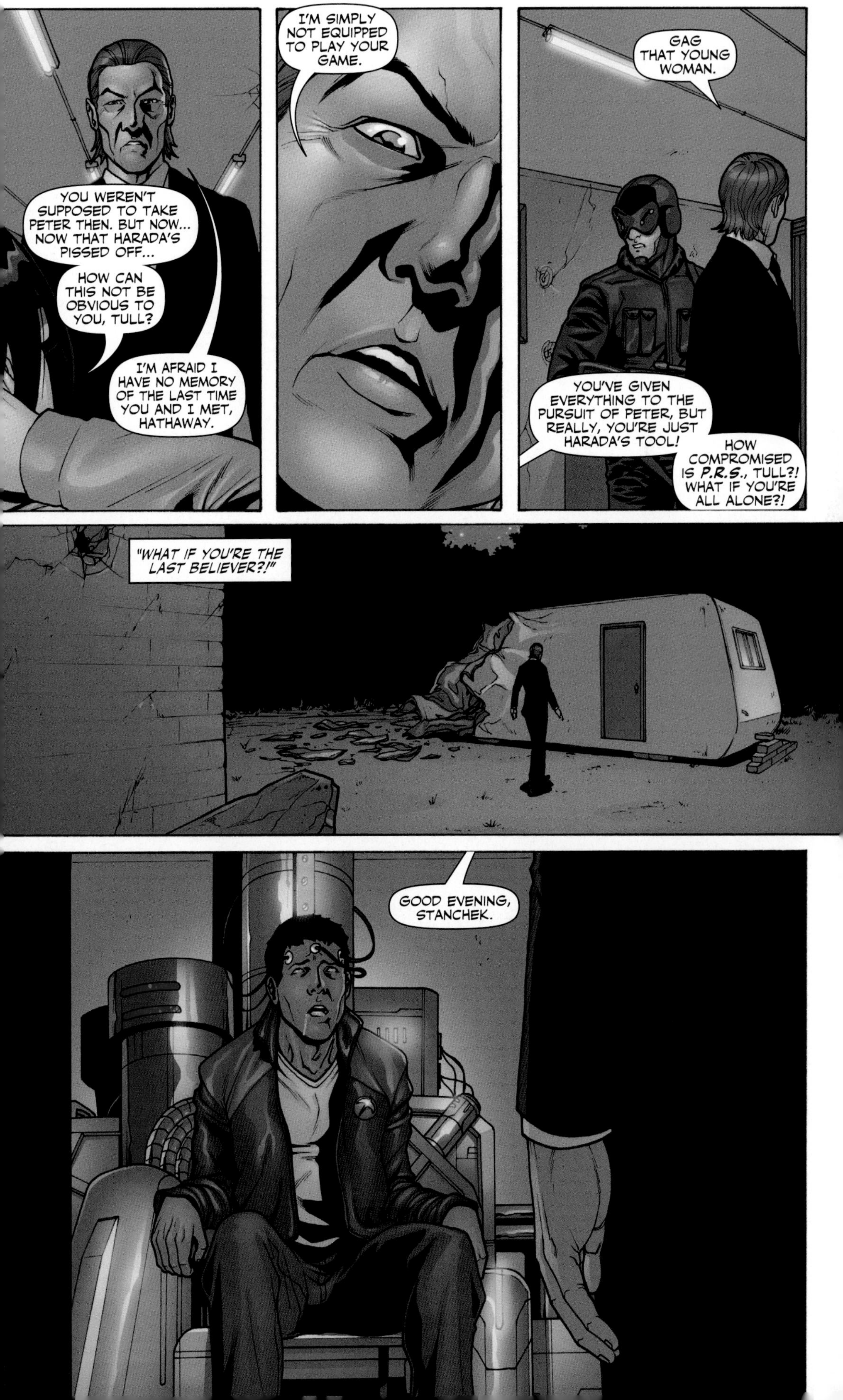
YOU WEREN'T SUPPOSED TO TAKE PETER THEN. BUT NOW... NOW THAT HARADA'S PISSED OFF...
HOW CAN THIS NOT BE OBVIOUS TO YOU, TULL?
I'M AFRAID I HAVE NO MEMORY OF THE LAST TIME YOU AND I MET, HATHAWAY.
I'M SIMPLY NOT EQUIPPED TO PLAY YOUR GAME.
GAG THAT YOUNG WOMAN.
YOU'VE GIVEN EVERYTHING TO THE PURSUIT OF PETER, BUT REALLY, YOU'RE JUST HARADA'S TOOL!
HOW COMPROMISED IS P.R.S., TULL?! WHAT IF YOU'RE ALL ALONE?!
"WHAT IF YOU'RE THE LAST BELIEVER?!"
GOOD EVENING, STANCHEK.

IT'S THE REAL ME THIS TIME. IN THE FLESH.

LOOKING BETTER THAN YOU. DO YOU KNOW WHAT A *DELTA WAVE* IS? IT'S A HIGH-AMPLITUDE BRAIN WAVE MOSTLY ASSOCIATED WITH SLEEP...

FOR THE OTHERS, JUST STANDARD ELECTROMAG TECH KEEPS THEM RELATIVELY IN CHECK.

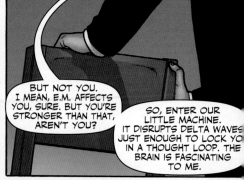

BUT NOT YOU. I MEAN, E.M. AFFECTS YOU, SURE. BUT YOU'RE STRONGER THAN THAT, AREN'T YOU?

SO, ENTER OUR LITTLE MACHINE. IT DISRUPTS DELTA WAVES JUST ENOUGH TO LOCK YO IN A THOUGHT LOOP. THE BRAIN IS FASCINATING TO ME.

MY SUPERIORS TELL ME THIS IS MY MOMENT. THAT I'VE BEEN CHASING YOU FOR SOME TIME.

THEY INFORM ME YOU'VE REPEATEDLY WIPED MY MEMORY. LEAVING NOTHING BUT THE MOST LITERAL ASPECTS OF LANGUAGE.

THEN TAKE ME IN. THEY TEACH ME, AGAIN AND AGAIN... ABOUT YOU. AND WHEN I'VE LEARNED ALL THEY NEED ME TO LEARN, THEY PUT ME BACK ON THE HUNT.

EVEN A PERSON WITH SEVERE AMNESIA IS CAPABLE OF EMOTION. BUT NOT ME. YOU'VE WIPED IT CLEAN.

THEY TELL ME THAT THIS IS FREEDOM. NO HISTORY. NO DESIRE. NO...PERSONALITY.

PERHAPS IT IS. HOW WOULD I KNOW?

THE QUESTION IS, AM I ANGRY ABOUT WHAT YOU'VE DONE TO ME, PETER? AGAIN... I JUST DON'T KNOW.

ALL I KNOW... IS YOU.

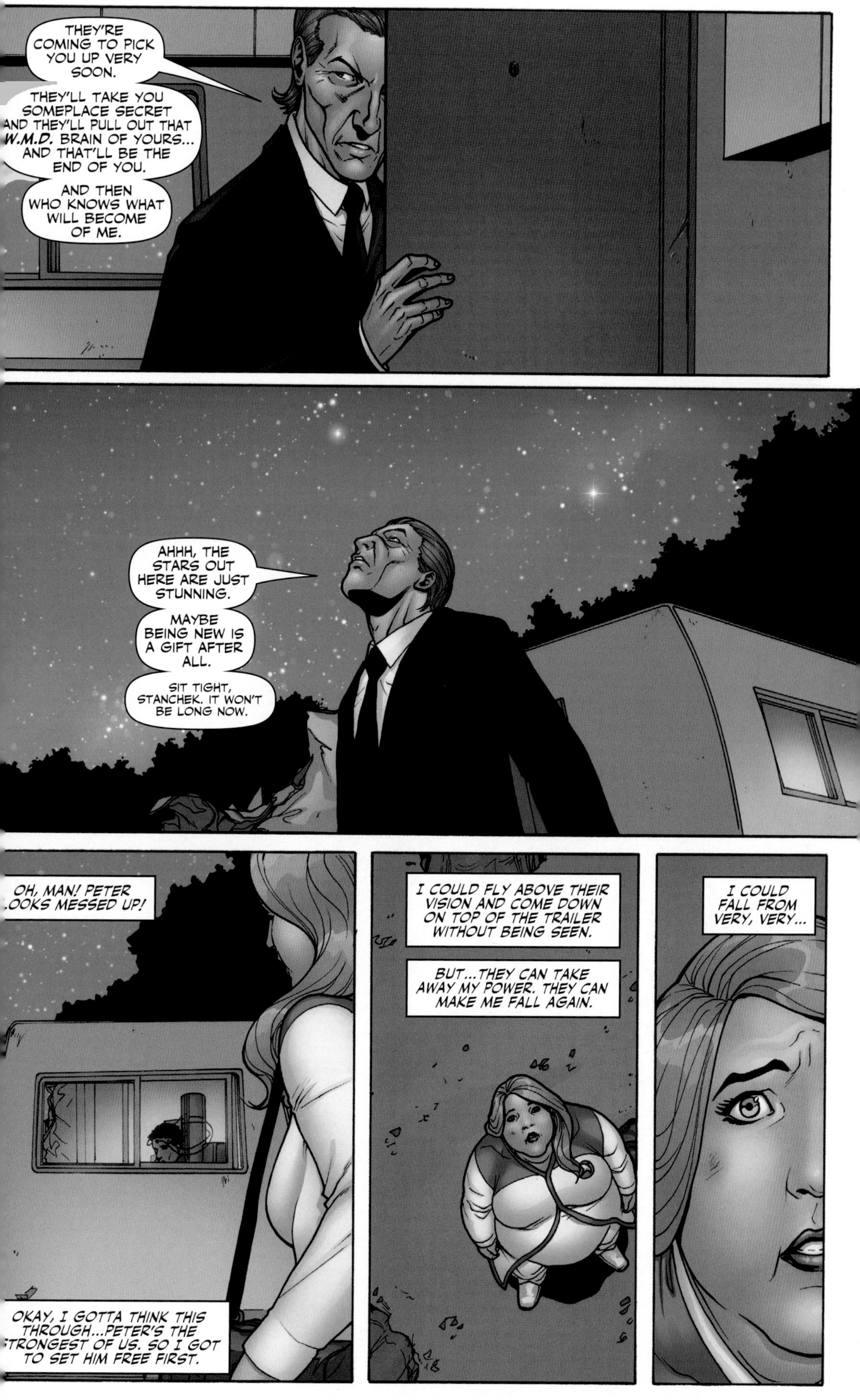
THEY'RE COMING TO PICK YOU UP VERY SOON.
THEY'LL TAKE YOU SOMEPLACE SECRET AND THEY'LL PULL OUT THAT W.M.D. BRAIN OF YOURS... AND THAT'LL BE THE END OF YOU.
AND THEN WHO KNOWS WHAT WILL BECOME OF ME.
AHHH, THE STARS OUT HERE ARE JUST STUNNING.
MAYBE BEING NEW IS A GIFT AFTER ALL.
SIT TIGHT, STANCHEK. IT WON'T BE LONG NOW.
OH, MAN! PETER LOOKS MESSED UP!
OKAY, I GOTTA THINK THIS THROUGH...PETER'S THE STRONGEST OF US. SO I GOT TO SET HIM FREE FIRST.
I COULD FLY ABOVE THEIR VISION AND COME DOWN ON TOP OF THE TRAILER WITHOUT BEING SEEN.
BUT...THEY CAN TAKE AWAY MY POWER. THEY CAN MAKE ME FALL AGAIN.
I COULD FALL FROM VERY, VERY...

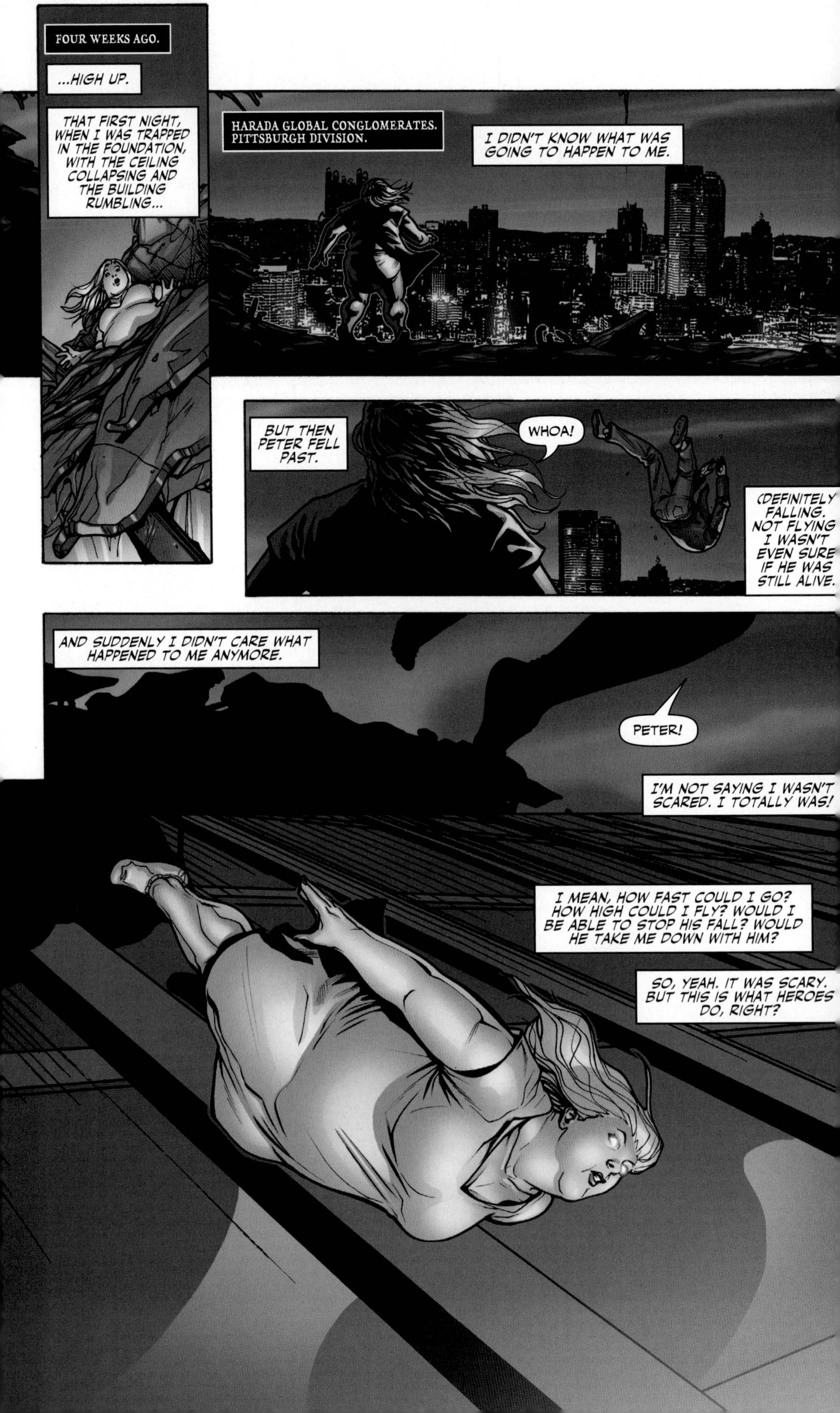
FOUR WEEKS AGO.
...HIGH UP.
THAT FIRST NIGHT, WHEN I WAS TRAPPED IN THE FOUNDATION, WITH THE CEILING COLLAPSING AND THE BUILDING RUMBLING...
HARADA GLOBAL CONGLOMERATES. PITTSBURGH DIVISION.
I DIDN'T KNOW WHAT WAS GOING TO HAPPEN TO ME.
BUT THEN PETER FELL PAST.
WHOA!
(DEFINITELY FALLING. NOT FLYING. I WASN'T EVEN SURE IF HE WAS STILL ALIVE.
AND SUDDENLY I DIDN'T CARE WHAT HAPPENED TO ME ANYMORE.
PETER!
I'M NOT SAYING I WASN'T SCARED. I TOTALLY WAS!
I MEAN, HOW FAST COULD I GO? HOW HIGH COULD I FLY? WOULD I BE ABLE TO STOP HIS FALL? WOULD HE TAKE ME DOWN WITH HIM?
SO, YEAH. IT WAS SCARY. BUT THIS IS WHAT HEROES DO, RIGHT?

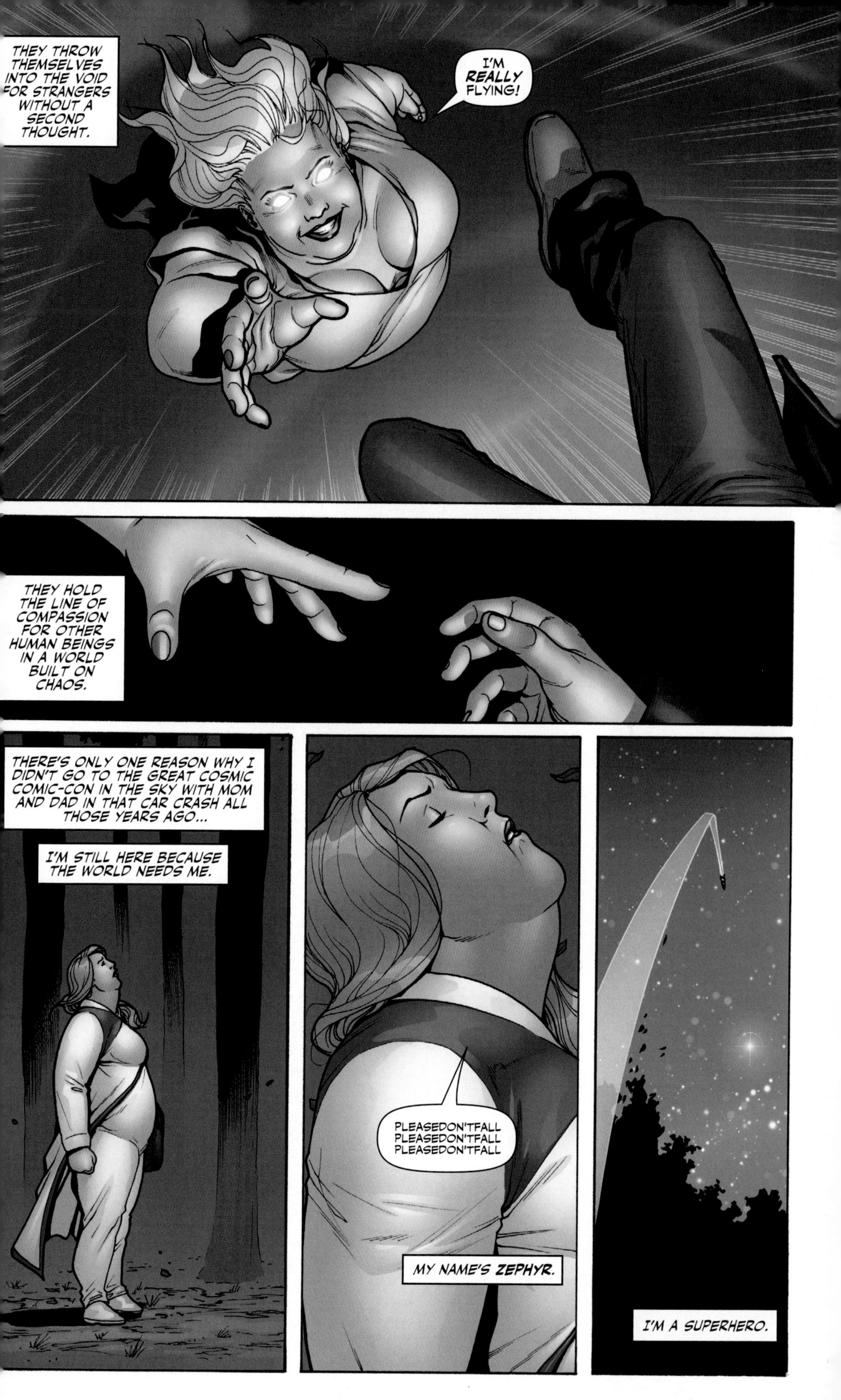
THEY THROW THEMSELVES INTO THE VOID FOR STRANGERS WITHOUT A SECOND THOUGHT.
I'M REALLY FLYING!
THEY HOLD THE LINE OF COMPASSION FOR OTHER HUMAN BEINGS IN A WORLD BUILT ON CHAOS.
THERE'S ONLY ONE REASON WHY I DIDN'T GO TO THE GREAT COSMIC COMIC-CON IN THE SKY WITH MOM AND DAD IN THAT CAR CRASH ALL THOSE YEARS AGO...
I'M STILL HERE BECAUSE THE WORLD NEEDS ME.
PLEASEDON'TFALL PLEASEDON'TFALL PLEASEDON'TFALL
MY NAME'S ZEPHYR.
I'M A SUPERHERO.

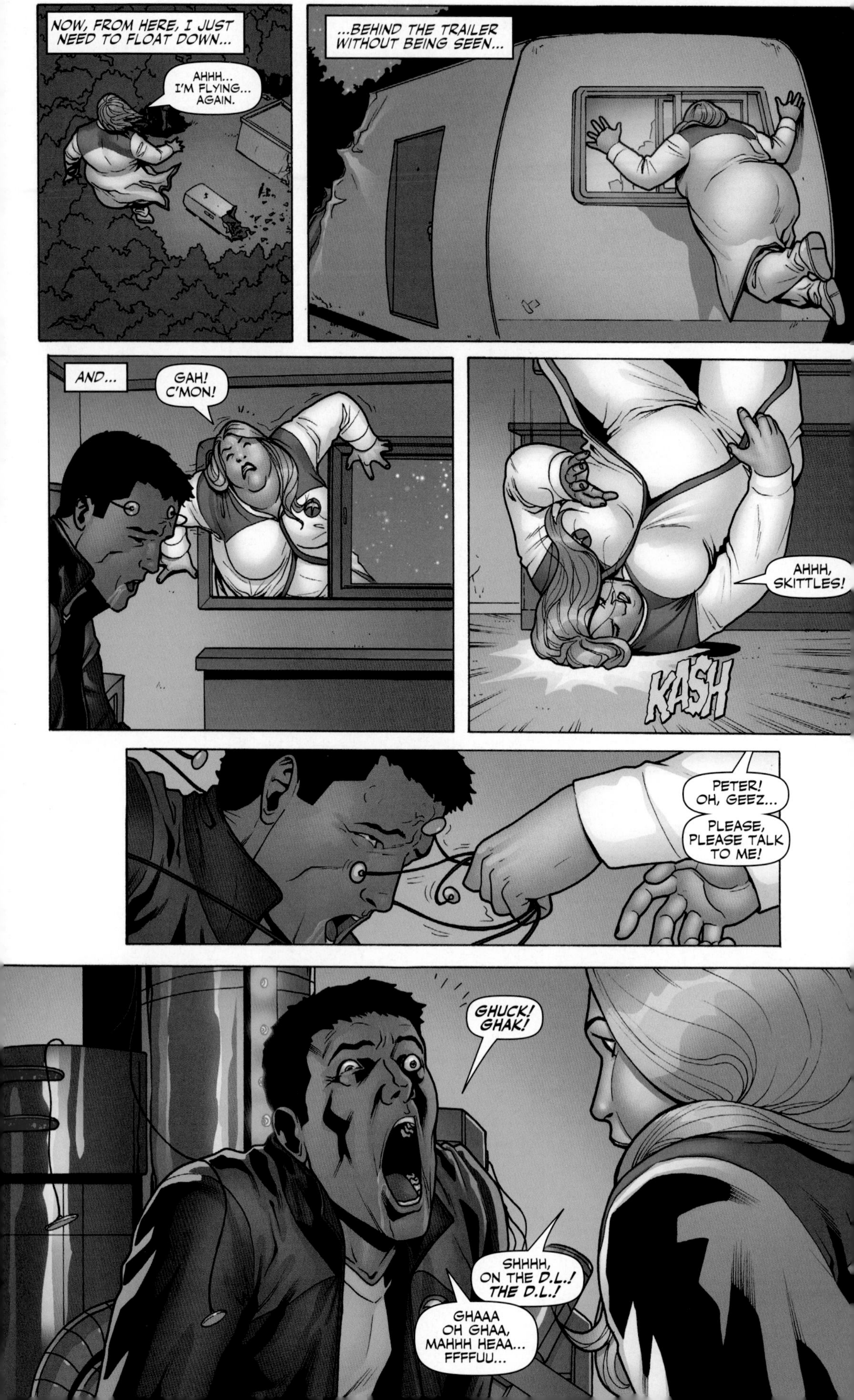
NOW, FROM HERE, I JUST NEED TO FLOAT DOWN...
AHHH... I'M FLYING... AGAIN.
...BEHIND THE TRAILER WITHOUT BEING SEEN...
AND...
GAH! C'MON!
AHHH, SKITTLES!
KASH
PETER! OH, GEEZ...
PLEASE, PLEASE TALK TO ME!
GHUCK! GHAK!
SHHHH, ON THE D.L.! THE D.L.!
GHAAA OH GHAA, MAHHH HEAA... FFFFUU...

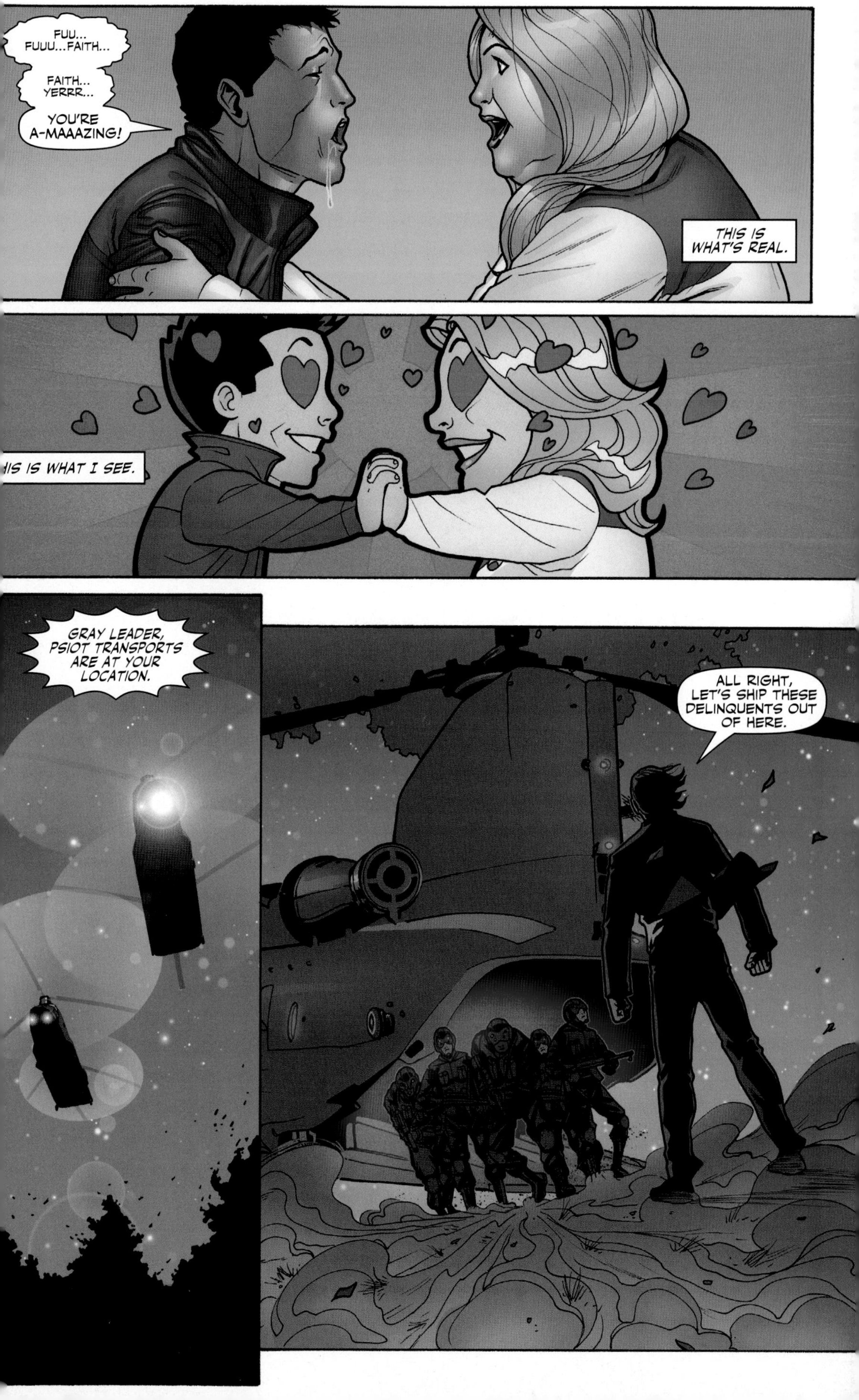
FUU... FUUU...FAITH...
FAITH... YERRR...
YOU'RE A-MAAAZING!
THIS IS WHAT'S REAL.
HIS IS WHAT I SEE.
GRAY LEADER, PSIOT TRANSPORTS ARE AT YOUR LOCATION.
ALL RIGHT, LET'S SHIP THESE DELINQUENTS OUT OF HERE.

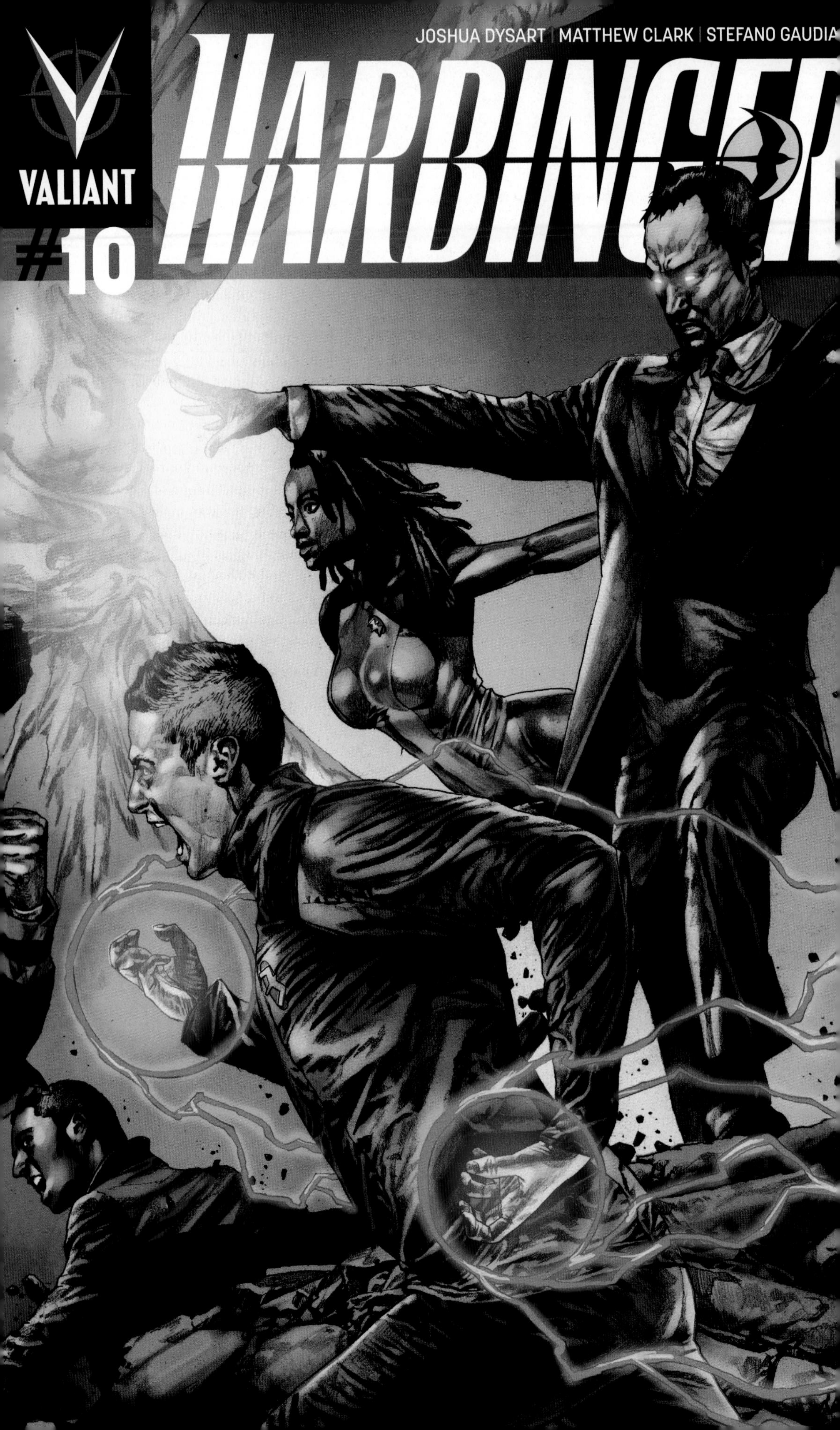

VALIANT
#10
JOSHUA DYSART | MATTHEW CLARK | STEFANO GAUDIANO
HARBINGER

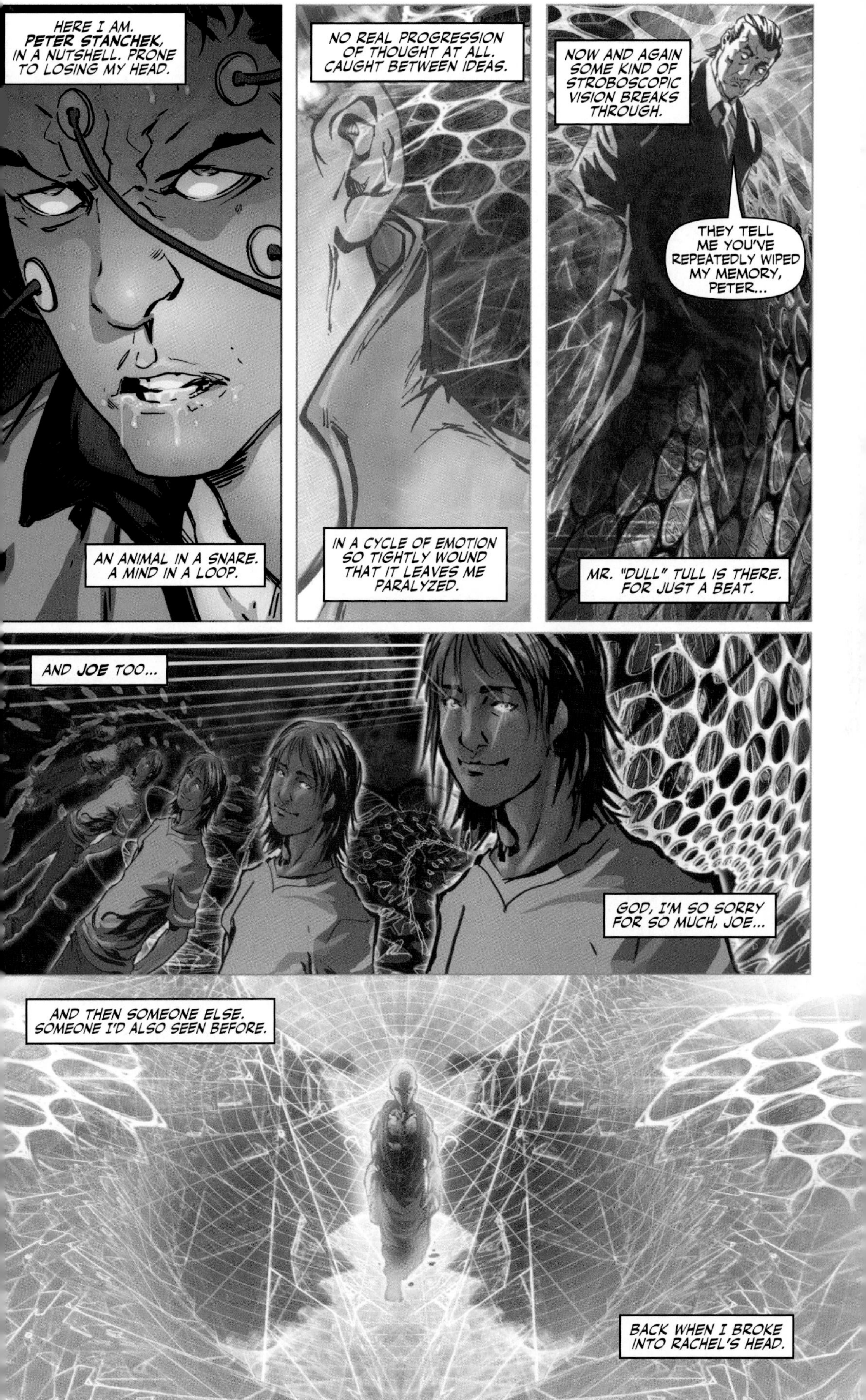
HERE I AM. PETER STANCHEK, IN A NUTSHELL. PRONE TO LOSING MY HEAD.
AN ANIMAL IN A SNARE. A MIND IN A LOOP.
NO REAL PROGRESSION OF THOUGHT AT ALL. CAUGHT BETWEEN IDEAS.
IN A CYCLE OF EMOTION SO TIGHTLY WOUND THAT IT LEAVES ME PARALYZED.
NOW AND AGAIN SOME KIND OF STROBOSCOPIC VISION BREAKS THROUGH.
THEY TELL ME YOU'VE REPEATEDLY WIPED MY MEMORY, PETER...
MR. "DULL" TULL IS THERE. FOR JUST A BEAT.
AND JOE TOO...
GOD, I'M SO SORRY FOR SO MUCH, JOE...
AND THEN SOMEONE ELSE. SOMEONE I'D ALSO SEEN BEFORE.
BACK WHEN I BROKE INTO RACHEL'S HEAD.

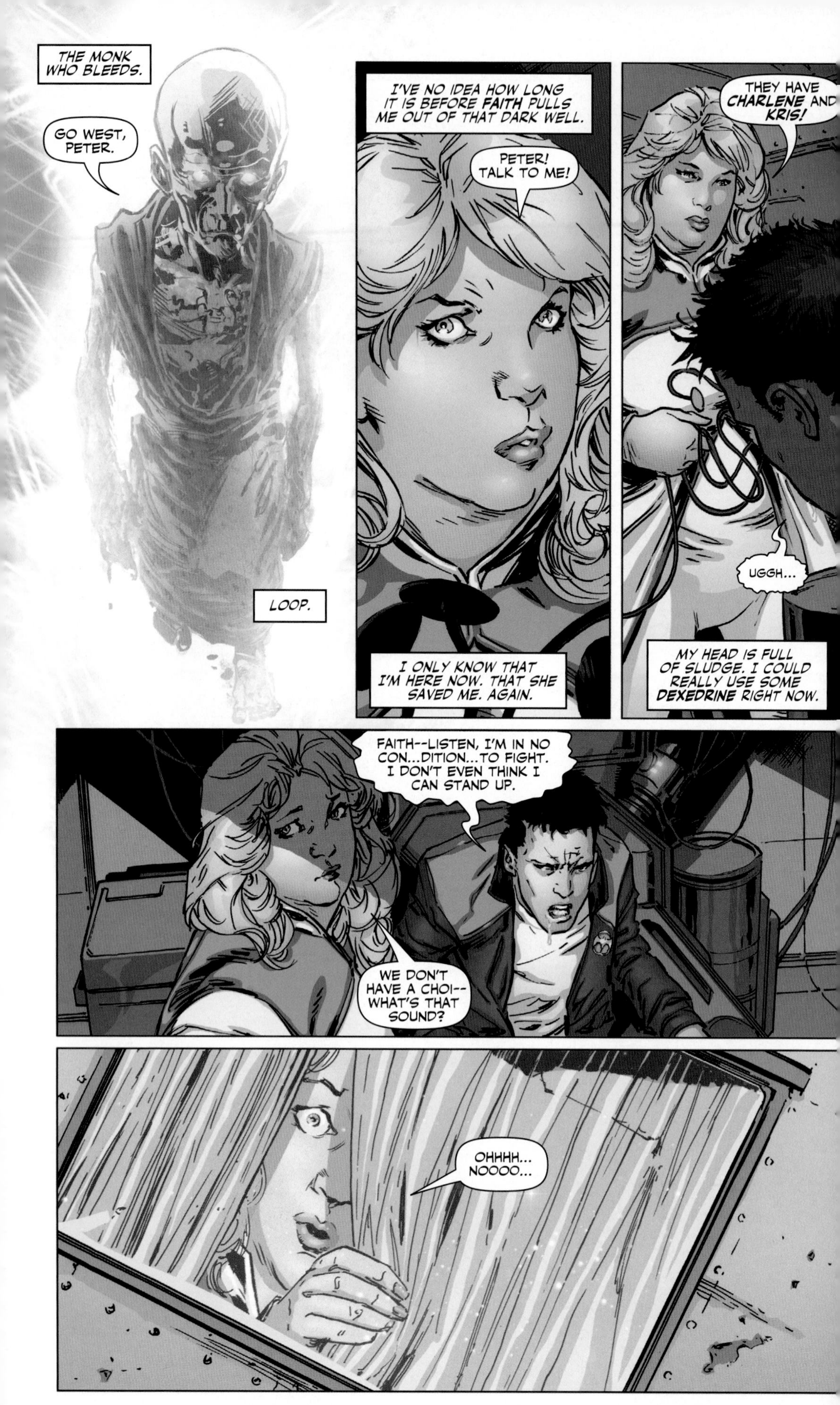
THE MONK WHO BLEEDS.
GO WEST, PETER.
LOOP.
I'VE NO IDEA HOW LONG IT IS BEFORE FAITH PULLS ME OUT OF THAT DARK WELL.
PETER! TALK TO ME!
I ONLY KNOW THAT I'M HERE NOW. THAT SHE SAVED ME. AGAIN.
THEY HAVE CHARLENE AND KRIS!
UGGH...
MY HEAD IS FULL OF SLUDGE. I COULD REALLY USE SOME DEXEDRINE RIGHT NOW.
FAITH--LISTEN, I'M IN NO CON...DITION...TO FIGHT. I DON'T EVEN THINK I CAN STAND UP.
WE DON'T HAVE A CHOI-- WHAT'S THAT SOUND?
OHHHH... NOOOO...

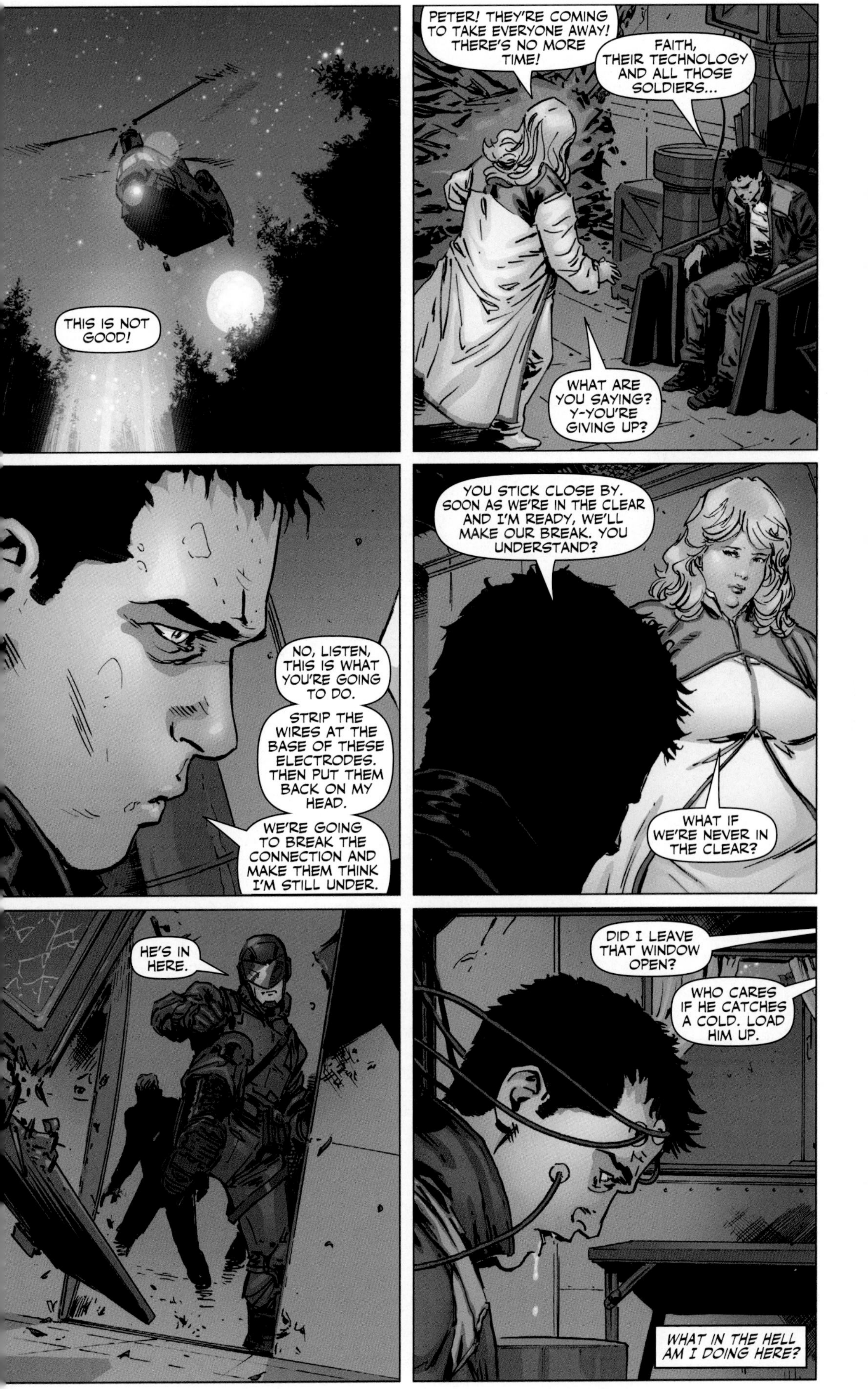
THIS IS NOT GOOD!
PETER! THEY'RE COMING TO TAKE EVERYONE AWAY! THERE'S NO MORE TIME!
FAITH, THEIR TECHNOLOGY AND ALL THOSE SOLDIERS...
WHAT ARE YOU SAYING? Y-YOU'RE GIVING UP?
NO, LISTEN, THIS IS WHAT YOU'RE GOING TO DO.
STRIP THE WIRES AT THE BASE OF THESE ELECTRODES. THEN PUT THEM BACK ON MY HEAD.
WE'RE GOING TO BREAK THE CONNECTION AND MAKE THEM THINK I'M STILL UNDER.
YOU STICK CLOSE BY. SOON AS WE'RE IN THE CLEAR AND I'M READY, WE'LL MAKE OUR BREAK. YOU UNDERSTAND?
WHAT IF WE'RE NEVER IN THE CLEAR?
HE'S IN HERE.
DID I LEAVE THAT WINDOW OPEN?
WHO CARES IF HE CATCHES A COLD. LOAD HIM UP.
WHAT IN THE HELL AM I DOING HERE?

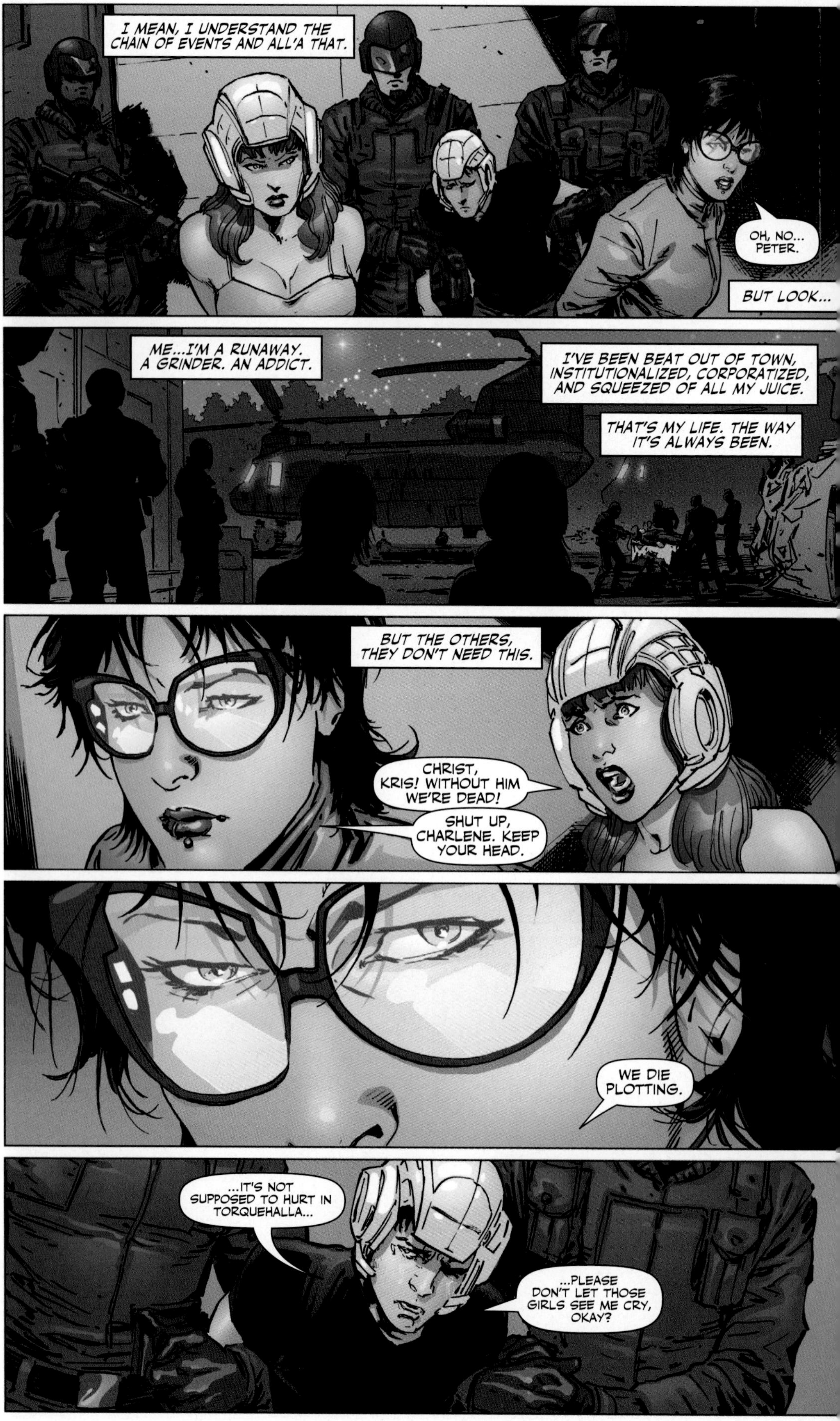
I MEAN, I UNDERSTAND THE CHAIN OF EVENTS AND ALL'A THAT.
OH, NO... PETER.
BUT LOOK...
ME...I'M A RUNAWAY. A GRINDER. AN ADDICT.
I'VE BEEN BEAT OUT OF TOWN, INSTITUTIONALIZED, CORPORATIZED, AND SQUEEZED OF ALL MY JUICE.
THAT'S MY LIFE. THE WAY IT'S ALWAYS BEEN.
BUT THE OTHERS, THEY DON'T NEED THIS.
CHRIST, KRIS! WITHOUT HIM WE'RE DEAD!
SHUT UP, CHARLENE. KEEP YOUR HEAD.
WE DIE PLOTTING.
...IT'S NOT SUPPOSED TO HURT IN TORQUEHALLA...
...PLEASE DON'T LET THOSE GIRLS SEE ME CRY, OKAY?

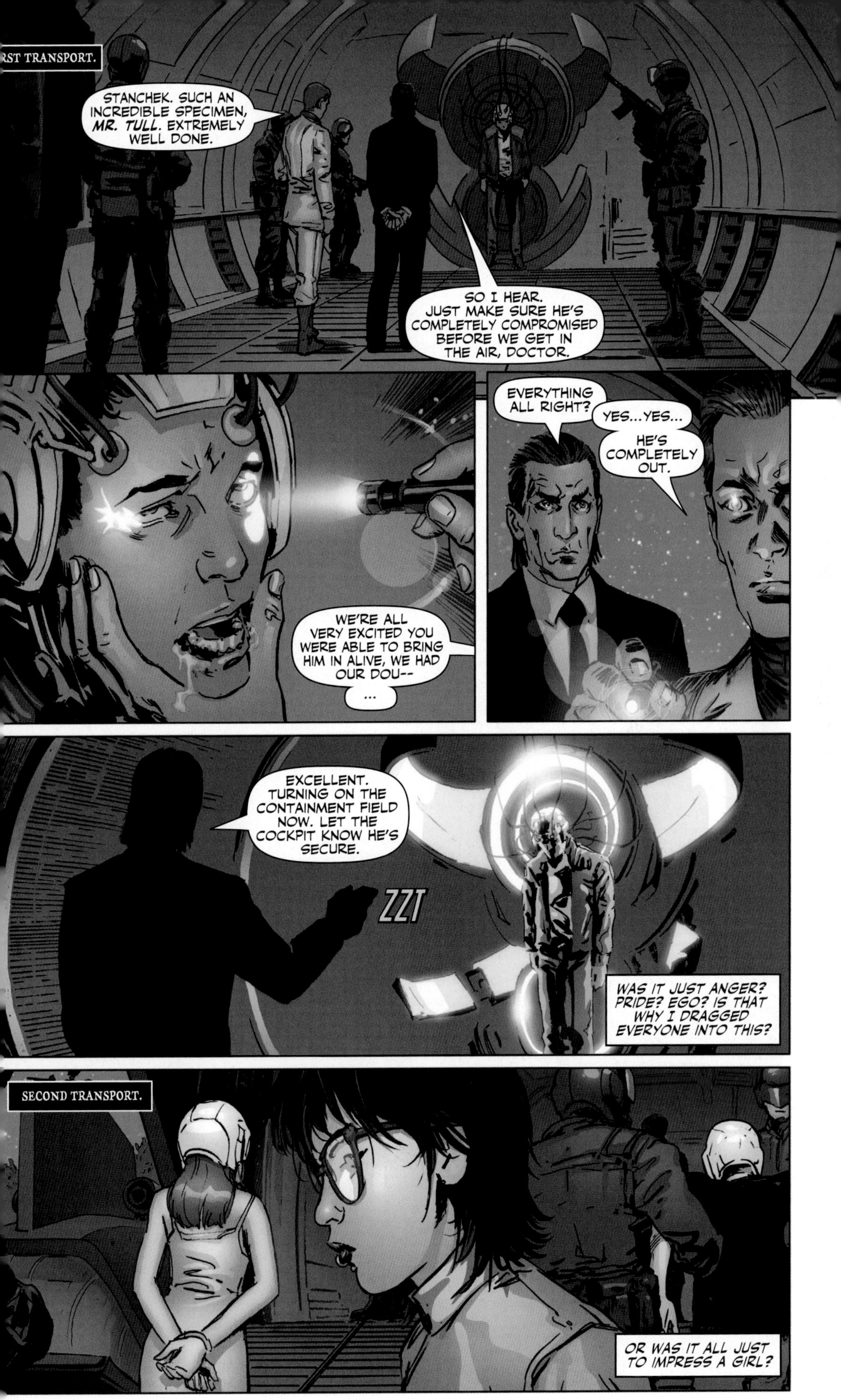
RST TRANSPORT.
STANCHEK. SUCH AN INCREDIBLE SPECIMEN, MR. TULL. EXTREMELY WELL DONE.
SO I HEAR. JUST MAKE SURE HE'S COMPLETELY COMPROMISED BEFORE WE GET IN THE AIR, DOCTOR.
WE'RE ALL VERY EXCITED YOU WERE ABLE TO BRING HIM IN ALIVE, WE HAD OUR DOU--
...
EVERYTHING ALL RIGHT?
YES...YES...
HE'S COMPLETELY OUT.
EXCELLENT. TURNING ON THE CONTAINMENT FIELD NOW. LET THE COCKPIT KNOW HE'S SECURE.
ZZT
WAS IT JUST ANGER? PRIDE? EGO? IS THAT WHY I DRAGGED EVERYONE INTO THIS?
SECOND TRANSPORT.
OR WAS IT ALL JUST TO IMPRESS A GIRL?

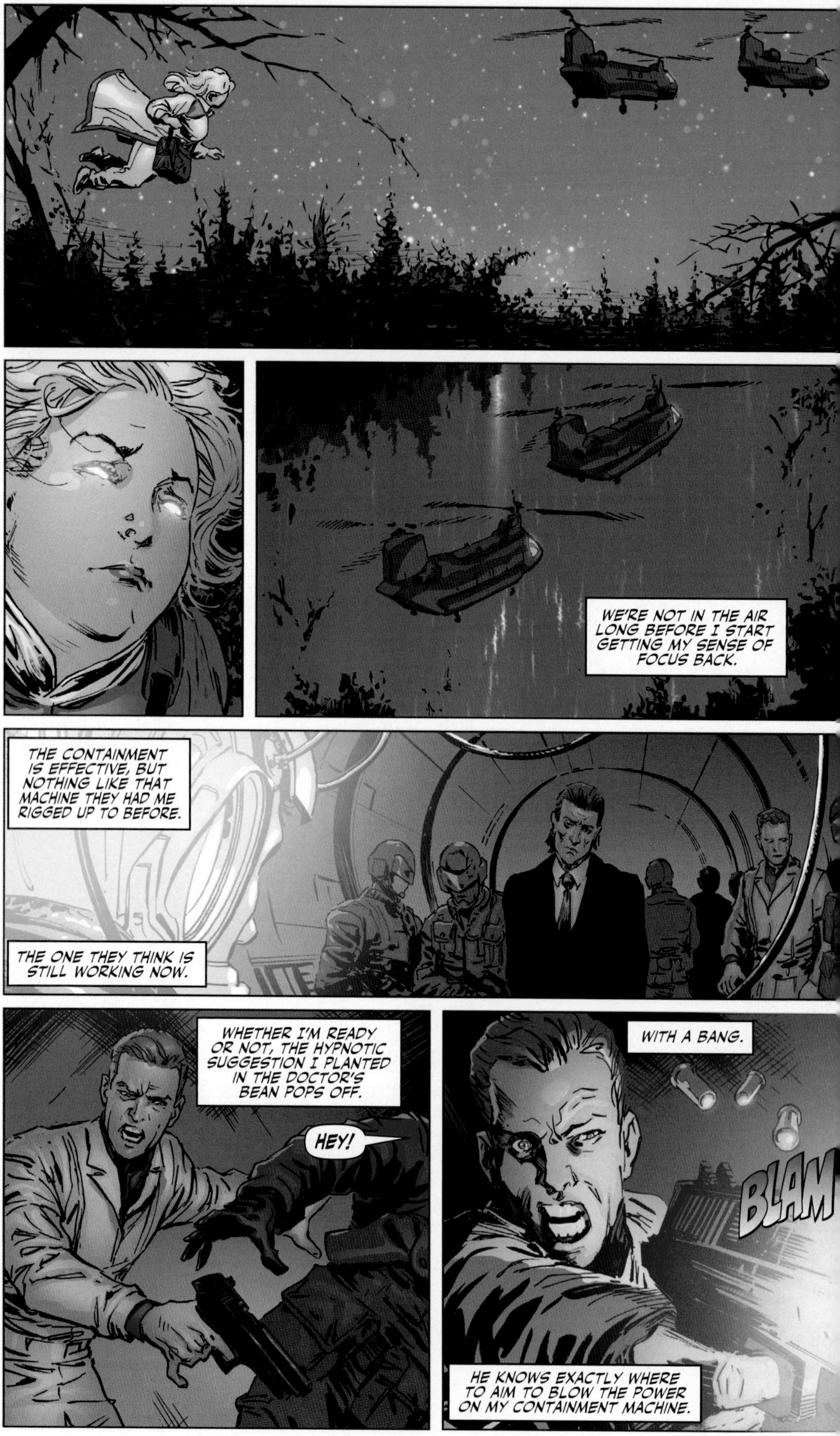
WE'RE NOT IN THE AIR LONG BEFORE I START GETTING MY SENSE OF FOCUS BACK.
THE CONTAINMENT IS EFFECTIVE, BUT NOTHING LIKE THAT MACHINE THEY HAD ME RIGGED UP TO BEFORE.
THE ONE THEY THINK IS STILL WORKING NOW.
WHETHER I'M READY OR NOT, THE HYPNOTIC SUGGESTION I PLANTED IN THE DOCTOR'S BEAN POPS OFF.
HEY!
WITH A BANG.
BLAM
HE KNOWS EXACTLY WHERE TO AIM TO BLOW THE POWER ON MY CONTAINMENT MACHINE.

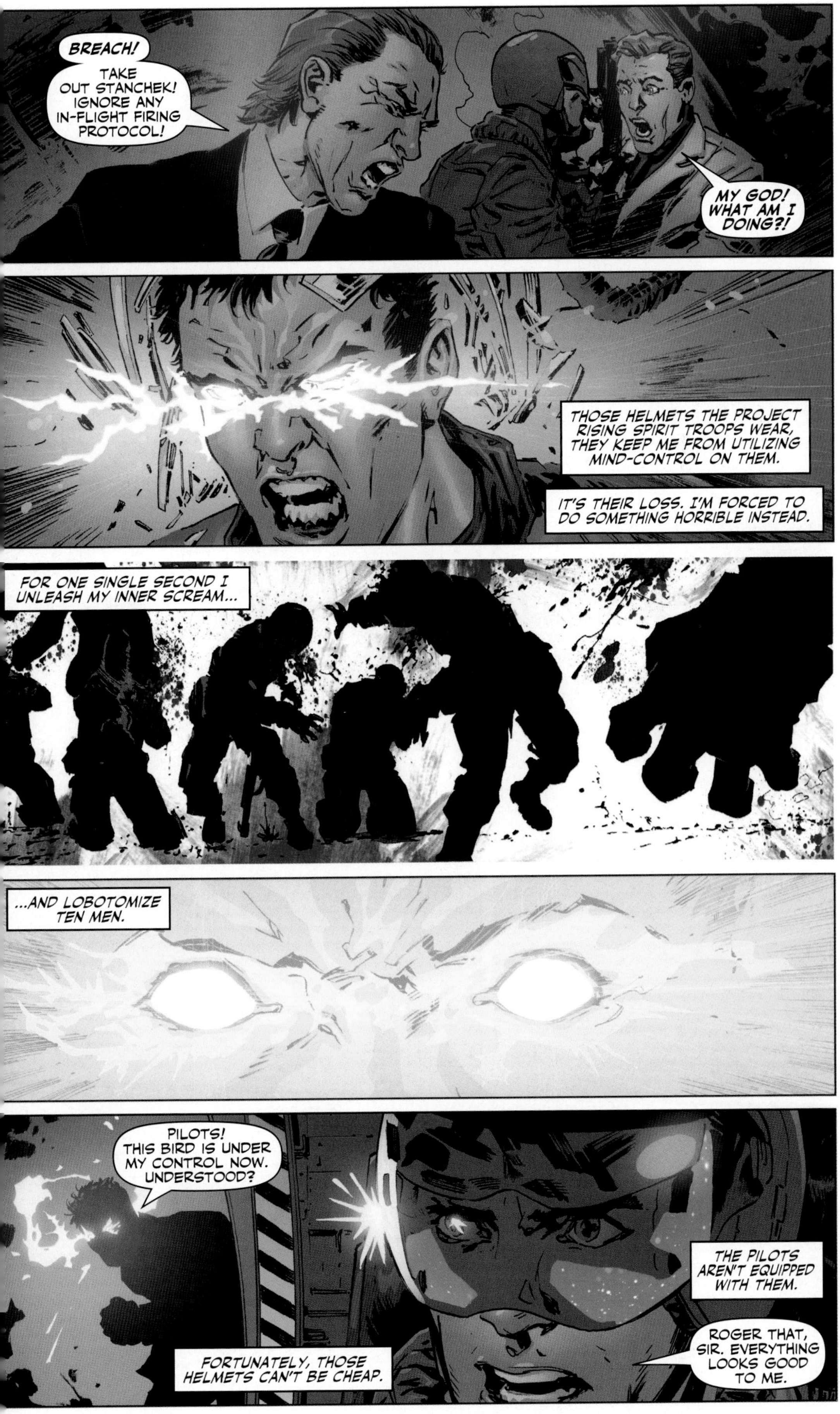
BREACH!
TAKE OUT STANCHEK! IGNORE ANY IN-FLIGHT FIRING PROTOCOL!
MY GOD! WHAT AM I DOING?!
THOSE HELMETS THE PROJECT RISING SPIRIT TROOPS WEAR, THEY KEEP ME FROM UTILIZING MIND-CONTROL ON THEM.
IT'S THEIR LOSS. I'M FORCED TO DO SOMETHING HORRIBLE INSTEAD.
FOR ONE SINGLE SECOND I UNLEASH MY INNER SCREAM...
...AND LOBOTOMIZE TEN MEN.
PILOTS! THIS BIRD IS UNDER MY CONTROL NOW. UNDERSTOOD?
THE PILOTS AREN'T EQUIPPED WITH THEM.
ROGER THAT, SIR. EVERYTHING LOOKS GOOD TO ME.
FORTUNATELY, THOSE HELMETS CAN'T BE CHEAP.

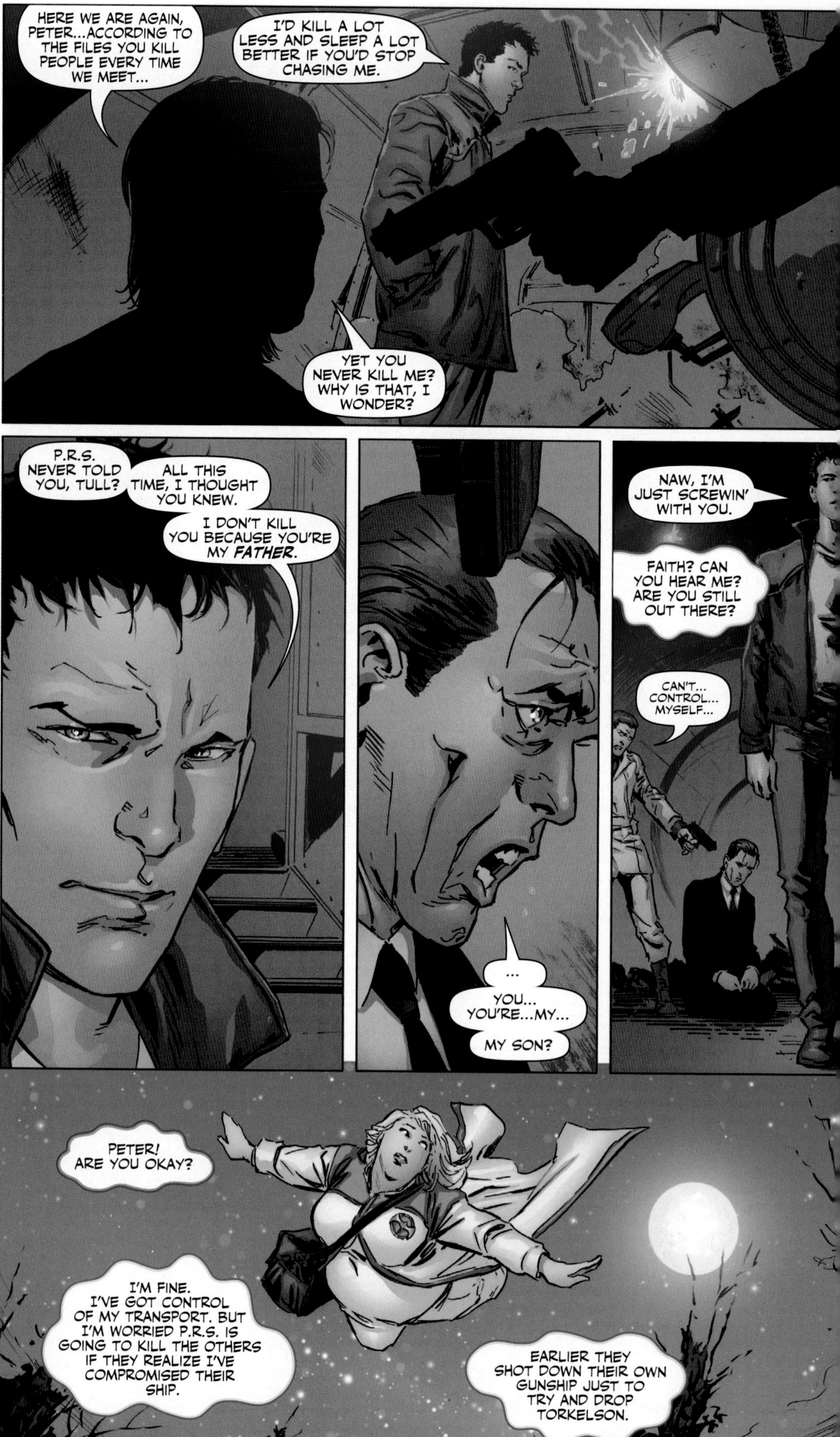
HERE WE ARE AGAIN, PETER...ACCORDING TO THE FILES YOU KILL PEOPLE EVERY TIME WE MEET...
I'D KILL A LOT LESS AND SLEEP A LOT BETTER IF YOU'D STOP CHASING ME.
YET YOU NEVER KILL ME? WHY IS THAT, I WONDER?
P.R.S. NEVER TOLD YOU, TULL?
ALL THIS TIME, I THOUGHT YOU KNEW.
I DON'T KILL YOU BECAUSE YOU'RE MY *FATHER*.
...
YOU... YOU'RE...MY...
MY SON?
NAW, I'M JUST SCREWIN' WITH YOU.
FAITH? CAN YOU HEAR ME? ARE YOU STILL OUT THERE?
CAN'T... CONTROL... MYSELF...
PETER! ARE YOU OKAY?
I'M FINE. I'VE GOT CONTROL OF MY TRANSPORT. BUT I'M WORRIED P.R.S. IS GOING TO KILL THE OTHERS IF THEY REALIZE I'VE COMPROMISED THEIR SHIP.
EARLIER THEY SHOT DOWN THEIR OWN GUNSHIP JUST TO TRY AND DROP TORKELSON.

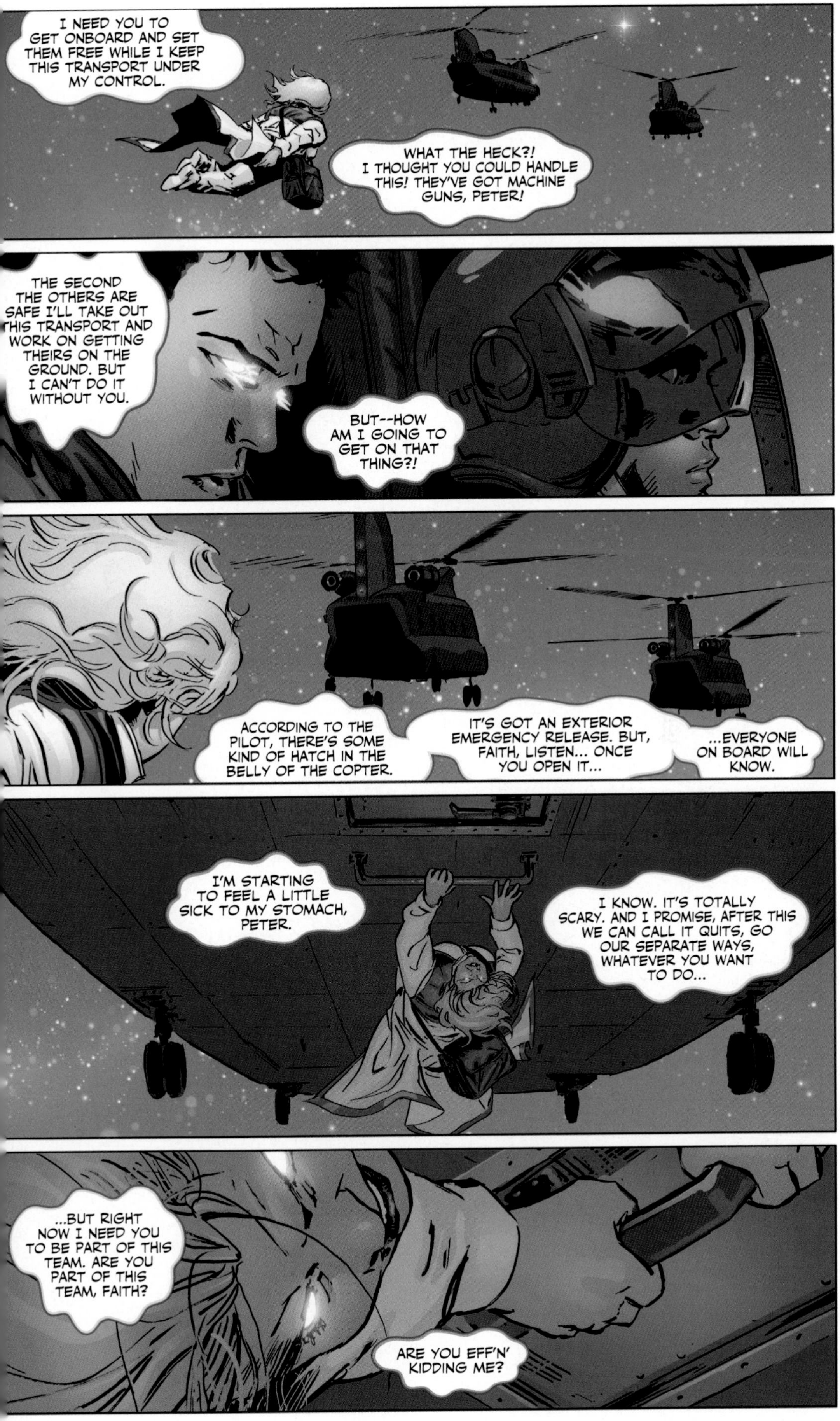
I NEED YOU TO GET ONBOARD AND SET THEM FREE WHILE I KEEP THIS TRANSPORT UNDER MY CONTROL.
WHAT THE HECK?! I THOUGHT YOU COULD HANDLE THIS! THEY'VE GOT MACHINE GUNS, PETER!
THE SECOND THE OTHERS ARE SAFE I'LL TAKE OUT THIS TRANSPORT AND WORK ON GETTING THEIRS ON THE GROUND. BUT I CAN'T DO IT WITHOUT YOU.
BUT--HOW AM I GOING TO GET ON THAT THING?!
ACCORDING TO THE PILOT, THERE'S SOME KIND OF HATCH IN THE BELLY OF THE COPTER.
IT'S GOT AN EXTERIOR EMERGENCY RELEASE. BUT, FAITH, LISTEN... ONCE YOU OPEN IT...
...EVERYONE ON BOARD WILL KNOW.
I'M STARTING TO FEEL A LITTLE SICK TO MY STOMACH, PETER.
I KNOW. IT'S TOTALLY SCARY. AND I PROMISE, AFTER THIS WE CAN CALL IT QUITS, GO OUR SEPARATE WAYS, WHATEVER YOU WANT TO DO...
...BUT RIGHT NOW I NEED YOU TO BE PART OF THIS TEAM. ARE YOU PART OF THIS TEAM, FAITH?
ARE YOU EFF'N' KIDDING ME?

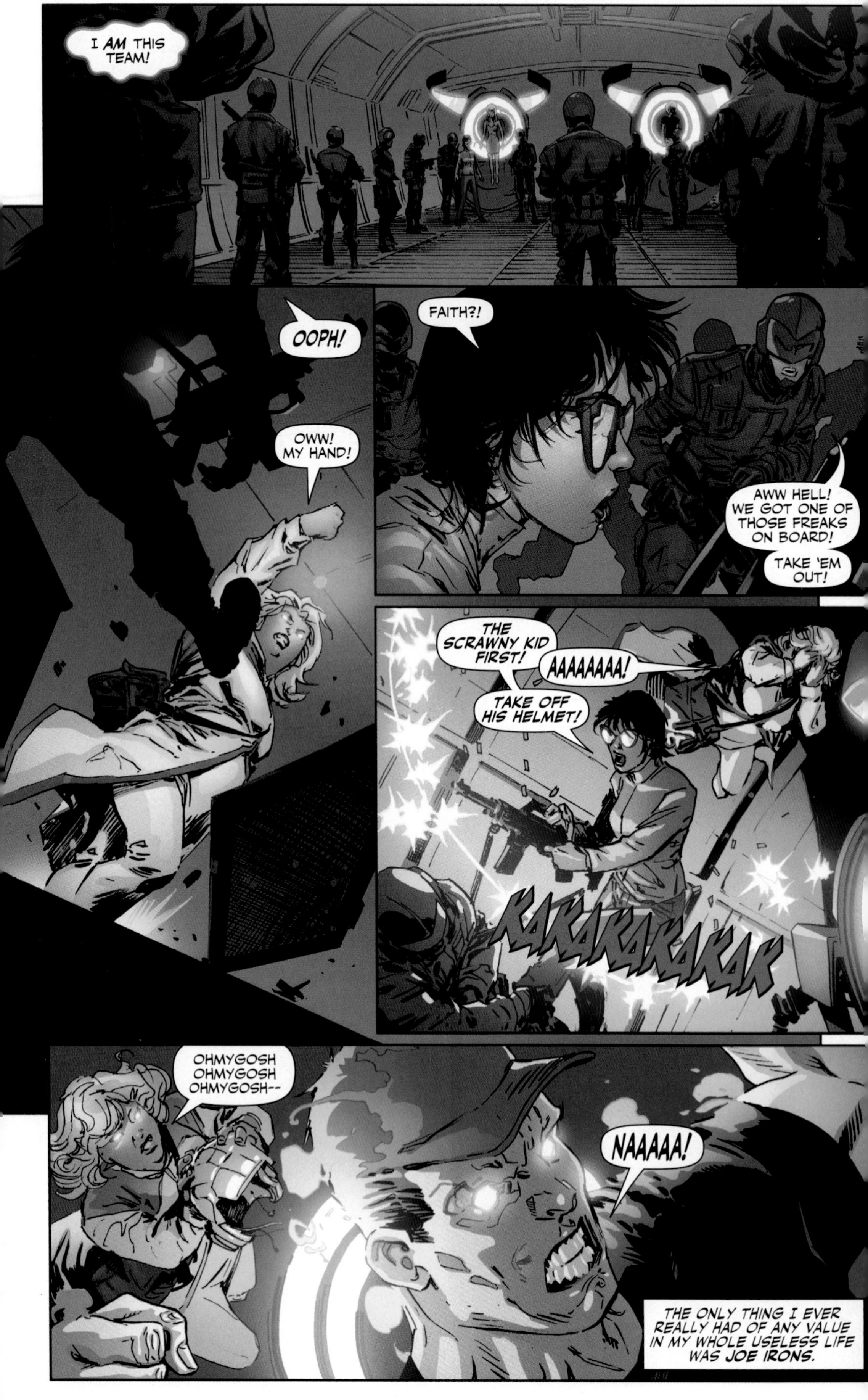

I AM THIS TEAM!
OOPH!
OWW! MY HAND!
FAITH?!
AWW HELL! WE GOT ONE OF THOSE FREAKS ON BOARD!
TAKE 'EM OUT!
THE SCRAWNY KID FIRST!
TAKE OFF HIS HELMET!
AAAAAAAA!
KAKAKAKAKAKAK
OHMYGOSH OHMYGOSH OHMYGOSH--
NAAAAA!
THE ONLY THING I EVER REALLY HAD OF ANY VALUE IN MY WHOLE USELESS LIFE WAS JOE IRONS.

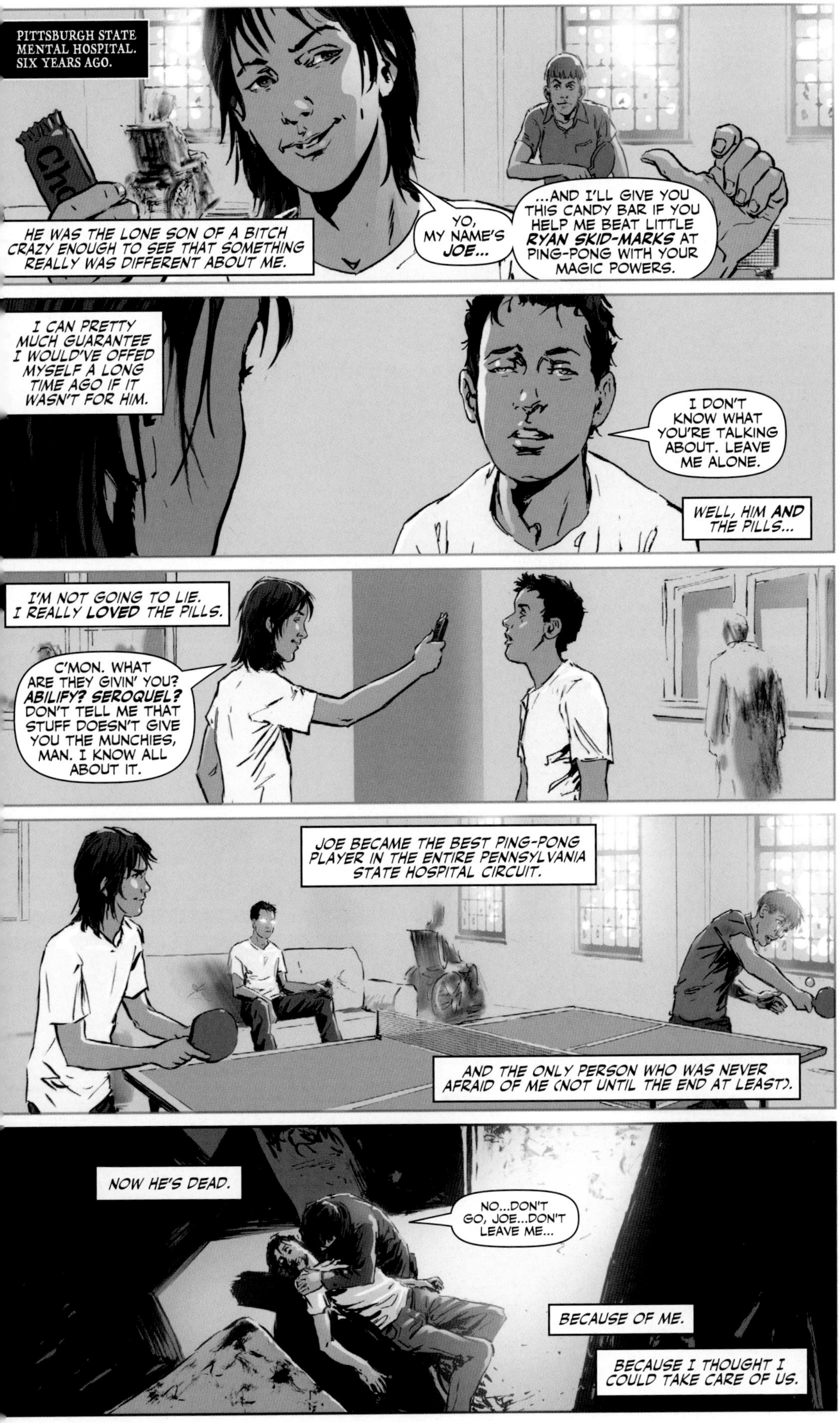
PITTSBURGH STATE MENTAL HOSPITAL. SIX YEARS AGO.
HE WAS THE LONE SON OF A BITCH CRAZY ENOUGH TO SEE THAT SOMETHING REALLY WAS DIFFERENT ABOUT ME.
YO, MY NAME'S JOE...
...AND I'LL GIVE YOU THIS CANDY BAR IF YOU HELP ME BEAT LITTLE RYAN SKID-MARKS AT PING-PONG WITH YOUR MAGIC POWERS.
I CAN PRETTY MUCH GUARANTEE I WOULD'VE OFFED MYSELF A LONG TIME AGO IF IT WASN'T FOR HIM.
I DON'T KNOW WHAT YOU'RE TALKING ABOUT. LEAVE ME ALONE.
WELL, HIM AND THE PILLS...
I'M NOT GOING TO LIE. I REALLY LOVED THE PILLS.
C'MON. WHAT ARE THEY GIVIN' YOU? ABILIFY? SEROQUEL? DON'T TELL ME THAT STUFF DOESN'T GIVE YOU THE MUNCHIES, MAN. I KNOW ALL ABOUT IT.
JOE BECAME THE BEST PING-PONG PLAYER IN THE ENTIRE PENNSYLVANIA STATE HOSPITAL CIRCUIT.
AND THE ONLY PERSON WHO WAS NEVER AFRAID OF ME (NOT UNTIL THE END AT LEAST).
NOW HE'S DEAD.
NO...DON'T GO, JOE...DON'T LEAVE ME...
BECAUSE OF ME.
BECAUSE I THOUGHT I COULD TAKE CARE OF US.

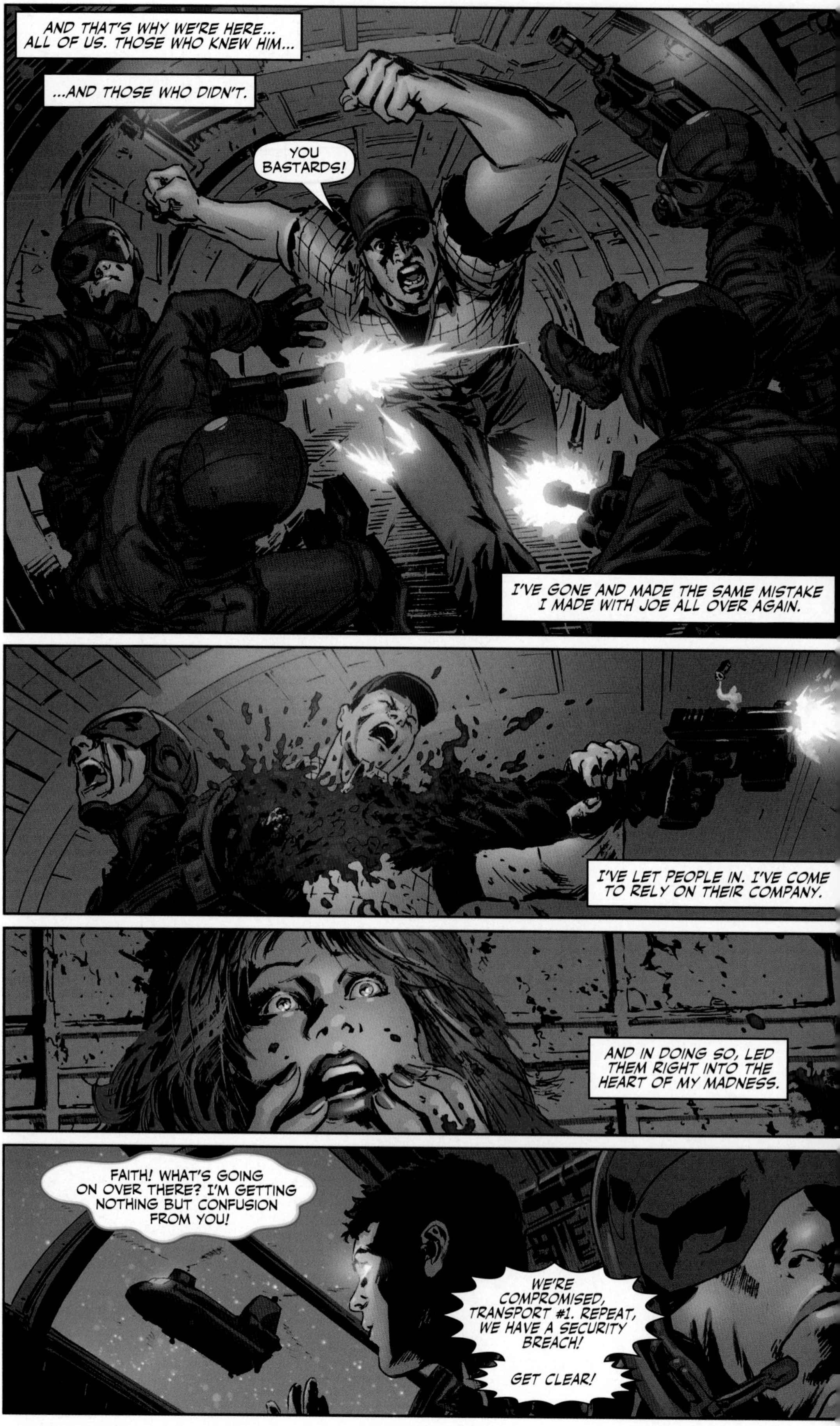
AND THAT'S WHY WE'RE HERE... ALL OF US. THOSE WHO KNEW HIM...
...AND THOSE WHO DIDN'T.
YOU BASTARDS!
I'VE GONE AND MADE THE SAME MISTAKE I MADE WITH JOE ALL OVER AGAIN.
I'VE LET PEOPLE IN. I'VE COME TO RELY ON THEIR COMPANY.
AND IN DOING SO, LED THEM RIGHT INTO THE HEART OF MY MADNESS.
FAITH! WHAT'S GOING ON OVER THERE? I'M GETTING NOTHING BUT CONFUSION FROM YOU!
WE'RE COMPROMISED, TRANSPORT #1. REPEAT, WE HAVE A SECURITY BREACH!
GET CLEAR!

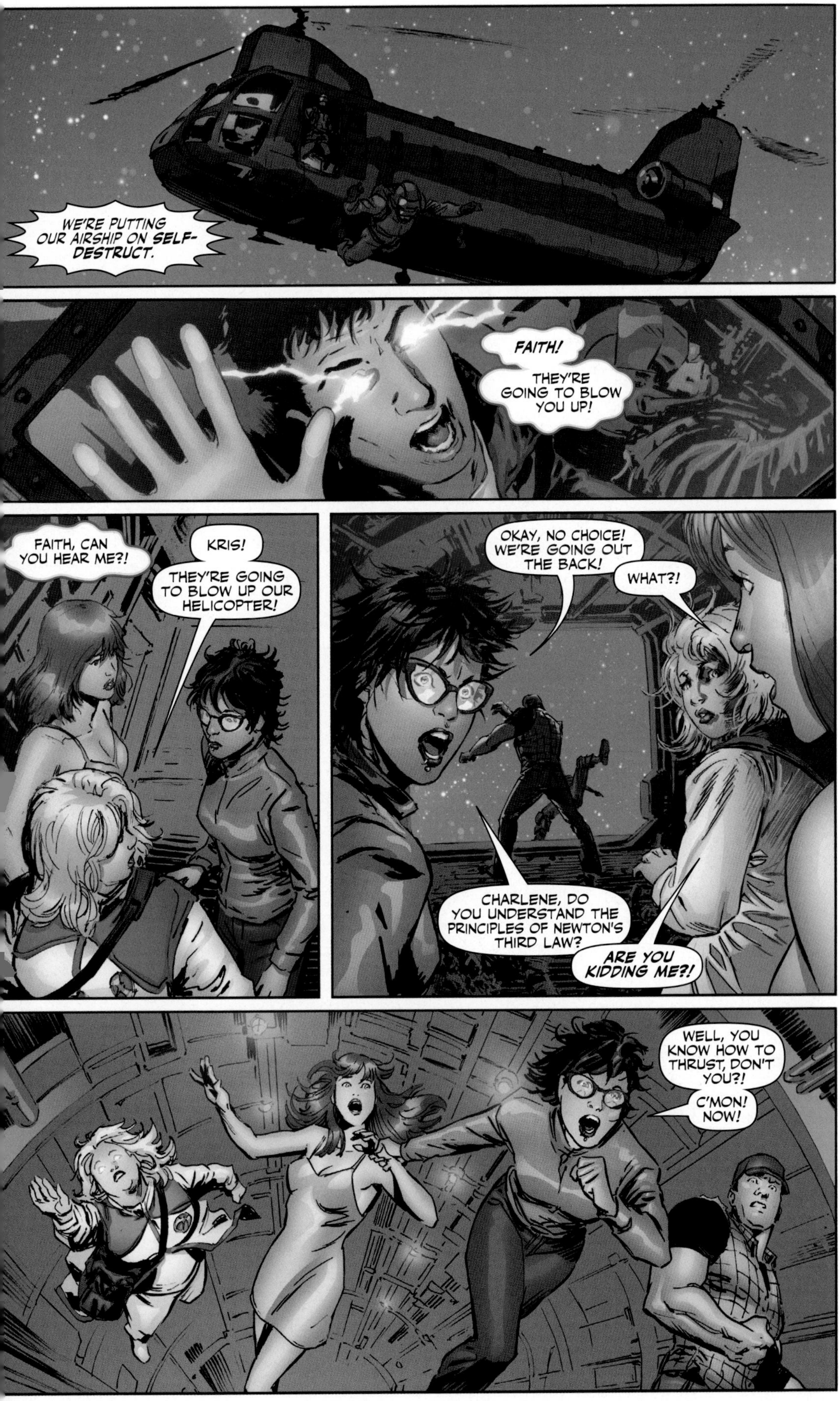

WE'RE PUTTING OUR AIRSHIP ON SELF-DESTRUCT.
FAITH!
THEY'RE GOING TO BLOW YOU UP!
FAITH, CAN YOU HEAR ME?!
KRIS!
THEY'RE GOING TO BLOW UP OUR HELICOPTER!
OKAY, NO CHOICE! WE'RE GOING OUT THE BACK!
WHAT?!
CHARLENE, DO YOU UNDERSTAND THE PRINCIPLES OF NEWTON'S THIRD LAW?
ARE YOU KIDDING ME?!
WELL, YOU KNOW HOW TO THRUST, DON'T YOU?!
C'MON! NOW!

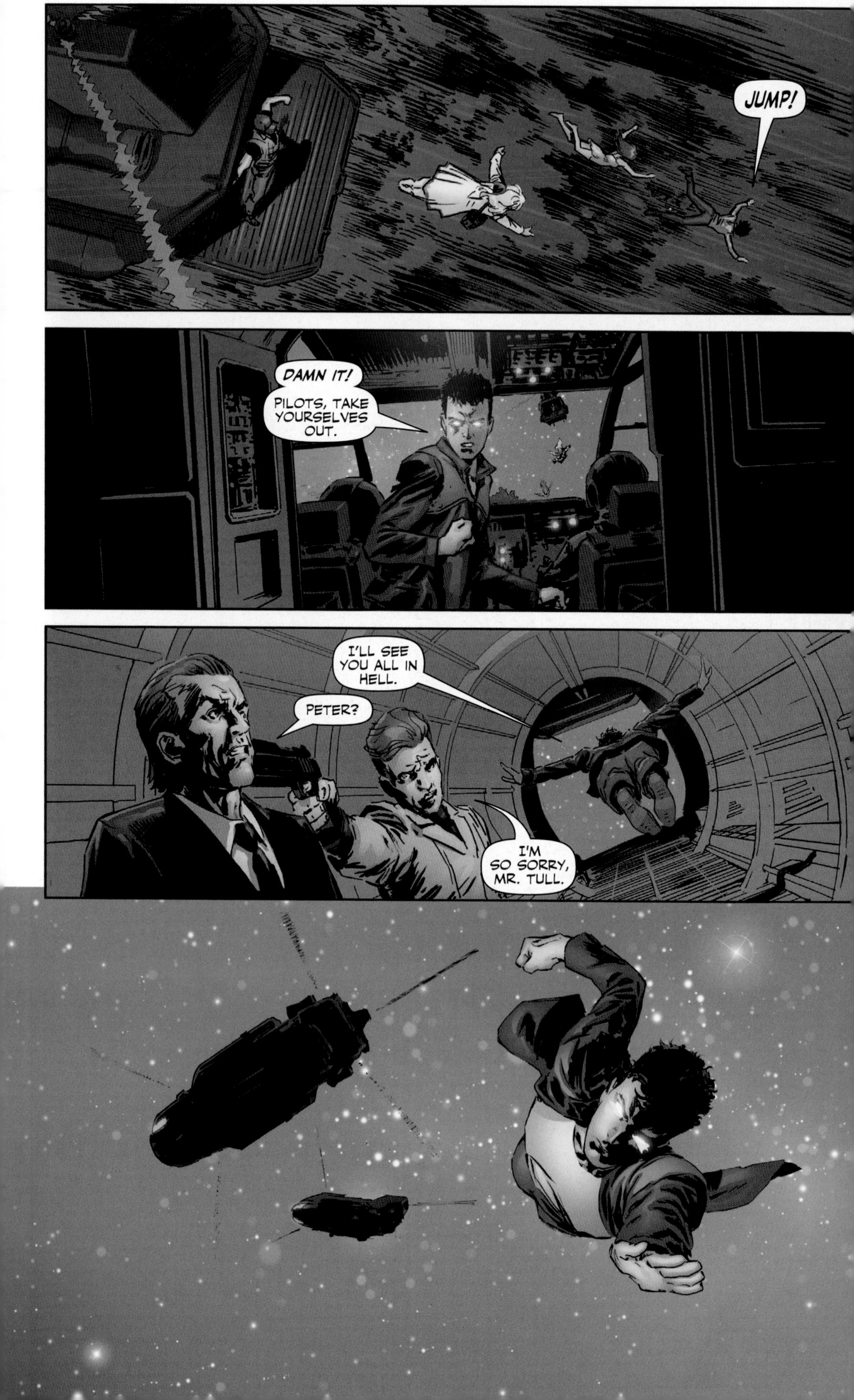
JUMP!
DAMN IT!
PILOTS, TAKE YOURSELVES OUT.
I'LL SEE YOU ALL IN HELL.
PETER?
I'M SO SORRY, MR. TULL.

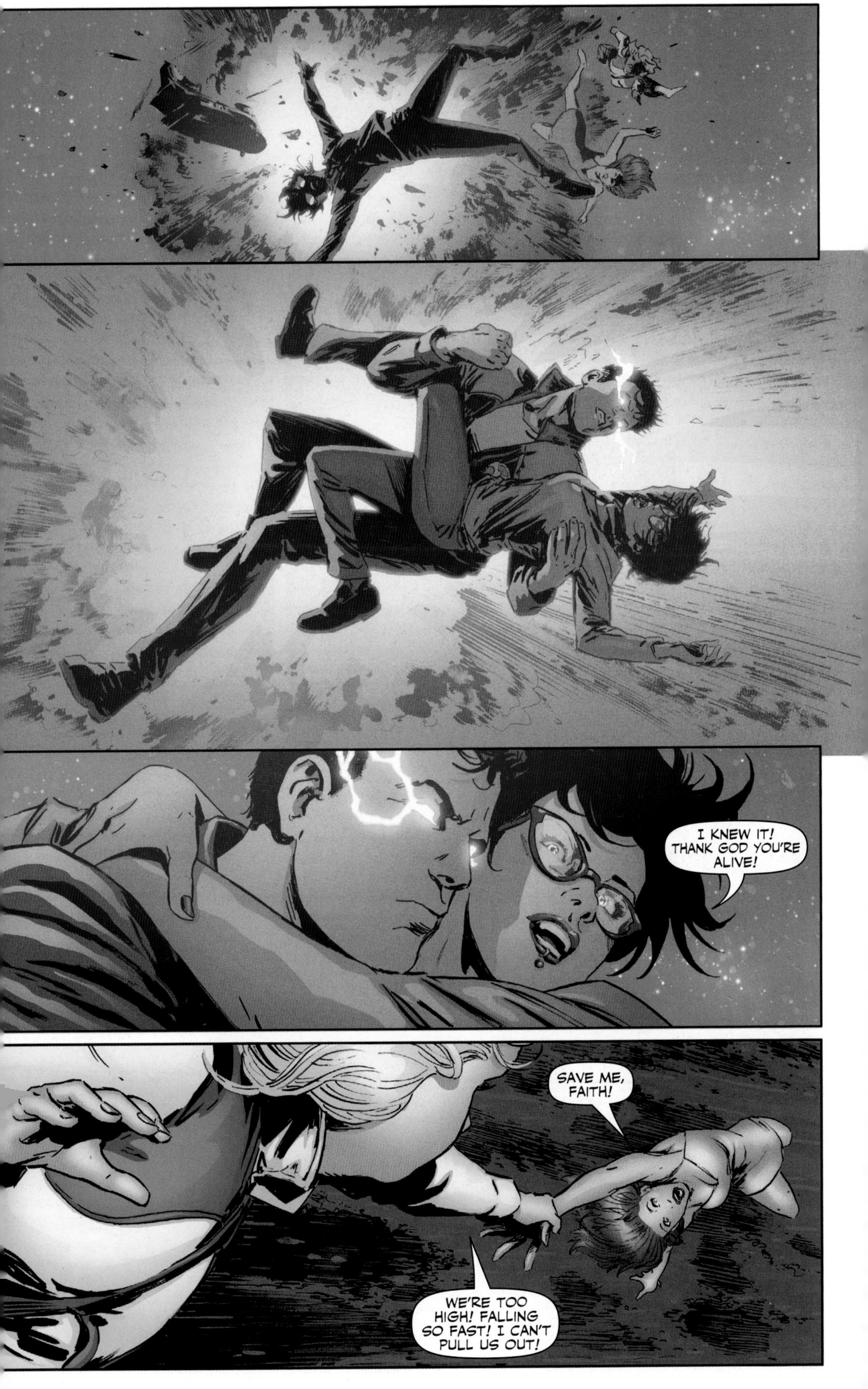
I KNEW IT! THANK GOD YOU'RE ALIVE!
SAVE ME, FAITH!
WE'RE TOO HIGH! FALLING SO FAST! I CAN'T PULL US OUT!

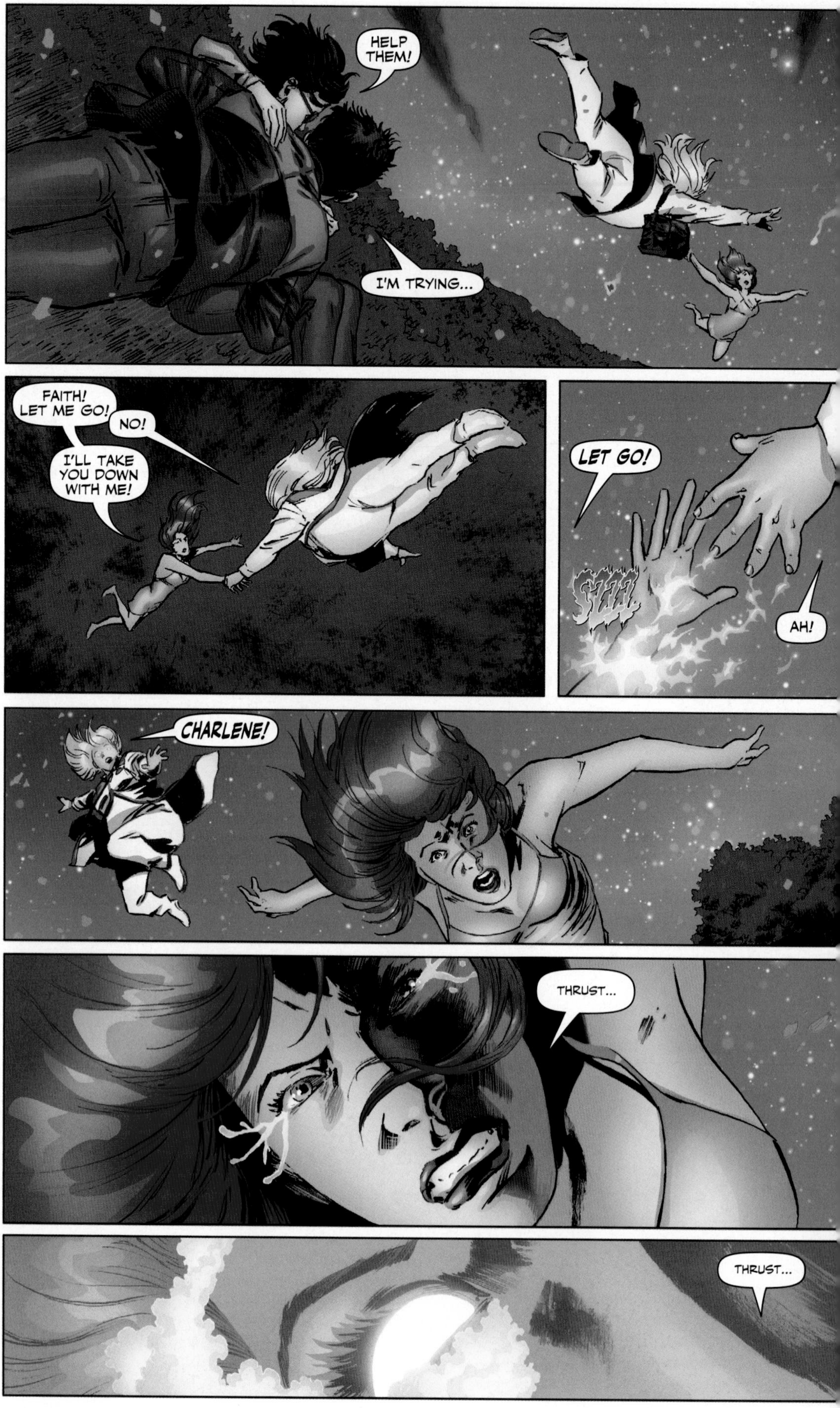
HELP THEM!
I'M TRYING...
FAITH! LET ME GO!
NO!
I'LL TAKE YOU DOWN WITH ME!
LET GO!
SZZZ
AH!
CHARLENE!
THRUST...
THRUST...

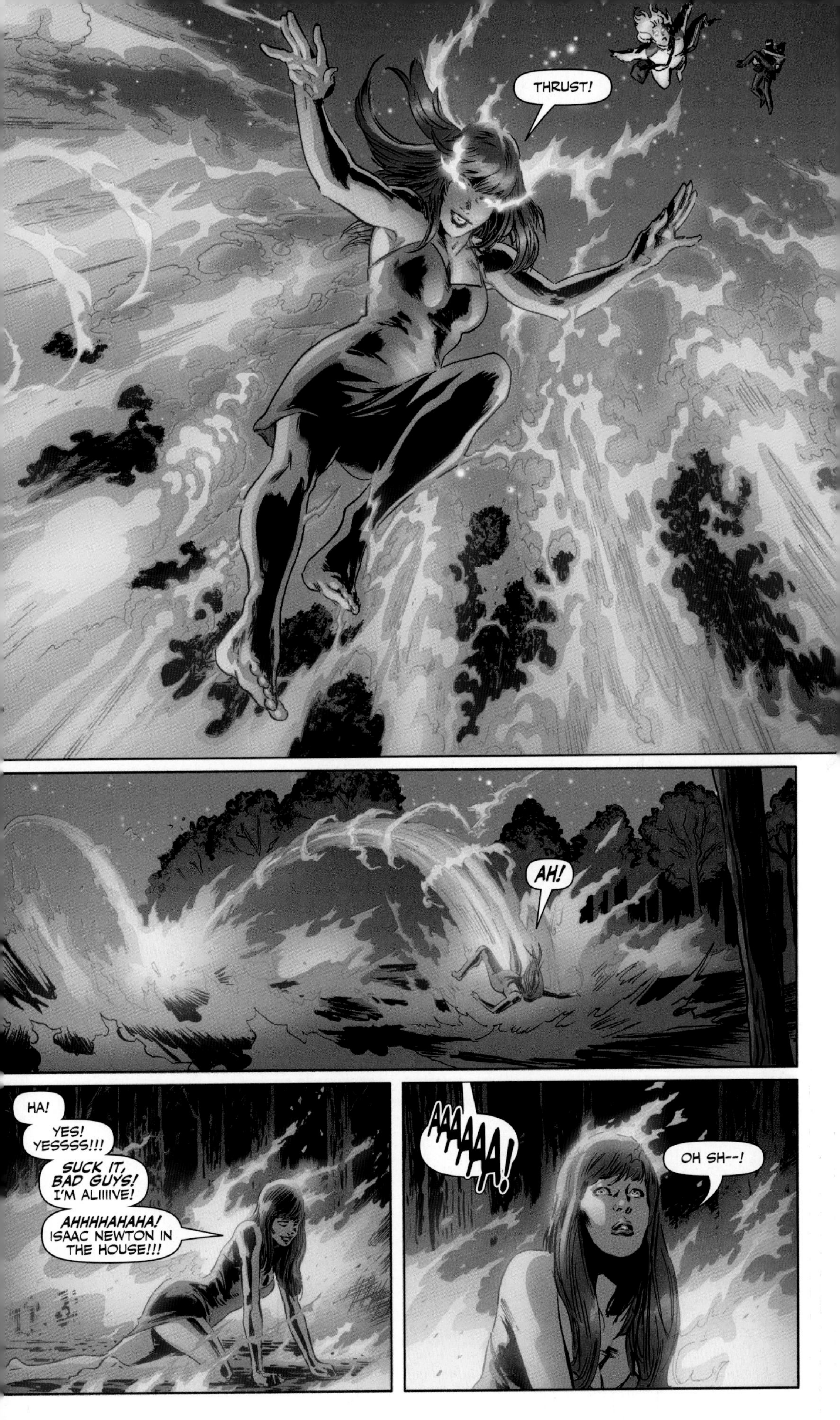
THRUST!
AH!
HA!
YES! YESSSS!!!
SUCK IT, BAD GUYS! I'M ALIIIIVE!
AHHHHAHAHA! ISAAC NEWTON IN THE HOUSE!!!
AAAAAAA!
OH SH--!

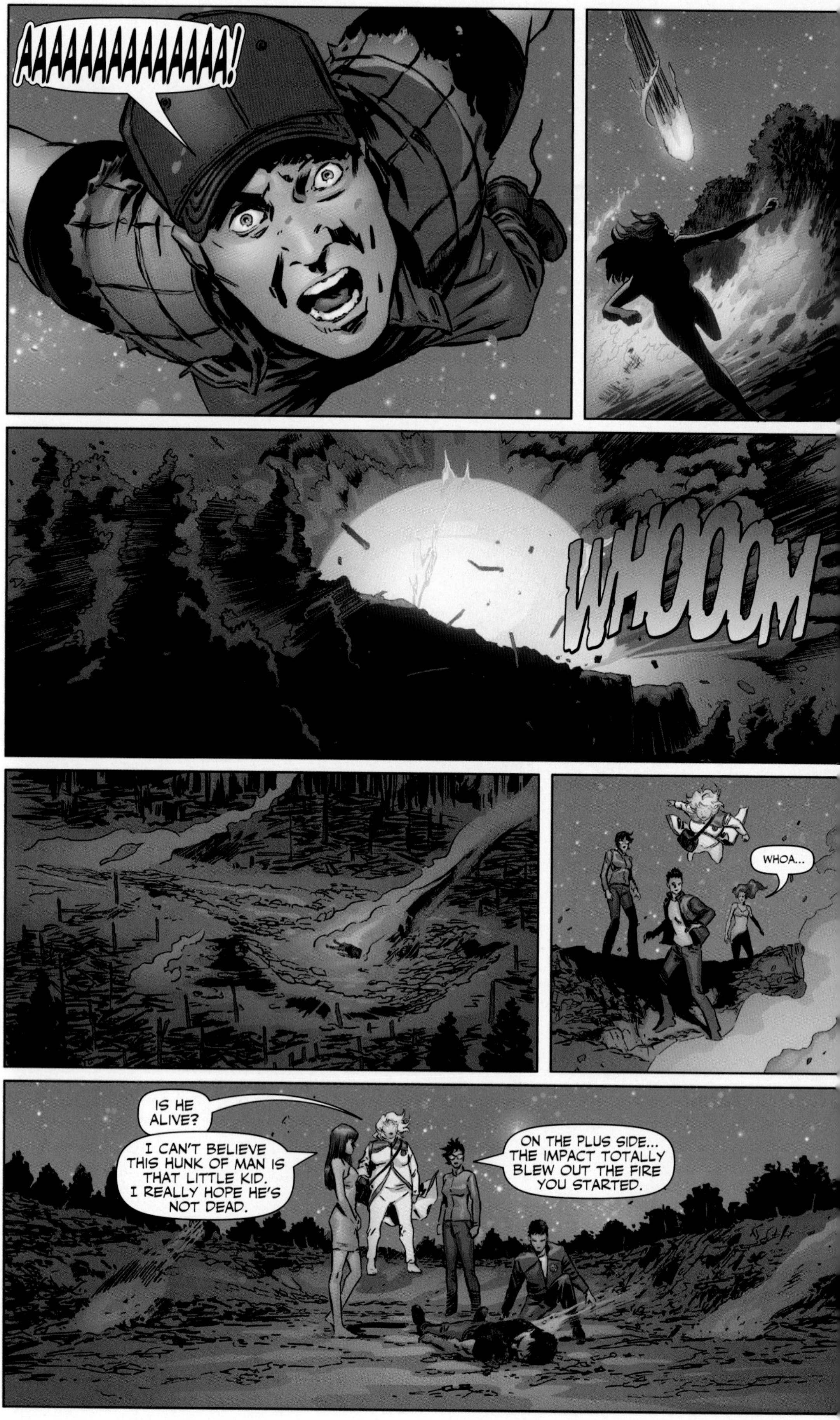
AAAAAAAAAAAAA!
WHOOOM
WHOA...
IS HE ALIVE?
I CAN'T BELIEVE THIS HUNK OF MAN IS THAT LITTLE KID. I REALLY HOPE HE'S NOT DEAD.
ON THE PLUS SIDE... THE IMPACT TOTALLY BLEW OUT THE FIRE YOU STARTED.

OHHHH GAAAA... FAAA!

IT'S NOT SUPPOSED TO HURT!

WH...WHAT HAPPENED?

IT LIVES!

YOU JUMPED OUT OF A HELICOPTER. WE ALL DID. IT WAS WICKED.

OH... I--I WOW-- YOU...YOU'RE PRETTY.

I KNOW. IT'S A BURDEN.

IS THIS...? THIS IS ALL... YOU'RE ALL... REAL?

CAN YOU WALK? WE NEED TO GET OUT OF HERE. LIKE, NOW.

I-I DON'T KNOW.

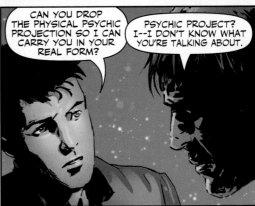

CAN YOU DROP THE PHYSICAL PSYCHIC PROJECTION SO I CAN CARRY YOU IN YOUR REAL FORM?

PSYCHIC PROJECT? I--I DON'T KNOW WHAT YOU'RE TALKING ABOUT.

DUDE, WE TOTALLY SAW YOU--

IT DOESN'T MATTER. JUST TRY TO WALK, TORKELSON. OKAY?

WE'RE NOT OUT OF THE WOODS YET.

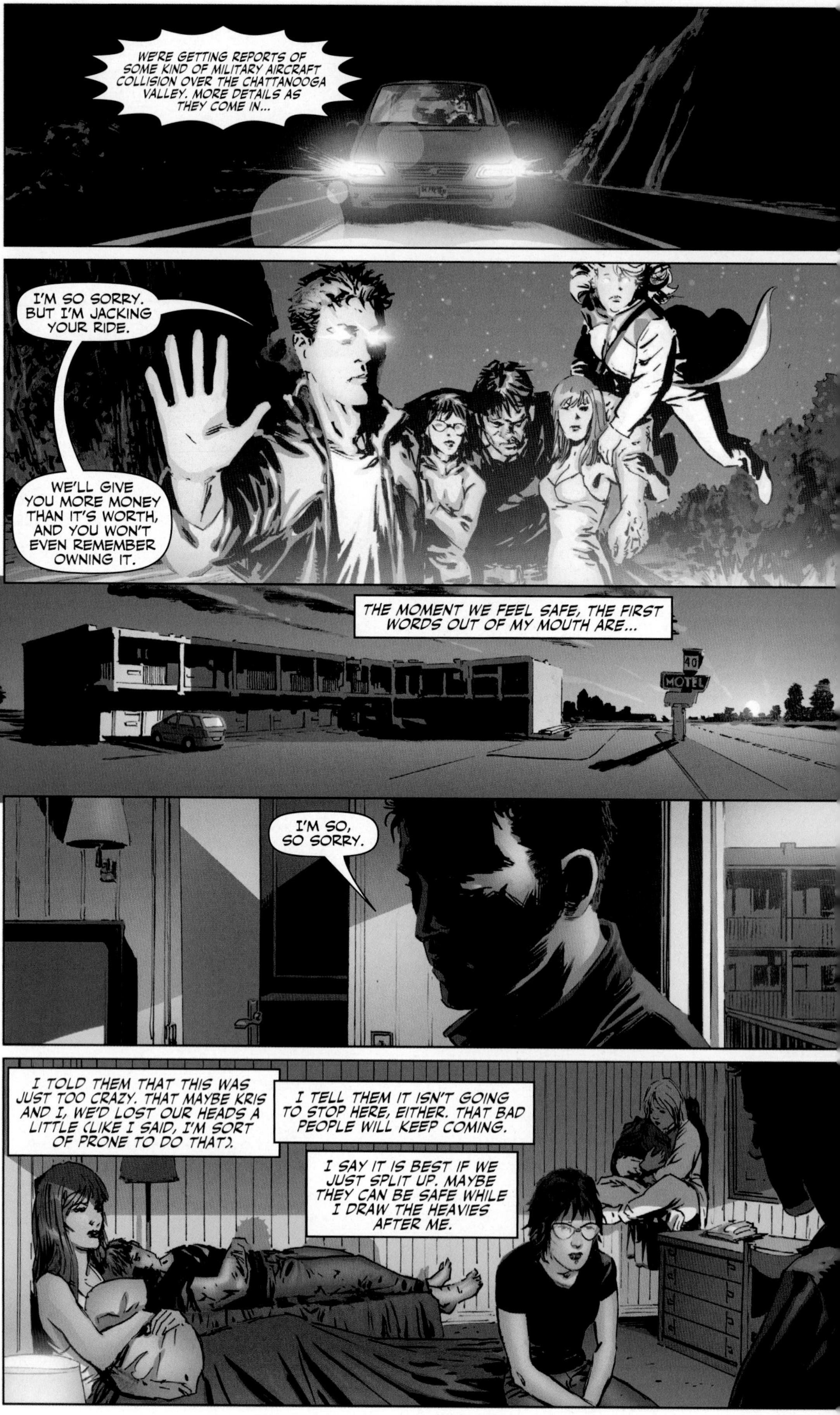

WE'RE GETTING REPORTS OF SOME KIND OF MILITARY AIRCRAFT COLLISION OVER THE CHATTANOOGA VALLEY. MORE DETAILS AS THEY COME IN...
I'M SO SORRY. BUT I'M JACKING YOUR RIDE.
WE'LL GIVE YOU MORE MONEY THAN IT'S WORTH, AND YOU WON'T EVEN REMEMBER OWNING IT.
THE MOMENT WE FEEL SAFE, THE FIRST WORDS OUT OF MY MOUTH ARE...
40
MOTEL
I'M SO, SO SORRY.
I TOLD THEM THAT THIS WAS JUST TOO CRAZY. THAT MAYBE KRIS AND I, WE'D LOST OUR HEADS A LITTLE (LIKE I SAID, I'M SORT OF PRONE TO DO THAT).
I TELL THEM IT ISN'T GOING TO STOP HERE, EITHER. THAT BAD PEOPLE WILL KEEP COMING.
I SAY IT IS BEST IF WE JUST SPLIT UP. MAYBE THEY CAN BE SAFE WHILE I DRAW THE HEAVIES AFTER ME.

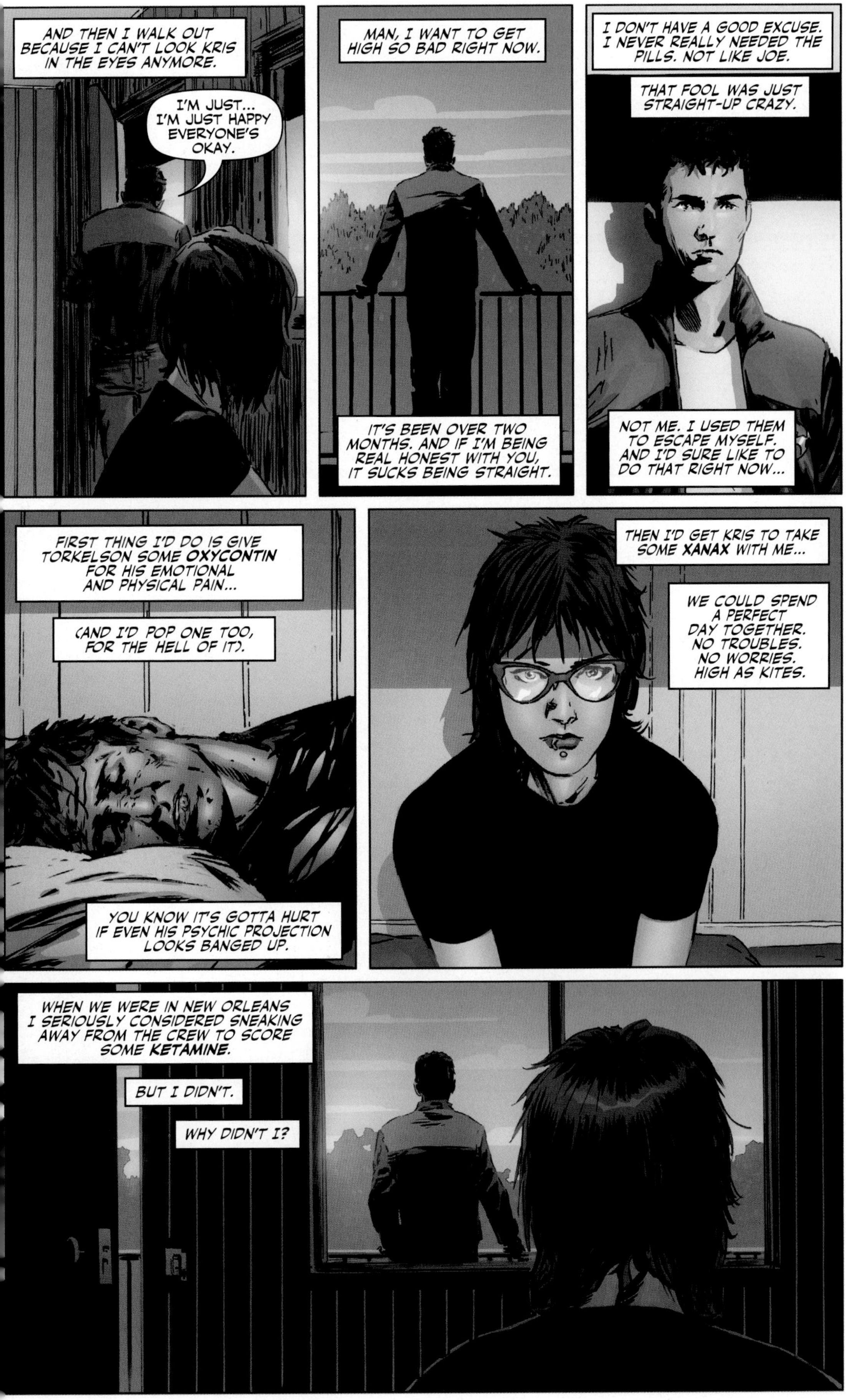
AND THEN I WALK OUT BECAUSE I CAN'T LOOK KRIS IN THE EYES ANYMORE.
I'M JUST... I'M JUST HAPPY EVERYONE'S OKAY.
MAN, I WANT TO GET HIGH SO BAD RIGHT NOW.
IT'S BEEN OVER TWO MONTHS. AND IF I'M BEING REAL HONEST WITH YOU, IT SUCKS BEING STRAIGHT.
I DON'T HAVE A GOOD EXCUSE. I NEVER REALLY NEEDED THE PILLS. NOT LIKE JOE.
THAT FOOL WAS JUST STRAIGHT-UP CRAZY.
NOT ME. I USED THEM TO ESCAPE MYSELF. AND I'D SURE LIKE TO DO THAT RIGHT NOW...
FIRST THING I'D DO IS GIVE TORKELSON SOME **OXYCONTIN** FOR HIS EMOTIONAL AND PHYSICAL PAIN...
(AND I'D POP ONE TOO, FOR THE HELL OF IT).
YOU KNOW IT'S GOTTA HURT IF EVEN HIS PSYCHIC PROJECTION LOOKS BANGED UP.
THEN I'D GET KRIS TO TAKE SOME **XANAX** WITH ME...
WE COULD SPEND A PERFECT DAY TOGETHER. NO TROUBLES. NO WORRIES. HIGH AS KITES.
WHEN WE WERE IN NEW ORLEANS I SERIOUSLY CONSIDERED SNEAKING AWAY FROM THE CREW TO SCORE SOME **KETAMINE**.
BUT I DIDN'T.
WHY DIDN'T I?

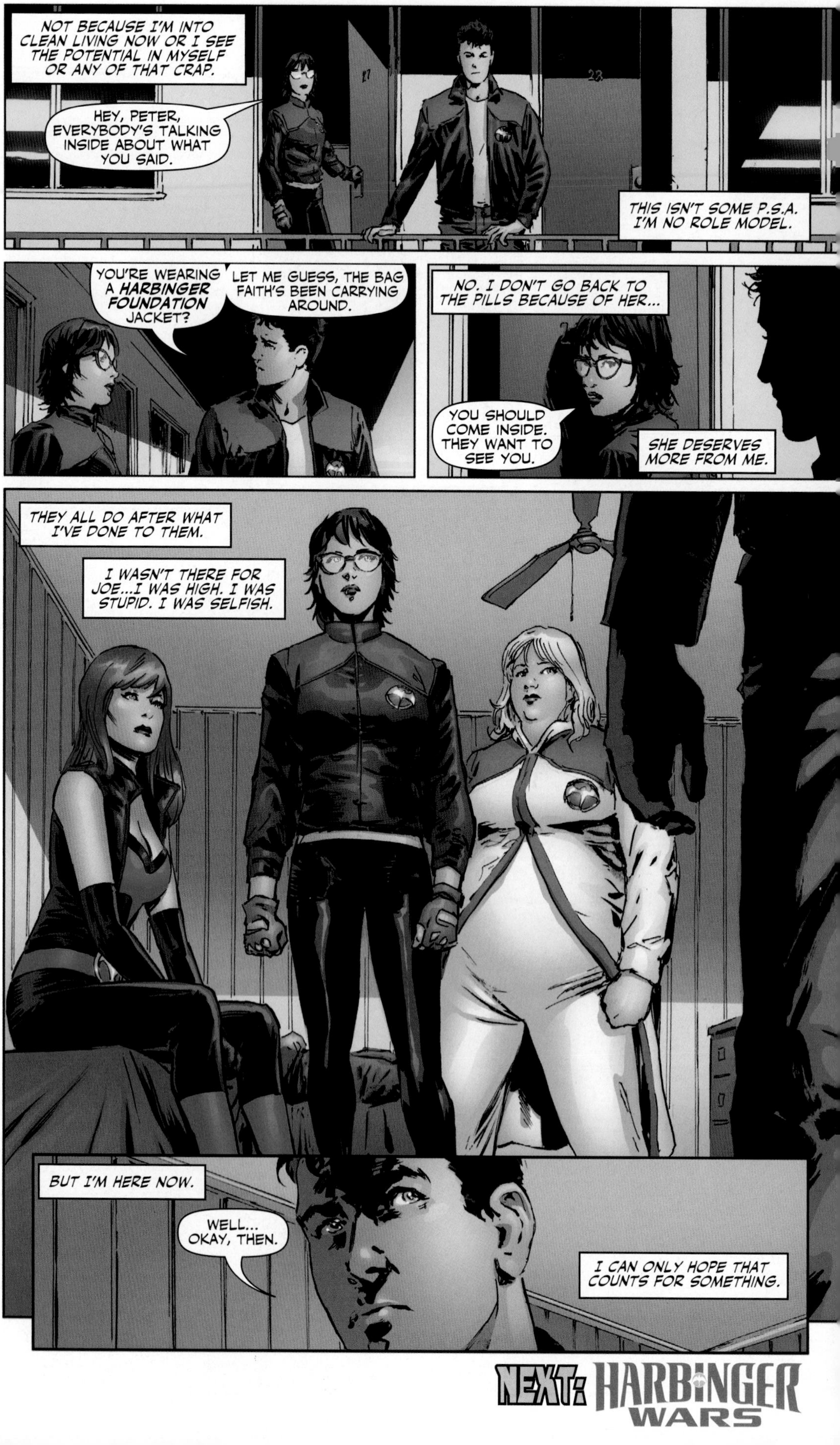
NOT BECAUSE I'M INTO CLEAN LIVING NOW OR I SEE THE POTENTIAL IN MYSELF OR ANY OF THAT CRAP.
HEY, PETER, EVERYBODY'S TALKING INSIDE ABOUT WHAT YOU SAID.
THIS ISN'T SOME P.S.A. I'M NO ROLE MODEL.
YOU'RE WEARING A HARBINGER FOUNDATION JACKET?
LET ME GUESS, THE BAG FAITH'S BEEN CARRYING AROUND.
NO. I DON'T GO BACK TO THE PILLS BECAUSE OF HER...
YOU SHOULD COME INSIDE. THEY WANT TO SEE YOU.
SHE DESERVES MORE FROM ME.
THEY ALL DO AFTER WHAT I'VE DONE TO THEM.
I WASN'T THERE FOR JOE...I WAS HIGH. I WAS STUPID. I WAS SELFISH.
BUT I'M HERE NOW.
WELL... OKAY, THEN.
I CAN ONLY HOPE THAT COUNTS FOR SOMETHING.
NEXT: HARBINGER WARS

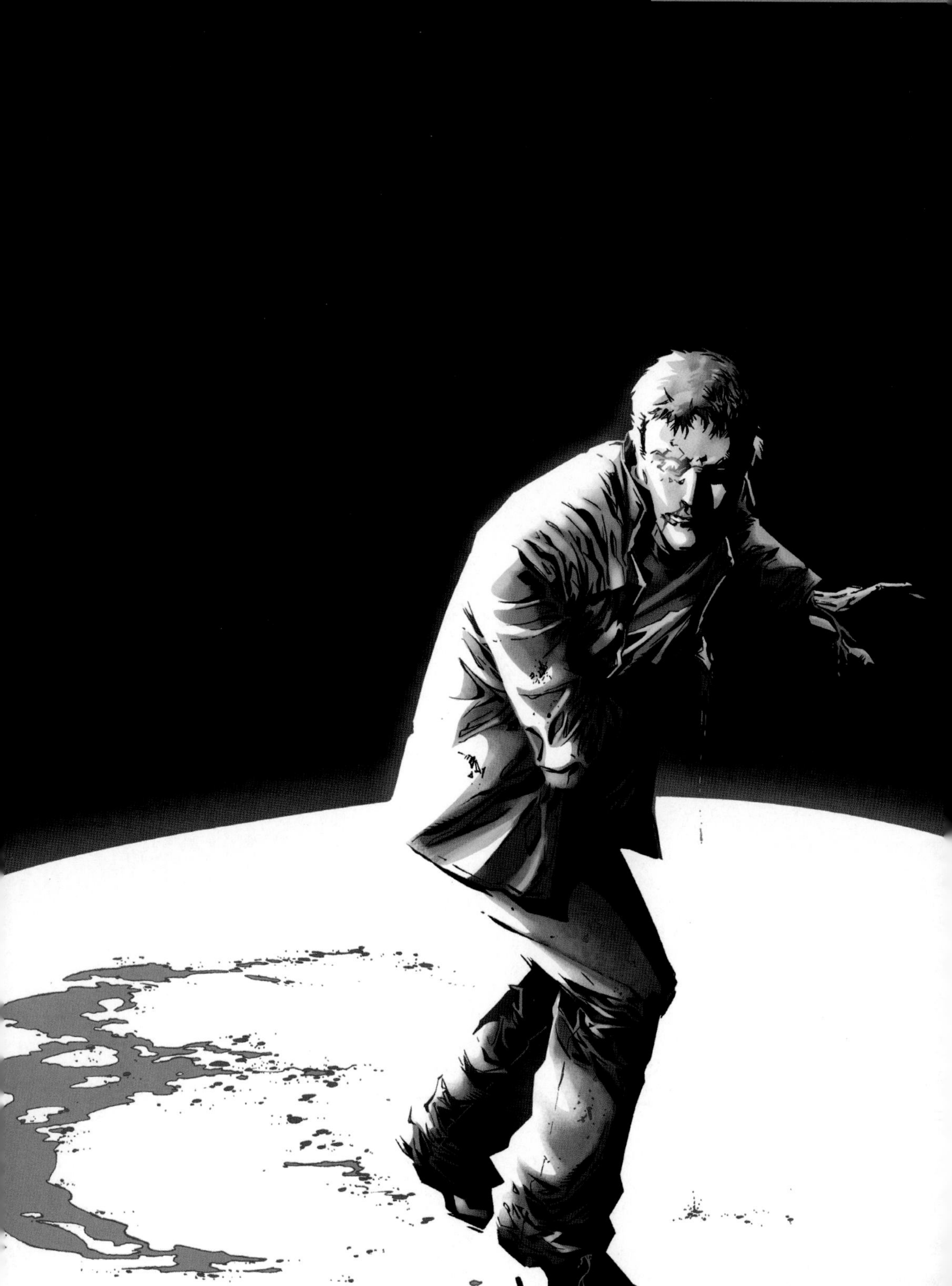

*HARBINGER* #6 VARIANT
Cover by MATTHEW CLARK

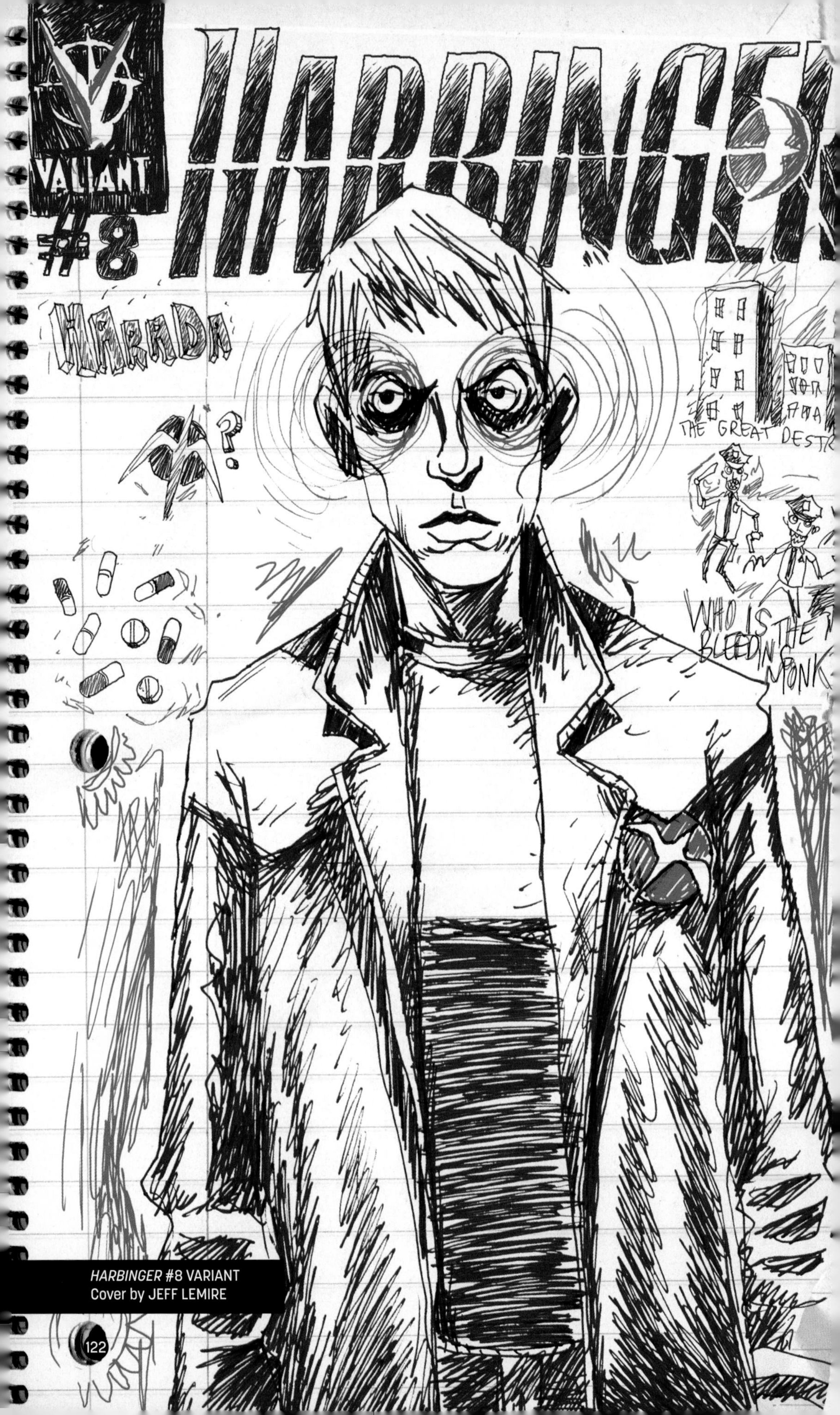
VALIANT
#8
HARADA
THE GREAT DESTR
WHO IS THE BLEEDING MONK

*HARBINGER* #8 VARIANT
Cover by JEFF LEMIRE

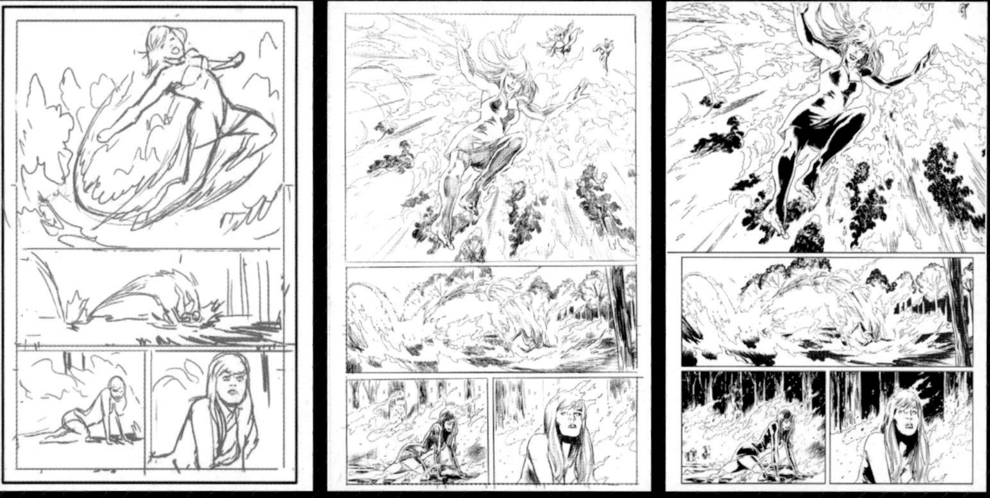

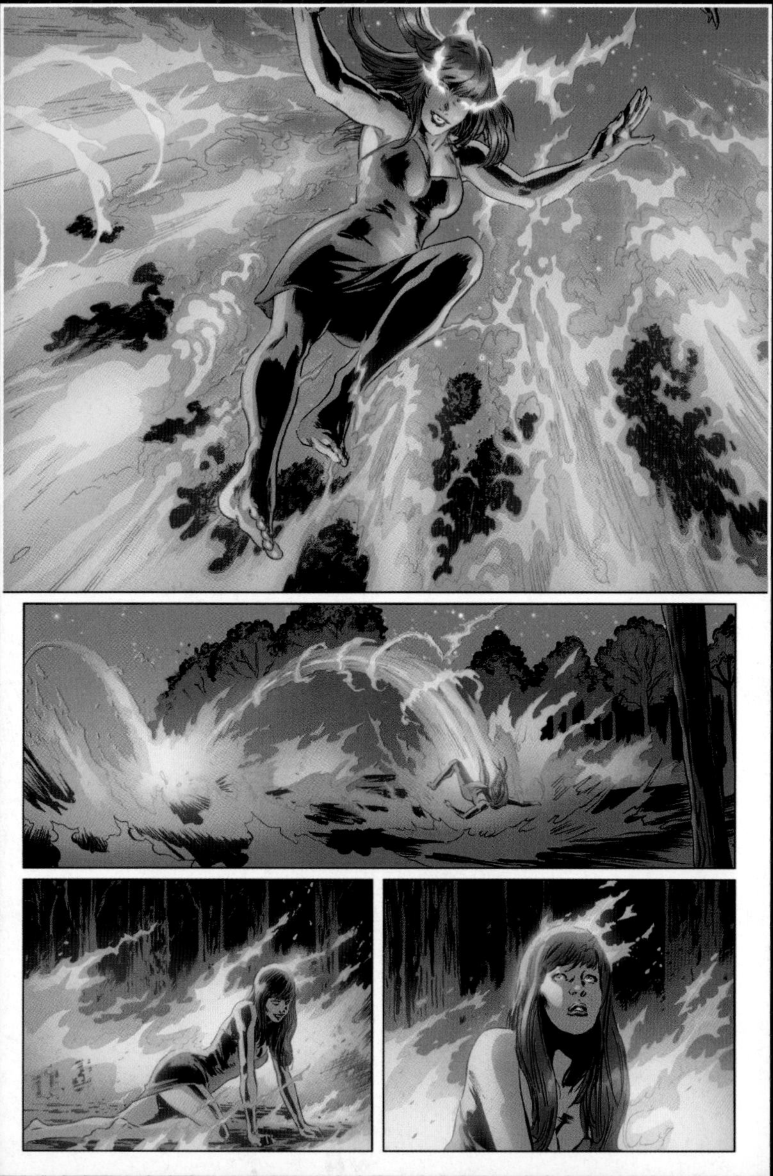

*HARBINGER* #10 Page 17
Layout and pencils by
ALVARO MARTÍNEZ
Inks by
STEFANO GAUDIANO
Color by IAN HANNIN

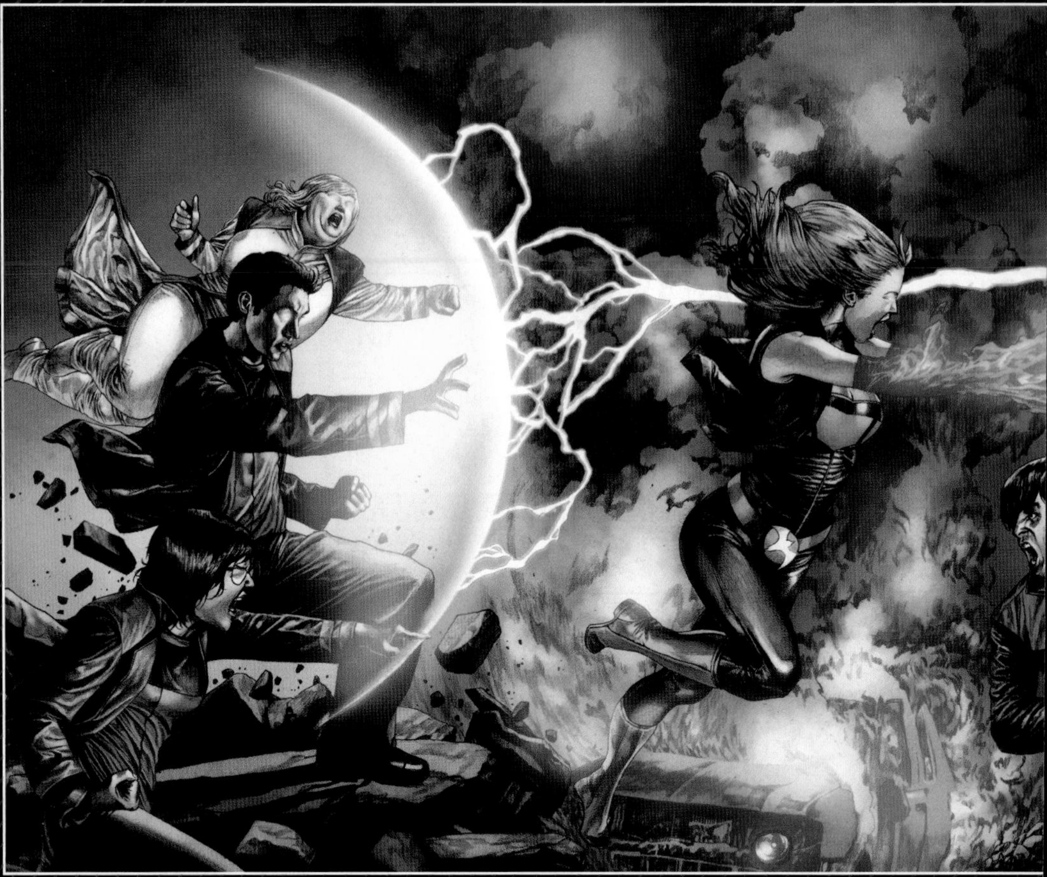

*HARBINGER #7-10* interlocking covers by MICO SUAYAN

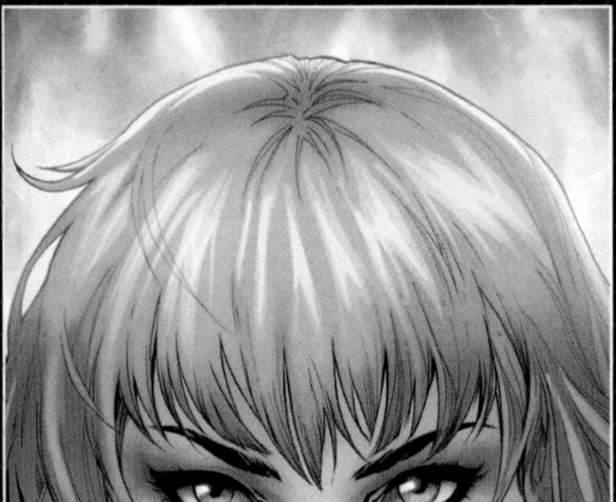

*HARBINGER* #7 VARIANT
Cover by EMANUELA LUPACCHINO

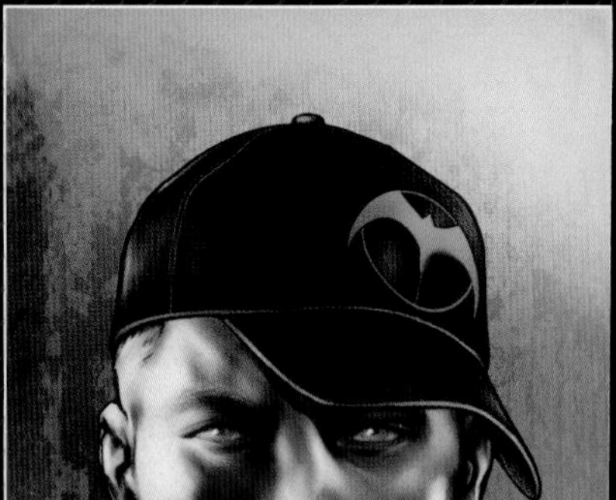

*HARBINGER* #8 VARIANT
Cover by KHARI EVANS